A DAMNED SERIOUS BUSINESS

A *Damned* SERIOUS BUSINESS

REX HARRISON

BANTAM PRESS

LONDON · NEW YORK · TORONTO · SYDNEY · AUCKLAND

TRANSWORLD PUBLISHERS LTD
61-63 Uxbridge Road, London W5 5SA

TRANSWORLD PUBLISHERS (AUSTRALIA) PTY LTD
15-23 Helles Avenue, Moorebank, NSW 2170

TRANSWORLD PUBLISHERS (NZ) LTD
Cnr Moselle and Waipareira Aves,
Henderson, Auckland

Published 1990 by Bantam Press
a division of Transworld Publishers Ltd
Copyright © Mercia Harrison 1990

"I'm An Ordinary Man", "Why Can't The English",
"I've Grown Accustomed To Her Face",
"Without You" and "You Did It".
© Chappell & Co. Inc. Reproduced by permission of
Warner Chappell Music Ltd.

The Appendix is an adapted version of the
Complete List of Stage and Screen Appearances
in Rex Harrison by Allen Eyles
published in 1985 by W. H. Allen and reproduced
with kind permission.

British Cataloguing in Publication Data
Harrison, Rex, 1908–1990
    A damned serious business: My life in comedy.
    1. Acting biographies
    I. Title
    792.028092

ISBN 0–593–02070–3

Typeset in 11 on 12pt Caslon
by Falcon Typographic Art Ltd
Wallington and Edinburgh
Printed in Great Britain by
Mackays of Chatham, PLC, Chatham, Kent

Any fool can play Tragedy, but Comedy, Sir, is a damned serious business

DAVID GARRICK

CONTENTS

ACKNOWLEDGEMENTS

I should like to acknowledge my debt, in writing this book, to Alan Jay Lerner's autobiography *The Street Where I Live*, first published in 1978 by W. W. Norton, New York, and Hodder & Stoughton, London, and now, sadly, out of print; to one entry in Richard Burton's diaries, quoted in *Rich* by Melvyn Bragg, published by Hodder & Stoughton in 1988; and to Allen Eyles's *Rex Harrison*, published by W. H. Allen in 1985.

I should also like to acknowledge the help I have been given with my research, and in finding photographs, by the newspaper archives of the *Liverpool Echo*, Liverpool, and The Theatre Museum, 1E Tavistock Street, London WC2.

And finally, my thanks to Judith Burnley, for helping me put these pages – and these memories – together.

LIST OF ILLUSTRATIONS

(between pages 116 and 117)

CHAPTER 1

LIVERPOOL DAYS

Acting is an extraordinarily difficult thing, and the easier it looks to the layman, the more difficult it is to do. This is a paradox which lies at the very heart of my career, because all my life as an actor I have aimed, above all, at naturalism. I've always tried to make my acting look very simple – as natural as possible, and as truthful. I've striven not to appear to be striving for anything, and this takes a lot of inner energy, and experience, to achieve. Without that special charge of inner energy, everything, the whole performance, will be wasted. It will – as we actors say – all go down your shirt front, and into the stage.

People often ask me when I first knew I wanted to act, and what made me so sure about it. I can only say I don't really know. I don't remember a time *before* I wanted to be an actor. I seem to have grown up knowing that this was what I was going to do. This is strange, really, because, as far as I know, there has never been anyone else in my family who went on the

1

stage. A bit of family folklore had it that my mother's family was descended from the great actor Edmund Kean (1787–1833), who was, in turn, descended from the poet–composer Henry Carey. Carey's best-known poem provided the lyric for the song "Sally in our Alley", made famous by Gracie Fields, and he is also thought to have written the words for the national anthem, "God Save the Queen", (or King, as the case may then have been). It is true that Carey was my mother's maiden name, but the Kean connection is just a bit of family nonsense, if you ask me, and remains an unsubstantiated rumour.

I was born in Huyton, outside Liverpool, on 5 March 1908, into the final flamboyant years of the Edwardian era, for King Edward VII, better remembered as Queen Victoria's fun-loving son, The Prince of Wales, was reigning monarch for a mean nine years, and died in 1910, when I was two years old. My father was William Reginald Harrison, sportsman, engineer, and businessman, and my mother Edith Carey Harrison. I was actually christened Reginald Carey Harrison, but at the early age of six or seven, decided that I was not a Reggie or a Reginald, and asked my mother if she would be so kind as to address me as Rex in future. She complied, and so I became known as Rex. It would be nice to think that this regal choice was influenced by the heroic deeds of some ancient king or other, or even by admiration of the reigning King of England at that time, King George V. It might even be amusing to think that perhaps I'd passed some early picture palace or place of entertainment called The Rex. Alas, I believe it was but a childish, arbitrary choice, which may, at best, have occurred because I heard someone calling his dog to heel.

LIVERPOOL DAYS

My parents already had two daughters when I was born. My sister Sylvia is four years older than I am, and Marjorie was eight, and if there is any fairly simple reason why anyone becomes an actor, it may have been partly to do with this. There was too large an age-gap between us for my sisters to be much company for me, so I was, to all intents and purposes, an only child, and played by myself a lot, making up my own games. Such children do learn to live in their imaginations.

With that minor exception, it was a normal, fairly boring, English middle-class childhood, enlivened by visits to my eccentric grandmother Harrison, who lived in a grand house, Bellvale Hall, Gateacre, with stables, tennis courts and a cricket ground, where she had brought up her large family of seven boys and a girl, and the upkeep of which she was no longer able to afford. I can still vividly remember her tearing through the house at a great pace in an electrically driven wheelchair yelling: "Got to eat hash, got to eat stew. No money, no money, no money!"

Apart from eating stew, or hash, and playing in the large rooms and larger gardens of Bellvale Hall, I can remember enjoying our family holidays on the beaches of Penmaenmawr, North Wales. Because I was not very strong as a small boy, and had had several illnesses, including a bad case of measles, which left me with permanently damaged sight in my right eye, I was not sent away to Harrow, like my father, but kept at home and sent to a local school called Liverpool College.

Naturally, being so much at home, and being the youngest, and the only son, I became something of a mother's boy, and I have often wondered since, whether that was how I first grew accustomed to having women around in my life. In direct contradiction to my famous song from *My Fair Lady*, "You Should NEVER Let a Woman in Your Life!", I have *always* had a woman in my life, and I've generally enjoyed the experience very much. Whether this "little weakness" is attributable to my mother, I do not know, but the fact remains that my mother was a very attractive, very feminine woman, with an ample, curvaceous figure, and I adored her. I can still remember the seductive shape and smell of her as she bent over to tuck me in at night. So perhaps it is because of her that I have always liked women so much. And perhaps not. Perhaps it is simply that I like their companionship. I like their understanding. I like them because you don't have to explain everything to them. They know. They're intuitive – and realistic.

I don't think it would be fair to say that I've been dependent on the women in my life – they've looked after me, and I've looked after them. Damn well, too! I mean, I never kept them bottled up anywhere, they went everywhere with me. They shared my boats, my holidays, my house in Portofino, when I had it. I like women to have fun. I like *people* to have fun. I've always liked spirited, funny women, who know how to enjoy themselves. Some of my chums have been a bit mystified, from time to time, quite understandably, about what women saw in me, and I can't say I know, either. I don't remember that I went out of my way to pamper them, or anything. I was generally having a fairly amusing time myself, and I suppose they enjoyed being part of it.

My friend, the film producer James Hill, (of Hecht, Hill and Lancaster fame) who was no slouch himself in these matters (having once been married to Rita Hayworth), remembers meeting two of my wives in a limousine in Hollywood – they must have been my first two wives, Collette and Lilli, by the sound of it – and he reported in some amazement that instead of scratching each other's eyes out, as anybody else's first two wives would have done, they sat there worrying if I would be all right without them – and whether I had enough woollen winter underwear – I must have been going on some location trip! Jim was clearly outraged at their unconventional behaviour, but to me it's just another example of the warmth, the sheer practicality of women.

My father, as I have said, was quite an athlete, and had a pretty impressive record. He had run the hundred yards in 10.05 seconds – and as a member of West Derby Hockey Club had played hockey for England. He and I played cricket together, and under his tuition I became a good enough left-handed bowler to get into the school First Eleven. My scholastic career, however, remained unmarked by brilliance, but, predictably, I appeared in our school plays, in Maeterlinck's *The Blue Bird*, in which I played the Cat and had one "Mee-ai-ow"; and *A Midsummer Night's Dream* as Flute, the bellows-maker who doubles as the fair maiden Thisbe. I decided to portray Thisbe with a large bosom and a lisp, and thus got the first laughs of my career. At sixteen, to everyone's relief I think, I was allowed to leave school and start my training for the stage.

It is surprising, I suppose, that my non-theatrical and rather conventional parents did not try to stop me, but they did not. Perhaps they thought my choice of career was at least partly their own fault. They had always taken us to see everything at the theatre, and they must have been aware of what a passion, if not what ambitions, this had provoked in me. My sister Sylvia,

5

now the Dowager Countess Delawarr, and a Dame of the British Empire, reminds me that I was always sitting Mother and Father on chairs in our drawing room, while I drew the curtains in the bow windows and took curtain calls. I never questioned the warmth of their applause when I made my bow, though as I never seemed to think it necessary to give any kind of performance before my curtain calls, it seems to me now that they were demonstrating a degree of tolerance — and humour — remarkable even among parents.

Of my two sisters, Marjorie never married, but stayed at home to look after our parents, while Sylvia had a long career at least as theatrical as mine — but not on stage! Still formidable, and still going strong, at eighty-six, Sylvia has always been smart and elegant, and was notable for her taste in fashionable hats. I've no idea whether she was a beauty — how can one tell such things about one's sister? — but she generally wore a look of hauteur suitable to the well-dressed beauty, and she made two quite illustrious marriages. Her first husband was a brilliant young Scottish lawyer, David Maxwell Fife, who had already attracted enough attention to himself as a student at Oxford to have rhymes written about his habit of appearing gloomy at all times:

> The nearest thing to death in life
> Is David Patrick Maxwell Fife
> But underneath his gloomy shell
> He does himself extremely well.

Despite his gloomy manner, however, Maxwell Fife was a terrific character, of whom I became extremely fond. He

6

was an immensely able barrister and Queen's Counsel, with a much publicized criminal practice at a time when England still had the death sentence, and criminals were hanged. After the war he became one of the judges of war criminals at the terrifying Nuremburg trials, and later on he became Home Secretary and then, as Lord Kilmuir, Lord Chancellor.

Then, one day, Sylvia behaved like some dotty aristocratic lady from one of the comedies I didn't play in. She got herself pursued across the fields and meadows of her country house by another peer of the realm, Lord Delawarr, who was famous, amongst other things, for having once turned up at a State Opening of Parliament in a mine-sweeper's uniform. He had been a conscientious objector in the First World War, had been drafted down the mines, and wanted no-one to forget it! Actually, Delawarr had no right to pursue Sylvia at all, nor Sylvia to listen to him, for he had a large family by his first wife, Diana Delawarr, all of whom were outraged at this behaviour, but he was rather the attractive wastrel type, whereas Kilmuir, though a very important man, a man in whom Churchill put his trust, had a much more sober personality. Anyway, for better or worse, Sylvia left Lord Kilmuir and married Lord Delawarr, which is why she is now the Dowager Countess Delawarr, and not the Dowager Countess Kilmuir. Nowadays, Sylvia lives in a pretty part of the English countryside, and whenever I'm in England we still meet and bicker in the amiable manner of brothers and sisters, even when they are both in their ninth decades. Besides, I shall always be indebted to Sylvia and David Kilmuir for providing me with two delightful nieces, which was particularly thoughtful of them, as I only have sons of my own.

Being four years my elder, Sylvia had embarked on her own type of "theatrical" career while I was still a schoolboy, but when it came to the time for me to leave school, my parents were wonderfully supportive to me. In spite of the ghastliness of my childish drawing-room performances, their encouragement remained unshaken, and it was my father who helped me get an interview with the Director of the Liverpool Repertory Theatre, a Mr William Armstrong. After my interview, there were months of waiting and hoping, and then at last a postcard headed THE PLAYHOUSE, LIVERPOOL appeared saying

Please attend rehearsals, 10.30. 30 May 1924.

Signed:
William Armstrong

It was the most exciting document I had ever seen in my life.

In those days a young man who went into rep was paid 30 shillings a week (about $2). You were allowed to understudy and watch, and you played any kind of part that was handed out to you. Sixteen-year-old boys were required to play men of sixty. It was great training because you really had to learn your job. My elation at getting into the theatre was not destined to last very long, however. Cast, early on, as a messenger with one line in John Drinkwater's *Abraham Lincoln*, I tried to give some realism to the part and, at the first rehearsal, came on stage reeling, and completely out of breath. Out of the darkness of the stalls came the voice of Mr Armstrong, calling, "What's the matter, Harrison, are you ill?"

"No, sir, I am acting," I replied, with as much dignity as I could.

*

When I first went on the stage there were two kinds of repertory companies in England, both running for a season of six or eight months each. One was the weekly Rep, where plays are done for one week only, then taken off again, and the other was the Repertory where plays ran for as long as there was an audience for them. Liverpool Rep was the second kind of repertory theatre, where plays were put on for a normal commercial run. The theatrical use of the word "repertory" must, I think, be derived from the French "repertoire" – the store of songs or plays an actor or singer has at his command, or the command of his memory. *The Oxford English Dictionary*'s definition of "a repertory theatre" is "a theatre to which is attached a permanent company of actors who perform plays belonging to a certain repertory," and that's exactly what we were at Liverpool: a group of actors employed for a season or a number of seasons, alternating the playing of a chosen group of plays.

The first provincial repertory company was opened in Manchester in 1907 by Miss Annie Horniman, the tea heiress, who was, I believe, responsible for having formed the very first repertory company at the Abbey Theatre, Dublin, in 1903. Her first venue in Manchester was The Midland Hotel, and from there she proceeded to The Gaiety Theatre in 1908. The next was Glasgow in 1908, and then came Liverpool in 1911. The famous Birmingham Repertory was established in 1913 under Barry Jackson, later Sir Barry Jackson, but the other well-known provincial Reps didn't get started until the Twenties, after the First World War. So popular was the repertory movement, however, that by 1935 there were fourteen repertory theatres throughout Great Britain.

At Liverpool, William Armstrong's policy was to do plays by good writers like J.M. Barrie, William Somerset

Maugham, Frederick Lonsdale, Harley Granville Barker, St John Ervine, Arnold Bennett, J.B. Priestley, Eugene O'Neill, Galsworthy, Chekhov, Ibsen and Shaw. Also farces by Ben Travers, and popular pieces of the day, such as *Hobson's Choice* by Harold Brighouse. He chose established playwrights and established plays hoping that they would run.

Actors were engaged for a season, and as far as I can remember a season was the best part of a year, certainly nine months, where the company would do plays by some of the playwrights I've mentioned and hope to get a four to five week run out of most of them. As far as the company was concerned, none of the actors who joined Liverpool Rep at the time I joined it became truly famous, but they were all quite well established actors of their time. The company was usually composed of two leading men, who were called leading men in spite of the fact that they were in their fifties and sixties, three or four juvenile actors, of which I was much the most juvenile presumably – they were mostly in their twenties and thirties – then there were the ladies. There would be a character lady, and there would be juvenile ladies, and that made up the company. Each group or company was designed to fit the parts in whichever of Shaw's plays or Ibsen's plays the management had chosen to put on that season.

When I joined Liverpool the company's two leading men were both in their sixties. One was Herbert Lomas, and the other was James Harcourt. Herbert Lomas was a very large bony man with a huge nose, and was probably the best actor I saw while I was there. Not that I ever wanted to be like him, but he was sort of an averagely good stock leading man who fitted into most of the plays. Harcourt, on the other hand, was a comedian. He was short and fat and round, and used to do some rather vulgar things, like cocking his leg, and other strange pieces of business which made the less sophisticated members of the audience laugh. I never thought him as good an actor as Herbert Lomas, but don't forget I'd only just begun to watch actors at work, and these were far too early days for me to make any judgements about the company. As far as the Liverpool public were concerned, however, the company's acting seemed to please them very much, for the plays went well.

The juveniles were a motley crew. One was a man called Robert Speaight who came to us straight from OUDS, which is the Oxford University Dramatic Society. He made himself distinguished by always coming to rehearsals wearing dirty old bedroom slippers. How he got himself through the dirty streets of Liverpool to the theatre in bedroom slippers I shall never know. It is only surprising they weren't even dirtier! But he was never out of them when he was rehearsing. It was all quite funny. Then there was Hugh Williams, a good-looking Welsh actor in his mid-twenties, or early thirties, whose wife, Gwynne Whitby, was also with the company – they were a nice couple, and I liked them. Jack Minster was an older actor and director, an unmarried and rather bitter man whom I didn't like very much, though later on when I met him again in London soon after I left Liverpool, he very kindly tipped me off about where to go to meet other theatrical hopefuls, and how to go about finding jobs in the big city. There were also a young brother and sister I became friends with, Basil and Doreen Moss, and an older actress, Marjorie Fielding who, I always thought, was good. She was a character actress, a sort of cardiganed lady in her fifties or sixties, who fitted very well into the character parts, while the young women's parts were played by Gwynne Whitby and Doreen Moss.

These actors were mostly reasonably competent at their job but there was nothing at all distinguished about them. God knows what happened to them afterwards because I never heard anything of them, and it seems that none of them did anything much of note with their lives. Only Herbert Lomas had a reputation of any size, and he was undoubtedly the biggest personality at Liverpool Rep when I joined the company.

When you first go on the stage it's very difficult to assess people's qualities as actors or actresses. I wasn't acting with them, you see, I was playing tiny little parts, drifting on and off with nothing to say, or sometimes with one line to say. Looking back I can see that considering every time I did drift on or off with one line to say I got it wrong, William Armstrong was probably absolutely correct to advise me to give it up. "Oh Harrison for God's sake don't go on with this," he used to say. "It's no good. Go into your father's business, do anything, but don't go on with acting." So naturally I thought – oh dear, oh dear, perhaps I'd better stop. I knew I didn't show any particular talent.

The first thing I did when I was called to join the company as a student, I remember, was in a play called *Thirty Minutes in a Street*, which was half an hour's entertainment about the people who passed by in a street. I was cast – somewhat prematurely at sixteen! – as "The Husband". The husband had to run across the stage dishevelled, with his hair standing up on end, saying: "Fetch a doctor! Baby!" The wife of this poor man was presumably in the process of delivering a child, and he was in a high state of excitement. Anyway I got it wrong, and I rushed on the stage, highly dishevelled, and said: "Fetch a baby! Doctor!" Well, as baby-doctors weren't in vogue at the time – I don't know whether they are now, actually –

it didn't make any sense, so William Armstrong, who was sitting in front must have thought: "This is terrible!"

The other appearance I made was as a coloured man which I enjoyed making up to do very much. I had to be blacked up all over, and I took hours painstakingly putting the blacking on, making sure it was evenly spread everywhere, even between my toes. My role called for me to wear nothing but a loin cloth and a couple of shark's teeth round my neck. Jimmy Kanaka, I was called, in a play of Eugene O'Neill's called *Gold*. I came on with a lot of pirates in the first act, one of them sighted a sail on the horizon (we were supposed to be in the Caribbean somewhere), and the only thing I had to do was to climb up the palm tree which was centre stage, sight the ship, and come down and report that I'd seen a sail or something. That palm tree was my undoing. No-one had thought to warn me that the trunk of the damned thing had been fireproofed just before we went on, and was still wet, so I went up with all my coloured make-up on, and came down with it all off. I mean the whole of my front was white as the day I was born! Oh God! I thought, and I sat there trying to cover the white bits of my body by keeping my legs crossed – my legs were still fairly brown – but of course it didn't work and I feared this was the end of my short career, which was obviously what William Armstrong thought too. What made it worse was that my mother and father and sisters were all in the audience watching the disaster. In fact as far as I can remember every time I had to say something on stage in Liverpool, particularly on the opening nights, something went wrong for me.

There were, however, some plays I was in where I don't think I made any mistakes – because I didn't have anything to say. One was a play called *Old English* by John Galsworthy (of *Forsyte Saga* fame), where I played "Another Clerk"; *Doctor Knock* by Jules Romains where I played "A Country Fellow"; *A Kiss for Cinderella* by J.M. Barrie (author of *Peter Pan*), where I played a Court Gentleman without lines; and *Abraham Lincoln* by John Drinkwater, where I played three parts without lines. The first of these was to be part of a Deputation from the Republican Convention, the second was a messenger from Fort Sumtner, and the third was an aide de camp to Lincoln, called Captain Malins. William Armstrong couldn't find fault with any of these, as I didn't speak, but all in all I can't say that my career at Liverpool Rep was any kind of a success.

Without realizing it, however, and almost by default, I suppose I was getting some sort of education in theatre. I still remember the pang of horror and the thrill of admiration I felt for Robert Speaight, who played Booth in *Abraham Lincoln*. One night he forgot to take his revolver on in the scene where he is supposed to shoot Lincoln. Showing great presence of mind, he drew an imaginary knife out of his pocket and stabbed Lincoln in the back instead, thus changing history overnight.

I was also able to watch and admire the technique of Herbert Lomas in his greatest part of Sylvanus Heythorp, Chairman of The Island Navigation Company in John Galsworthy's *Old English*, which was a play about shipping and shipowners set in Liverpool at a time when that port, the docks and the shipbuilding industry were at the height of their power. It was then that I first observed the potent aura surrounding the leading actors of the day, the aroma of cigars and port, the total absorption in the character. I think I must have been doubling my part as "Another Clerk" with that of "A Footman" because I remember having to stand behind Lomas's chair and fill up his glass with port. But the scene was long and I

14

became so entranced by him that when he said: "Fill up, fill up . . ." I simply stared at him and failed to move. He had to repeat the line, which got a laugh, and after that, he allowed me to keep this bit of business in. Lomas had a particularly rich, fruity voice, and when I got home I used to try to imitate him to amuse my parents – very poorly, I am sure.

When you are as young as I was then, every kind of experience is educational, and as the Roaring Twenties had hit even Liverpool, our recreational pursuits certainly qualified as education – of a kind. My friends and I used to go regularly to tea dances in the afternoon, and frequent the lively local dance halls at night, where amazing-looking flappers with bandanas round their hair and short skirts did the Charleston and the Black Bottom. I was very dressy in those days – I can still remember my favourite pair of fashionable beige Oxford bags. And I learned to dance.

It was probably also around this time that I began to affect a monocle with which to scrutinize pretty girls through my bad eye at popular meeting places like the Lyceum Café, where, apart from some ravishing actresses visiting Liverpool with touring companies, I also met the film director Carol Reed, later of *Third Man* fame, who was then a humble actor carrying on a spear in Shakespeare's *Henry VIII* and a pudding in Shaw's *Saint Joan*. Places like the Lyceum Café don't exist any more, and I don't know what young hopefuls do without them. It was a large room full of smoke – there was no cancer scare in those days, everyone smoked away like chimneys. There were lots of tables, no booze, just milky coffee and brewed tea, and those cakes that broke your teeth – the aptly named rock cakes, with currants and raisins – fairy cakes – little cakes with icing on top

– and cream puffs. The waitresses were very old or very young and wore black uniforms with white aprons, but you could sit there for hours over one coffee without them disturbing you.

Another product of the Roaring Twenties was a new, rather "fast" kind of night life in Liverpool. The Adelphi Hotel had opened a nightspot called The Bear Garden, where a noisy "Washboard" band played blues, and other early New Orleans jazz. I used to go there a lot with an art student friend of mine, Arthur Barbosa – he's still a friend, even though many years later he designed a flop I directed on Broadway, a play called *Nina* by the French playwright André Roussin. We used to dance, and listen, and absorb those powerful rhythms, and I think it must have been at The Bear Garden of The Adelphi Hotel in Liverpool that I became seriously addicted to this kind of music. To this day, I am notoriously fond of jazz.

CHAPTER 2

"I'VE GOT A TOUR!"

I stayed only one season in Liverpool, and then I decided that I'd better go to London to seek my fame and fortune. So my mother very sweetly took me in the train from Lime Street Station in Liverpool down to London where I was going to stay with my Aunt Evelyn in Leinster Gardens, W.2. My aunt had a lot of daughters, my cousins, and they were all delighted to see me, so I settled in there quite comfortably. Aunt Evelyn was a big cosy woman who mothered me and took care of me, so I had a very warm and secure base from which to start finding my way around London. This wasn't easy. I'd never been to London, and so, of course, it was all very strange and exciting. I loved it. My first priority was, of course, looking for work, and trying to get a job, and I found there was a place in London in Coventry Street called Sandy's Bar. I don't know how I heard of it, I think I bumped into Jack Minster who had also left Liverpool at the end of the season, and knew the ropes in London better than I did, and he said why don't you come along to Sandy's Bar, there are a lot of out-of-work actors there,

17

and they'll give you some tips. So I went along to Sandy's Bar and that became my home-from-home for a number of weeks, because there was a whole bunch of young kids there all looking for work.

It must have been at Sandy's Bar that I first heard about Connie. She was an agent who seemed to me at the time to be a comic figure about a hundred years old, but she knew the business very well, and most of the young hopeful actors in London found their way to her offices, and sat about there for hours when they got fed up with sitting in Sandy's Bar. I was lucky really, because I got quite a lot of little parts, not because I was any good, but because I was "presentable" – the type of "young gentleman" they needed in the plays of that period. And there is no doubt about it that the only way to learn how to act is to act. And then Jack Minster again befriended me, and we used to go to the theatre together. He took me under his wing, a slightly suspicious wing, I always felt, but as I was, even then, so earnestly devoted to the female sex, I was completely safe. We used to queue up for the gallery and go to see all the plays that were on, and that was the beginning for me of the magic of the theatre, when I began to see why I had wanted to do this extraordinary thing, because I was lucky enough to see a lot of wonderful actors of that period, who were all specializing in comedy.

There was Sir Gerald Du Maurier (1873–1934), there was Sir Charles Hawtrey (1853–1923), there was Ronnie Squire (1886–1958), there were Ralph Lynne and Tom Walls, there was A. E. Matthews, any number of these high comedy actors, who held the town. They were very popular. They were very immaculately dressed. They played comedy as if they weren't playing comedy at all. Unlike Mr Harcourt at Liverpool, they weren't forcing anything, they were very relaxed, very easy with it all, not apparently trying for one second to make an audience laugh, and yet succeeding triumphantly in entertaining audiences with the plays of Lonsdale and Maugham, and the plays I'd seen done very stiffly in Liverpool by, I suppose, looking back on it, some fairly second-rate actors. It was magical watching these men and wondering how they could come on and without apparently any effort at all, throw a line away and hit an audience right between the eyes, so that they fell off their seats with laughter. I watched spellbound from the galleries. It was a wonderful experience, and I think that was the beginning of my realizing what I would like to try to do with my career, if I had any luck.

Constantly watching such expert actors in such excellent productions was the best kind of education I could have had. It was the time of the carefully crafted theatrical vehicle, as often as not written around the personality of one of the great actors or actresses of the day. Acting then was much more a matter of the personality of the performer than it is today, and many great writers fashioned their plays with the sole purpose of exploiting these popular personalities. They were so relaxed on stage they appeared to me like drawing-room types who made you believe they had just popped into the theatre for a spot of acting on the way to the club. There was nothing at which these elegant men didn't seem at ease, whether it was wearing a dinner jacket, opening or closing the inevitable French windows, or manipulating a cigarette case, something which Du Maurier had made into a fine art on its own. These were men who thought nothing of balancing a cup of tea in one hand and a duchess in the other. What a nerve I had – pale, lanky, unsure lad that I was at the time – to try to model myself on them!

Well, what with all this watching and admiring, and getting the hang of the small parts I was offered, one thing led to another, and I heard from my friends in Sandy's Bar that Jevan Brandon Thomas, who was the son of the man who had written a play called *Charley's Aunt*, was looking for some juveniles. He lived in one of the big squares north of the park, so I bravely put on my only decent suit and sallied forth to give an interview to Mr Brandon Thomas. I rang the bell and I was ushered into the living room by a manservant, and Jevan Brandon Thomas came into the room. He was a tall, nice-looking man with whom I hit it off right away. He was very easy, very relaxed, and we chatted about one thing and another and he said he thought I'd be absolutely perfect to play the leading juvenile part in *Charley's Aunt*, the part of an undergraduate called Jack. As luck would have it, I didn't even have to audition for him, he was so sure that I was a gentleman, which was the only thing he was looking for, really. The Brandon Thomas family had become rather snobbish after the great success of *Charley's Aunt* and the fortune they'd made from it, and they liked to insist it was cast with well-bred juveniles. They wanted young ladies and gentlemen in the play, and presumably, even then, they were fairly hard to find. He was so sure, he didn't bother to read me, he just said, "Oh yes, you'd be excellent!" So I left Brandon Thomas's house in a whirl of excitement, thinking: "My God, I've got a tour!" And I had.

And that was just a piece of extraordinary good fortune, because *Charley's Aunt* – that tried and true old warhorse of a piece – was the perfect vehicle for learning the business of playing comedy. It was toured a great deal in those days, and had become something of a mainstay of the touring companies. Part of the play's great charm is that it is set in Oxford in the college rooms of two undergraduates, Jack Chesney and Charley Wickham. The two boys badly want to invite some girls up to their rooms, two properly brought up young ladies, as Jevan Brandon Thomas would say, and the rules were that undergraduates were not allowed to have young ladies in their rooms unless they had chaperones. Now Charley had an aunt who was coming over from Brazil to see him, and the boys planned to use the aunt's visit to have the girls up, making her seem the chaperone.

When Charley's aunt writes and tells them she can't come, they are terribly disappointed, and they are discussing how awful it all is with a friend called Babs (for Babbington-something) when Babs gets the idea that he'll dress up as Charley's aunt so the girls can come. He puts on a wig and a dress and becomes Charley's aunt from Brazil "where the Nuts come from". He's not very successful at pretending to be a Brazilian lady, but he finds it rather fun because he can flirt with the girls and pinch their bottoms and they don't seem to mind because, of course, they think he's another girl. They also think he's rather weird, but Jack and Charley don't care about this because they're able, at last, to have their girlfriends up into their rooms at Oxford.

This is going pretty well, and Jack and Charley think they've got it made, but then an older man called Spettigue, guardian to one of the boys, turns up, and into the middle of this comes the real aunt, who has decided that she mustn't let the boys down after all. Naturally, complications ensue from there being two aunts, and the boys trying to keep the two of them from bumping into one another, and also to keep the girls from meeting the real one. It becomes a question of keeping the real aunt out, and having the phoney aunt in, as much as possible, a typical but genuinely funny, farcical situation. And what is nice is that at the end of the play everybody matches

21

up – the two boys with the two girls, and Spettigue with the real aunt, though as far as I can remember the chap who dresses up as the phoney aunt doesn't get anybody. But it all ends happily, as farces did in those days – it's a pantomime, a wonderful pantomime, and such fun to do because the moment the undergraduate dresses up as the aunt it's a riot of fun, especially if the actor playing the phoney aunt is good. We had an awfully good one, who'd played it many times before.

I didn't get much of a chance to emulate my urbane heroes, Du Maurier, Hawtrey & Co. in *Charley's Aunt*, not only because it's a pretty broad and rather simple-minded farce, but because we had a dullish company full of "ladies and gentlemen", and the ladies who played Kitty and Amy – you probably remember the song "Once in love with Amy" from the musical made of *Charley's Aunt* – were so ladylike they bored the tears out of me. The person I do remember, though, was James E. Page, the funny old bird who played the undergraduate's guardian, Spettigue. He wore a frock coat and a top hat, and he used to do extraordinary things on stage with his top hat to try to make us youngsters laugh. James E. Page had originated the part of Spettigue, which meant that he must have been playing it for about thirty years. He was, understandably, bored out of his mind, so he used to turn his back to the audience, take his false teeth out and throw them up in the air and catch them in his top hat, then turn on us with a beaming, toothless smile. Naturally, this made us all laugh non-stop, and, in fact, as far as I can remember I spent the entire tour in stitches of laughter at the antics of James E. Page.

Laughter on stage is a very dangerous thing – I had first come across it at Liverpool one night when Cecil Parker had been seized by an uncontrollable fit of laughter on stage, and was to be seen helplessly waving a handkerchief about in an absolute paroxysm. He left the stage in order to regain control of himself, and then re-entered, only to collapse again with mirth, and because I could not see what he was laughing at (I was in the audience, not on stage), I remember thinking his behaviour quite extraordinary. Nothing alienates an audience quite so much as actors laughing at a private joke which they, the audience, cannot see, but I hadn't learned that lesson yet. Jevan Brandon Thomas kept coming up and reprimanding us for giggling on the stage, and at one point he had a long talk with me, the essence of which was that I would have to leave the cast if I didn't stop laughing on stage. As a result of this I suppose I did learn to control myself a little more, but I was, like so many novice actors, using laughter on stage, however subconsciously, to relieve my tension at being on stage at all. Latterly, I have been accused – by the young actors and actresses I worked with at the Haymarket in J.M. Barrie's *The Admirable Crichton* – of making *them* laugh uncontrollably on stage! They, however, seemed to cope with my bad behaviour a great deal better than I did with that of James E. Page.

During the *Charley's Aunt* tour I got so fed up with the ladies and gentlemen of the cast that when we were playing a town called Whitby which is a seaside watering place on the east coast of England, I decided to go in for a local dancing competition. I couldn't bear to go in for it with either of the two young ladies in the company so I asked the barmaid at the local hotel in Whitby – I think it was called The Talbot Arms – if she'd come and dance with me. She did – she was a very sweet little thing – we did the Fox Trot, and I won The East Coast Dancing Championship while I was playing Whitby! I needed relief from the monotony of the company. My attitude to work was still pretty light-hearted, I suppose, and I hadn't yet learned the gentle art of concealment. I hadn't learned very much at all, I'm afraid, and I will have to continue the narrative to find out when I did start this extremely difficult thing of being able to act properly.

I suppose I did, without realizing it, learn quite a lot when I was touring in *Charley's Aunt* because there were all sorts of things you couldn't help learning. Just by going on stage eight times a week you learned the differences in audiences, for instance. You learned things like how to fill different-sized theatres with your voice, and you began to realize that there was such thing as a back wall which you had to reach. You couldn't just be inaudible. I don't think we were inaudible in that company, though the company was pretty awful, as I remember it – ladylike and gentlemanlike, but audible. The juvenile lead in *Charley's Aunt* is really a supporting role, and the job of a supporting actor is to "feed" the star his lines. On that tour I learned that you cannot "feed" lines unless you are audible. I had to "feed" the Aunt, and I soon saw that if I could not be heard, the other poor chap couldn't get his laughs. To be a good feed, every word must be heard. When I started, I think I was appalling because I was far too confident. I simply had no idea how difficult the whole thing was. I don't think any of us realizes when we first go on stage how very difficult good acting is. It looks so easy when it's done well – enthralling, exciting – and easy!

I did about ten years of touring after *Charley's Aunt*, and the sum total was learning a great deal about audience reactions. One difference I always found very fascinating was the difference between North Country audiences and audiences in the south of England, because the North Country audience is on the whole a dour thing. They are pretty dour people in the north, they can't help it, poor darlings, the weather is so bloody awful up there, and the towns in those days were pretty bleak. It was the industrial period where there were a few wealthy people who lived in large houses outside these towns, and the towns themselves, in which we lived in digs run by landladies, were rows and rows and rows of dark dingy little houses, no sign of much foliage, and people just went to work in the pits or in the docks every day.

But the south was always better. The people who visited our productions in the country towns in the south of England were farmers, they had livestock, owned farms some of them, and their surroundings weren't so dismal, therefore they were much more relaxed as audiences, had much more fun in the theatre, and were more easily amused. They would be hysterical with laughter at *Charley's Aunt* a lot of the time in the south. In the north they treated it all much more seriously because they themselves were having such a rotten time with their lives, and I suppose that's why it was that they were so tough to move in any direction.

One has to remember, of course, that the provincial theatre was enormously lively in those days, certainly in the south, because, for every London success, two companies went out to the provinces. There were managements in London – Barry O'Brien was the name of one – who made a very good living by sending out such touring companies. Naturally, it depended on how good the play was, and how successful it had been in London, but if the play was good, and the manager got a good company together, he made a lot of money in the provinces. I was very lucky to be around at the time all this was happening, because movies and television later on squashed touring days, and the provincial theatres are no longer in the same state as when I was playing them in the Twenties, Thirties and Forties. Many beautiful old provincial theatres have been pulled down now, but in those days they were the centre of a booming business.

Among a lot of plays I did when I was touring was a play called *A Cup of Kindness*, by Ben Travers. Ben Travers was a marvellous farceur who wrote all the plays which Ralph Lynne and Tom Walls did at the Aldwych Theatre, and all three of them were amongst the people I admired more than almost anybody else. When I was going around seeing plays with Jack Minster, and seeing Du Maurier and Hawtrey, I used to go to the Aldwych regularly and fall off my chair laughing at Ralph Lynne and Tom Walls. They were total opposites. Ralph Lynne was very thin, he had an eye-glass and made a lot of hand movements, and was very funny in his own particular way: he played the youngish, "Silly Ass" type of character. Tom Walls was very fat with a huge moustache, didn't move much, was very static and relaxed, and played the older, rather more solid types. They were a marvellous foil for each other, they'd been acting together for so long, they had become the perfect combination. Their timing was incredible, and their talents had, by now, become entirely complementary. They were unforgettable. Ben Travers wrote his plays especially for them, and one play after another came off his pen. They all ran for about a year, they were wonderfully funny plays, and Ralph Lynne and Tom Walls were wonderfully funny together in them, and very celebrated.

By the time I had to play in a farce, I knew a lot about Ralph Lynne, and I copied him, not slavishly, but I used to try to do some of his hand movements because they were so extraordinarily original, and not corny at all. He was so good that, in spite of being a farceur, he was getting into a form of naturalism, though you can never be truly naturalistic in farce. It is one of the extraordinary things that the difference between high comedy and farce is that farce is an unnatural medium and high comedy is a naturalistic medium. There are many different kinds of comedy, and I like, and have learned a lot from all of them. Farce, with its broad strokes and exaggerated, almost pantomime types for characters is at one end of the spectrum, and high comedy, subtle, sophisticated, often using wit to unfold a situation with as much substance in it as any straight play, is at the other. In drama, the spectrum runs from melodrama to high drama; in comedy it runs from farce to high comedy. The difference, therefore, between farce and high comedy is of paramount importance.

To put it in a nutshell, high comedy is a form of truth, and farce takes it beyond truth into the realms of idiocy.

Because farce is broad comedy, and the strokes are very broad, an actor has to go slightly overboard to get the best out of it. Farce is comedy's equivalent of melodrama, and if a farceur, an actor who generally plays farce, were to appear in a high comedy he would overdo it in the same way as a melodramatic actor would overact in a high drama. If he did that we'd describe him as a ham, someone who overacts. Overacting is as out of place in high comedy as it would be in the most subtle of dramas, and an actor can easily push a comedy piece over into farce by overacting. You can see farce acting on television every time you switch it on because most of the television writing is pretty broad, so actors in television almost always seem to be playing farce.

As you can probably tell from my tone, I don't like farce very much. Except when superbly done, it's very broad and very obvious to me, which means that a farcical actor doesn't have to be real; he can, if he wants to, be totally unreal, à la Mickey Rooney in the recent show, *Sugar Babies*. He can stick his tongue out, let his trousers down,

27

do everything to make the plebs laugh a lot. The average audience adores farce because they don't realize that it's fairly easy for an actor to let his drawers down, and they think it's amazingly funny, whereas I was always interested in keeping my drawers up and making an audience laugh by being a little subtler than that. Of course, the top-flight farceurs never took the easy option. Walls and Lynne were the height of farce, and they, to my certain knowledge, never stooped to letting their trousers down.

In acting terms, farceurs don't try to conceal the fact that they're being funny, whereas in high comedy we do try to conceal the fact that we're amusing the audience. The farceur will do it right into the audience's face, and it is much easier to do it right at them than to do it sideways on and pretend you aren't doing it at all. Good high comedy is as truthful as drama, but it needs a more intelligent audience. I've specialized in high comedy, but I've done an awful lot of other things, including tragedy. If somebody can play high comedy, they can play almost anything, I think. It's very difficult to achieve the appearance of not working terribly hard, but that's the object of the exercise, and that can apply to any form of drama, and to tragedy as well. You should be able to make an audience cry as apparently easily as you can make them laugh, and it is this apparent effortlessness which you have to master.

Acting is bad acting if the actor himself gets very emotional in the act of making the audience cry. The object of the exercise is to make the audience cry but not cry yourself, any more than it is to make the audience laugh, and laugh yourself. This is where the difficulty lies. The emotion has to be inside the actor, not outside. You have to feel it, or you won't be able to make an audience feel it, but you mustn't show you're feeling it. You must control your own emotion, so you let them feel it. If you stand up there on

28

stage weeping and wailing, all your emotion will go down your shirt, and nothing will go out across the footlights to the audience. Audience control is really about the actor's control of his own emotions. A good actor's tears remain at the back of his eyes.

Good actors do probably have to feel things more strongly than other people, but they have to control their feelings more, and this explains why quite often, in real life, they are withdrawn, and only really alive when they're on stage. You have to have a lot of emotion inside you to be an actor in the first place, but you can't afford to use it up in ordinary social life. You have to store up your most intense kind of energy, both emotional and physical, to achieve the kind of control we're talking about, and only let your feelings out on stage.

Mind you, I can remember one incident, fairly early on in my career, in which an actor did take his emotions out on the audience. We were playing the New Cross Empire, in south London, in a popular piece of the time called *The Chinese Bungalow*. An actor called Butler had the title role of a wicked Chinaman, for which he was dressed in Chinese robes, and held his hands in his sleeves. Suddenly, in the middle of the play, the rough London suburban audience turned violently anti-Chinese, and started barracking poor Butler.

When he could stand the heckling no longer, he pulled his hands out of his Chinese sleeves, marched down to the footlights, dropped his Chinese accent, and gave them an amazing earful in their own vivid Cockney. Not until they'd calmed down, did he walk back, put his hands back in his sleeves, resume his Chinese accent and go on with the play. I was on stage at the time, playing the planter, dressed in white ducks and solar topee, and I sat through all this amazed at his boldness.

*

Touring was a pretty tough life in those days – moving from one grim little town to another, staying in fairly grotty digs with motherly – or bossy! – landladies. They were characters, the landladies, some were old pro's – retired actresses – some were old biddies, but most of them were nice old things, and all of them gave my weak stomach the rough treatment by feeding it boiled beef and dumplings with overcooked cabbage, and revolting desserts like sponge rolypoly, spotted dick, or suet pudding with jam. Oddly enough, this coal heaver's diet of unremitting stodge seemed to cure my weak tummy, and also – up to a point – my lifelong hypochondria. I was always consulting doctors, and carrying round pills for every little twinge, and the touring life knocked all, or most of that out of me – like going away to boarding school, I suppose.

We travelled between towns by train, playing from Monday to Saturday, and on Sundays the whole company would board the train, and we'd eat our sandwiches or whatever, and try to find out if anyone knew of decent digs (or lodgings) to share in the next town. It sounds like fun, but it was too uncomfortable and we were probably too tired to enjoy it much. Apart from every provincial town that has a theatre, I think I've played every pier in every seaside town in Britain, including some deserted ones out of season. No families, or people with "real" jobs travelled on the trains on Sundays – even our scenery and costumes went separately, by night – so the trains we travelled on were full of fish and actors.

At the end of these gruelling journeys, we had always to find ourselves somewhere to stay. The managements were no help at all, and theatrical lodgings were always in the same dingy working-class areas of town, where landladies let out bedrooms and sitting rooms for thirty shillings (about $2) a week, plus food – breakfast, and supper left out for after the show – cold ham and salad, cold beef, perhaps stew, sometimes beer. Generally, a few of us shared digs, and ate supper together, so it wasn't in any way a solitary life. We drank beer for winding down after the show because it was the cheapest thing we could get.

You had to be careful of your health, too, because you couldn't afford to miss a performance. If you got 'flu and missed a week they'd replace you, and if you missed a day you'd be docked, which in those days meant quite a lot. I wasn't strong as a young boy, or when I was growing up, but somehow I kept going. You knew it could be very serious if you caught a cold, which in those northern climes it was easy enough to do. You still had to go on every night, get to the theatre, make up, and somehow find the energy to do your part. I was still very young and these were the "rigours of the profession", and this is where the motherly old landladies helped. They were very sweet, and tried to look after us, though the rackety old bathrooms in their houses didn't help, generally freezing cold, with ancient sinks, baths and lavatories, broken-down geysers called Ascots for hot water, of which there was never enough. By today's standards they were not even very clean, though I dare say, clean enough.

During these tours, as I have said, I was beginning to learn my trade, as well as its rigours, without really knowing I was learning anything. Until then the only theatre I'd known the feel of was the Liverpool Repertory Theatre, with the particular size and shape of its stage and auditorium, and its particular acoustics. Now I was learning the all-important trick of pitching my voice correctly for all kinds, shapes and sizes of theatres, and getting used to judging the level of projection which would make sure my voice carried to any auditorium back wall. Until you

31

know this, you can't begin to develop a style as an actor, let alone a naturalistic style. You are still too concerned with making yourself heard.

We got precious little help in this department, for the directors of tours were more like stage managers – often they had been the stage managers of the London production of the show. They were hired by the management for the duration of the tour, which meant they were able to give us the plotting of the London show, and the moves we were to make, but little more. So there was no real direction, as such.

The great value of my training, however, was that it was got in this hard school, and was not scholastic in any way. I didn't go to acting school, to voice coaches, or to doctors to see what was wrong with me, or to make sure I wouldn't lose my voice. I was very fortunate with my voice, in that I was born with a strong vocal box, and it has stood the rigours of time very well. I think this is because I have always produced it right. Once you produce your voice correctly, it is apt to serve you well, whereas if you constantly strangle it, it will not.

Tours are invaluable training grounds for this because they teach you to find the right pitch. You are forced to hold the attention of difficult, restless audiences, and keep them quiet, so you learn the hard way that audibility is the essence, and you learn to judge the back wall of most theatres, and reach, or hit that back wall with your voice. You get to know when the audience in the back rows and in the gallery can hear you, and after a while you become so experienced at this business of "bouncing off the back wall" of the house, you only have to look at a theatre to know how much pitch it needs. Then, and only then, are you free to work on your performance, and – in my case – start to polish up my favoured naturalistic style.

CHAPTER 3

A SENSE OF STYLE

Any amount of naturalistic style couldn't help me, though, in the next play I chose to do, because after my first long tour, I accepted a small part in Shakespeare in London in *Richard III*. I was taking anything that came along, at that point, and Balliol Holloway, who was a celebrated Shakespearean actor at the time, was playing the hunchback king, Richard III. I had several little parts. I played a soldier, and was asked the question:

Where is Lord Stanley quarter'd, dost thou know?

And I had to say:

His regiment lies half a mile at least
South from the mighty power of the king.

Well, that sounds very easy when you say it now, but I thought it was an awful line, so come the night, I get the question:

'Where is Lord Stanley quarter'd, dost thou know?'

And I said:

'His regiment lies half a mile at least East . . .
no . . .
South . . . from the power of the king of France.'

The King of France hadn't been heard of, of course, in
Richard III and I didn't know what to do.

Balliol Holloway gave me a funny look and the play
went on, but it worried me very much that I'd totally
fluffed this line, and I stayed awake all night thinking
about it, and saying it over and over to myself in my
head and out loud: "His regiment lies half a mile at
least/South of the mighty power of the king." But the
next night, as my cue approached, I panicked and I
thought: I can't do it, I can't go on, so I got lost in the
scene change. I hid behind the flat, I dodged around, I
missed my entrance on purpose, and I wasn't there. So
the chap said: "Where is Lord Stanley quarter'd, dost thou
know?" and got no answer. He looked round and saw I
wasn't there, and the play went on, he didn't wait for an
answer, he just went on. I think it was then that I learned
that there's one rather valuable thing about Shakespeare,
which is that it doesn't matter if you're off because nobody
understands it anyway! At least, I never did, and that's
one of the reasons why I find Shakespeare so difficult to
act, and also so difficult even to listen to, because a lot of
the time I don't understand what anybody's saying. It's
like listening to a lot of people sitting in a pub speaking
Welsh. I know he's a great playwright and all that –
"Our Beloved Shakespeare" – and I shouldn't be saying

this, but I do find him very difficult to understand, let alone play.

I also had another line in that production: "What is't o'clock?" somebody said to me, and I had to say: "Upon the stroke of four!" And everybody said that "Upon the stroke of four", I lifted up my chainmail and had a look at my wristwatch! This is totally incorrect, of course, because I do know that they didn't wear wristwatches in those days, but a sort of little joke went round. Anyway "Upon the stroke of four!" wasn't *declaimed* enough, I was told, so that line was taken away from me, and another man said, "UPON THE STROKE OF FOUR!", or, "UPON the STROKE of four!", or whatever it was, and I remember it was Bernard Miles who got the line. He was a nice chap and a good Shakespearean actor (as befits the founder of the Mermaid Theatre), so they gave him the line, and I was left with "His regiment lies South of the mighty power of the king – of France!"

Well, after that small brush with the Bard, I realized that my forte was not Shakespeare, and certainly not that extrovert acting that is needed for the Bard, and my mind went longingly back to Squire, and Matthews and Du Maurier and Hawtrey and their understated naturalistic style, though I was nowhere near getting it right. I was struggling towards that aim. It's not an easy aim, but for me it was easier than Shakespeare, and the forward and extroverted kind of acting which is the quintessence of Shakespeare. You have, of course, to be asked: "What is't o'clock?" to be able to answer it properly. I don't want anybody to ask me: "What is't o'clock?" because I don't enjoy the Elizabethan act of saying: "Upon the stroke of ten", or upon the stroke of anything. I don't know why. It's something to do with my genes, I suppose. If anything I prefer: "Got the time on yer, cock?" glancing nervously down at my flies. It amuses me more.

I think the first time I really found my feet in the theatre at all was on a tour of a very interesting play called *After All* written by John Van Druten. It was a story of the eternal conflict between the generations, in which the son and daughter of a middle-class English family in Kensington rebel against their parents. The daughter leaves home to live with a married man, and the son for an artist's studio and a Bohemian, night-club sort of life. But years later they both crave the peace and domesticity of their old home which once bored them to tears. My part was, of course, that of the rebellious son, Ralph, which had been played first by Laurence Olivier in the original production at The Arts Theatre Club in 1930, opposite an actress called Elissa Landi as the sister, with Helen Haye as the mother, and Cathleen Nesbitt as a girl called Greta. In 1931 the play transferred to the Criterion Theatre, where Robert Douglas played the part of Ralph opposite the beautiful Madeleine Carroll. I can't think why my old friend Larry Olivier didn't go on into the Criterion production. I can only suppose that he had got involved in one of his classical, or Shakespearean plays, and preferred doing that to what the *Daily Telegraph* critic Sydney W. Carroll described as "this exquisitely English comedy of middle-class life".

Anyway, the play was a great success at the Criterion, where, apart from Robert Douglas and Madeleine Carroll as the brother and sister, Lillian Braithwaite played the mother, and I got the part of Ralph for the first tour that went out. John Van Druten had written what turned out to be a marvellous part for me, and it was in that play that I began to find my way towards a degree of naturalism and, I think, to mobilize a certain amount of inner energy.

I enjoyed doing that play enormously, and it seemed to me the first time I hit my stride. I looked up some old reviews for the purpose of this book, and it was nice to find that some critics agreed with me! the *Birmingham Post* said that I played the part "with such charm and humour and humanity" that I made the best juvenile he had ever seen! "His impertinence is equally as good as his pathos," this perceptive man went on, "and he has the natural easy manner which makes the character one to remember."

The two women in the play with me were Violet Vanburgh and her daughter Prudence Vanburgh, who was a good six or eight inches taller than me, and I'm six foot! Auriol Lee, who had directed all three productions of the play, had clearly asked Prudence to do the part in order to get her mother, who was a leading actress of the day, and was ideal to play the mother, the part Lillian Braithwaite had played with Robert Douglas, and Helen Haye had played with Larry. The fact that as my sister Phyl in the play, Prudence towered over me quite a bit didn't seem to matter. We just weathered on, and as the provincial theatre was still booming at that time, and this was a play pleasing to both generations of playgoers, we did a very long and very successful tour, starting at the Princes Theatre, Manchester, in October 1931, going to the Princes Theatre, Birmingham, the Kings Theatre, Glasgow, the Lyceum at Edinburgh, the Grand at Leeds and the Theatre Royal at York. I enjoyed that tour enormously. It was really the first time I felt I was getting anywhere, and managing to do just a little bit towards the relaxation I wanted to get, and the inner energy I was striving for.

It is odd to think that at the same time I was trying for the greatest possible naturalism, a lot of my contemporaries were developing a completely different technique where they were obviously acting very hard. This may have been because they chose to act in dramatic plays rather than in the kind of high comedy parts which require the niceties of acting with which you disguise the fact that you *are* acting. Classical drama demands a very different approach which is often the reverse of mine, and it is obvious that in the great classical tragedies you cannot always go so far towards naturalism as to disguise the fact that you're acting at all. The truth is there have always been lots of different styles of acting in the theatre at any one time. Yet good acting is always good acting, and the rules for it haven't changed.

As I've said, my style derived from the high comedy style popular in the early years of this century, exemplified by Sir Charles Hawtrey and Sir Gerald Du Maurier, and is in a different tradition from the Olivier/Gielgud style which derived from the grand classical acting of the same period, as practised by Sir Henry Irving and Sir Herbert Beerbohm Tree. But those actors had other actors in their period, as I had Olivier and Gielgud in mine, who were acting away in neighbouring theatres in a different style, and both styles were popular and represented perfectly good acting of its kind. I suppose that when Hawtrey and Du Maurier were appearing in their polished high comedies, in the form of naturalism which I love, they had the Irvings and the Trees acting away in theatres down the road, and screaming and yelling and waving their arms about.

Sometimes I wonder whether, if I'd gone to see the classics when I was young and impressionable as assiduously as I went to the Aldwych farces or the plays Du Maurier was in, I'd have been influenced to go in a completely different direction altogether. I think that's a doubtful proposition, though, because temperament obviously has a lot to do with it. How you act depends, in the end, on your own personality, on yourself. And, more than anything, it depends on your sense of humour, and your sense of humour about yourself. Humour's relation to acting is a subject in itself, and it interests me very much. To do the kind of portentous acting the classical roles call for, however, you've got to take yourself very seriously indeed. And you've got to love the essence of Shakespeare, and of the Elizabethan theatre, which was so different, in every way, from ours.

Take, for example, Larry Olivier's rendition of the Elizabethan verse plays. Thinking back over those remarkable performances of his I feel that Larry excelled because he allowed a little of the twentieth century to creep in. Not much, just a touch – but enough to allow him to make Shakespeare very understandable. For instance, if he'd been in that production of *Richard III* where I did everything wrong, and he'd said "What is't o'clock?" you wouldn't have thought that was strange at all. You'd have thought he'd said "What's the time?" He had a gift for making Shakespeare sound contemporary, and though his style of acting was so completely different from mine, he achieved this effect by introducing a degree of naturalism into Shakespeare which made it immediately understandable to huge audiences.

In the hands of an old-fashioned Shakespearean actor, the line "What is't o'clock?" would be as bad as when I did it. Olivier knew how to refine that kind of thing. He was a very controlled actor, who may have gone into bravura acting in the big arias, but was generally very subtle. He was quite wonderful, I think, and one of the things I liked best about his work was that his humour always came through in it, especially in his *Richard III*. It was rather bizarre, black humour but it was certainly there in that play, and in the film he made of it.

I daresay that if Olivier had been fifty years older than

I was, and had been acting at the time I was young and pliable, his influence might have tempted me away from high comedy towards the classics. I think that, even then, I would have appreciated what he was doing when he played Shakespeare. Most of the other actors of his generation including Gielgud, declaimed Shakespeare, whereas Olivier did not. He was effective because he was truthful, and none of his contemporaries could come anywhere near him in the particular form of acting he'd perfected. Gielgud was always very mannered, and would speak the Shakespearean verse as though it should have been accompanied by music. There is no naturalism at all in his work. But it seems to me, looking back on Olivier's achievements, that the form of naturalism he brought to Shakespeare was quite original. I admired his acting very much.

Another actor among my contemporaries, whose approach to naturalism I liked, was Ralph Richardson. Richardson had a unique sense of humour which fitted him very well for naturalistic parts. He was very eccentric – almost the quintessential eccentric Englishman – and he understood that sense of self-deprecation, that special irony, to be found in so many English plays. He did some wonderful things. I remember him, especially, in a play I did myself on Broadway after he had done it first in London – William Douglas Home's *The Kingfisher*. He was marvellous! And very, very funny. The importance of humour to acting is exemplified, really, by Richardson. He was a unique character, both on and off the stage, and used to do quite crazy things, like drive his motorcycle to the theatre on the pavement, which wasn't only daring, it was downright dangerous!

There is a story that once, during rehearsals for a rather weird production of *Othello* at that exciting Old Vic season they did just after the war, Olivier suddenly grabbed Ralph and kissed him passionately on the mouth because he, Larry, had decided to play Iago as a homosexual in love with Othello. Richardson drew himself away with dignity and said soothingly: "There, there, dear boy! My dear, DEAR boy!" The idea for this homosexual Iago had come from the director, Tyrone Guthrie, who had been reading the psycho-analyst Ernest Jones, who in his turn had been applying the insights of Freudian psycho-analysis to the Shakespearean texts of *Hamlet* and *Othello*. But Ralph wasn't having any of it. The theatre is full of wonderful Richardson stories, and we all miss him very much indeed.

Richardson's special brand of madness makes me wistful. I have always admired the actors who had a touch of madness about them, and who could get it into their parts on stage. Another such actor I admired was Wilfred Lawson, who, among other things, had played Doolittle in *Pygmalion* in the theatre, early on. He certainly had a streak of madness in him, had Lawson, and this was compounded by the fact that he was a pretty good drinker. There's a story about him, that he was in the pub next to the theatre he was appearing in one day, drinking happily and chumming up with some of the chaps, and when the show was due to start he invited them all into the theatre with him. But he went and sat down with them in the stalls, and, as the play went on, he nudged them eagerly, and said: "Now watch this bit! This bit is good – it's where I come on!"

Talking about the techniques of acting, or the different styles of acting, is not something which comes naturally to me, as the reader may have gathered. This may be because I have spent so long actually acting, rather than thinking about it, and may also have to do with the peculiar nature of what I've spent so long doing. Making acting look like natural behaviour calls upon your instincts and your eye rather more than your analytic powers. I am reminded, here, of something my old friend James Hill said on this subject:

"Ask the hundred-yard-dash man how he runs faster than anyone else in the world. He can't tell you. Ask Joe di Maggio what he does when he gets out there on the field. He can't tell you. Or, at best he'd say: 'I watch the ball leave the pitcher's hand, that's all.' Well, asking Rex Harrison what he does when he gets on stage is like asking Joe di Maggio what he does when the ball leaves the pitcher's hand. Actually, Rex has quite a lot in common with the Joe di Maggios of the world – a great natural, instinctive talent, his own unique style, and unbelievable powers of concentration. He's a rarity in his profession, in that he has great athletic coordination, which Rita (Hayworth) and I used to see demonstrated when we all played golf."

The Broadway producer, Eliott Martin, who has produced many of the plays I've done in New York, including the current one, Somerset Maugham's *The Circle*, says that a great deal of my success is due to the sense of danger I convey. This may seem an odd kind of comment, but when you think of actors who can really hold an audience, grip them by the throat and capture their attention, this sense of danger – of unpredictability, and possibly, even, imminent violence of some sort – is one quality they all share. And a dangerous personality is clearly attractive to the opposite sex. Think of Richard Burton, or Peter O'Toole. Think, above all of Larry Olivier. In his kind of classical acting there were two kinds of danger – the danger of the rapier and the danger of the broadsword. Gielgud also conveyed this necessary sense of danger, but his was of the rapier variety. Richardson's was more the broadsword. Only Olivier combined them both.

The kind of style you develop as an actor has, of course, a lot to do with the kind of material you choose to act, and this is something on which an actor must bring all his intelligence to bear because it's very difficult to get it right. I've always tried to choose material that suited me, that I wanted to do and knew I could do, and the same thing applies to most leading actors. I'm sure Larry, who had a much more extrovert personality than mine, chose the material which would best suit his extrovert personality. Looking back, I think I can say that I enjoyed doing almost all the major parts I played, with the exception of certain unplayable characters like the warrior Pope in the film about Michaelangelo, *The Agony and the Ecstasy*, which I did with Charlton Heston, or the homosexual in the film *The Staircase* which I did with Richard Burton, and it is very satisfying to find that on the whole I did manage to select material which was not out of my range, or silly for me to do.

Some actors actually wrote the parts which fitted their own personalities, and the style they wanted to play, like Noel Coward, whose characters were him, and generally he played them on the stage himself the first time round. This made it pretty difficult to follow him, which I had to do in 1939 in *Design for Living*. He'd played himself in the first production on Broadway, opposite the Lunts, and I played his part at the Theatre Royal, Haymarket, London, opposite Anton Walbrook and Diana Wynyard. This was a situation you couldn't win, and may well have been when Noel first uttered his much quoted remark about me: "Rex Harrison is the best light comedian in the business – after me!" What most people don't know, however, is that there's another version of this, which goes: "If Rex

43

Harrison wasn't the best light comedian in the business after me, he'd be a car salesman!" It's a wonder, really, that he and I remained on speaking terms!

Richard Burton commented in his diaries on the first, and better known of those two Cowardisms, after seeing me in the revival of *My Fair Lady* I did in 1980. "I would say they were at least even, with Rex having the edge." Then Richard goes on to make some interesting observations about my style of acting. "Rex's brand of acting and his off stage personality are inextricably bound together. Most obviously, for instance, Rex's normal private-life voice is the same as the voice on stage – only projected a little more. I think mine is. So is George Scott's, so is Gielgud's, so was Coward's, so is Jason Robards', Fonda's, Richardson's. But Olivier's is totally different, as is Paul Scofield's and Alec Guinness's. Alec and Paul tend to 'boom' on stage, though cathedrically quiet off, and Larry Olivier develops a machine-gun rattle with an occasional shout thrown in 'to keep', as he once said to me, 'the bastards awake'.

"I'm not quite sure whether Larry meant his fellow-actors or the audiences, or both. But one has to be careful with Larry – he is a great dead-pan leg-puller and one is never quite sure whether he is probing very subtly for weak spots or majestically sending one up. Superb good value though, all of them. O'Toole's voice, too, eccentrically accented in private, is the same on stage. I wonder what it means. Does it mean that Olivier, Guinness and Scofield are basically and essentially character actors, while the rest of us mentioned above are simply extensions of ourselves. Well, the more I act and the more I think about it, (which is not very often), the less I know I know of the heart of its mystery. Why one believes absolutely in one actor and knows he's blazingly honest, and not in another equally

44

dazzling player is beyond my competence to explain. I can only accept it and hope for the best."

It was nice to come across that passage in Richard's diaries as it shows that I am not the only one who is mystified, at the end of a long career, at exactly how this peculiar acting magic works.

These ruminations on acting in general, and the different acting styles were brought about, I seem to remember, by my having reached 1931, or the age of twenty-three, in my narrative, and finding, at last, in John Van Druten's play *After All*, something of the right style for me, or at least, the beginnings of my style.

Like most young actors, I was permanently hard-up in those days of the early 1930s because, although I took all the suitable parts I could get, most of them didn't make much money. I remember one amusing play I appeared in by St John Ervine, called *Anthony and Anna*, in which I played a chap who is allergic to work, but graciously hires himself out occasionally for luncheons, dinners, or country weekends. My co-stars were all excellent actors: Carol Goodner, Herbert Lomas, and Bruce Belfrage, but all this was at a theatre called The Shilling Theatre, in Fulham, south-west London, long since gone dark, and its name was a reference to the fact that no seats cost more than a bob – one shilling, or ten cents. By this time, 1934, I had married my first wife, Collette, taken a flat in Bruton Mews, off Berkeley Square in Mayfair, and had my first son, Noel, so I had a family as well as an extremely fast but erratic motor car to support.

Then I got a small part in a play about doctors called *Man of Yesterday*, which went on at the St Martin's Theatre, and starred Leslie Banks and Ann Todd. I played the part of a young doctor. Before the curtain went up I had to go into Leslie Banks' dressing room and put a bandage on his head so that I would know how to take it off again during the action of the play. Banks was playing the leading part and I didn't know him very well, but I knocked politely on the door and went in and put the bandage on his head, and every evening I found him very monosyllabic and very tight and not able, or inclined, to communicate with me at all.

I suppose I was quite hurt by this at the time, but now I understand absolutely why he behaved like that. You have to concentrate very hard before a performance, and it is very difficult to make polite conversation, or indeed any conversation, especially with a young actor who is in the company with you. It is only now, towards the end of my career, that I understand why Leslie was so tense before he went on, because we all are. At the time I wondered why he was apparently so nervous, even though he was such an experienced actor and the play had been running quite a while. I thought that, in time, one would lose all that. I didn't know that you can never afford to slacken up on the intense concentration necessary to control and direct your inner energy. You have to give your utmost to each and every part, however experienced you may be.

At the beginning of your career, to come out in front of an audience and spend the evening pretending to be someone else fills you with tension and nervousness. The lights, the sea of unknown faces, the strangeness of it all are quite a shock to the budding actor's nervous system. He has trouble with the simplest things. The simplest movements seem to pose the most frightening difficulties. For some reason, this kind of early self-consciousness goes straight to the hands and feet, and in particular the hands. I had great trouble with my hands when I first started, and I discovered that the best thing is not to think about them, then they behave quite well, and do the right things for you. But if you start thinking about your hands, it's fairly fatal. It is also true that you feel less naked if your hands are tucked away safely in your trouser pockets, or – even better – doing something. Cigarettes, or drinks, can save an actor's life on stage, though, taken in excess, they may well destroy his off-stage life!

Props like cigars, or cigarettes, or drinks are probably the greatest single influence on timing, and actors find them indispensable. The movements required to take a cigar from a humidor and light and smoke it, for instance, and to pour a glass of port from a heavy cut-glass decanter and drink that, are far less jittery, and far more thoughtful, than those deployed in shaking a cocktail or lighting a cigarette. The actors I grew up admiring were definitely cigar and port actors, they were acting in plays written before the advent of the cigarette-holder and the dry martini, and their timing was different, their movements slower, more thoughtful and less hectic. Lighting a cigar could take endless time, because you would really light, and smoke, a real cigar – it's not something you can fake.

Now that smoking has gone out of fashion, the whole practice of timing your lines in between the actions dictated by it, has gone out too. This makes things rather more difficult for actors, because a great deal of acting skill, and certainly timing skill, depends on how adroit you are with *things*. Scenes can be pointed by using the objects *with* the lines. I mean, if you want to make a point, the cigarette-lighter can be quite amusing. If you want to be very polite, or very impolite, you can underscore it with the lighter. If you want to stop somebody talking, it's very easy to put your cigarette-lighter there – in front of their face, so they

47

have to put a cigarette in their mouths – and they have to shut up.

Altogether, self-consciousness – being conscious of one's self – is a very good description of what every inexperienced actor feels when he gets up in front of an audience. When you think about what he's doing, it's hardly surprising that he does. The average human being, if it's stared at by a lot of other human beings, does get self-conscious. And as, on the stage, we're constantly being stared at by bodies of people in auditoriums, we've got to love our self-consciousness, otherwise we won't be able to act. The great trick in losing it is in thinking right. If you're thinking the part right, you should be too occupied in your head to think about your own body.

People often ask me how I developed my sense of timing, and I can only say that it is a question of trial and error really – with audiences. Seeing where the laughs come. Seeing how the effects work, getting the rhythms right. Audiences have no idea what an important role they play in an actor's life, and would no doubt be most surprised if they could hear us talk about them while the play proceeds. For talk about them we do! We moan about them when they seem "puddingy" and dull, and adore them when they're quick and subtle and intelligent. This doesn't mean we like a great deal of guffawing from the audience – too many, or unexpected guffaws can irritate an actor. But a ripple of laughter is wonderfully rewarding.

The most difficult thing – and the one which takes longest to learn – is how an audience is reacting when it's *not* laughing, but being amused in a quieter, more sophisticated way. When you speak one of Shaw's wittiest lines, you can sometimes feel no-one appreciates it – it's a plum which you're pulling out almost for yourself. But every so often you get a bonus which makes it all worth while – with intelligent audiences, you do get an intelligent reaction, and you can *feel* it, even if it's only a murmur of delight.

Good acting is the result of this curious interaction between the actors and the audience, and I think it is very heartening that, today, when most forms of entertainment have been taken over by the higher technology, and become, to a greater or lesser extent, mechanized, or canned, theatre remains the interaction between two sets of people across the footlights, which changes, as those people change, every single night.

I was now getting small parts in London productions regularly enough to be able to turn down tours, and this was a great relief. It was lovely to work in London at such a rich and exciting time in the theatre, and it also allowed me to learn more about my crafts from the actors I admired. A.E. Matthews was one such actor, and I had a chance to observe him at close quarters in Robert Morley's first play *Short Story*, directed by Tyrone Guthrie. The reason I admired A.E. tremendously and learned so much from him was that although he was always terribly funny, he never looked as though he was being funny. In fact he never looked as if he thought what he said or did was even remotely amusing. He had become such a master at manipulating an audience that he had developed a habit of getting a good laugh with a line one night, then the next night, deliberately killing it, and trying for a different laugh. This boldness amazed and impressed me – only a supremely confident actor could have attempted it, and then only if he loved a perpetual challenge.

We had an illustrious cast in this production, but the average age was so high – apart from A.E. it included Marie Tempest, Margaret Rutherford and Sybil Thorndike

– that they chose me simply because I was young – to bring the ages down. H.M. Tennant were the management, and they had just taken on a new young man called Binkie Beaumont, who was determined to have some young blood in the cast. This was a bit of a problem since there were no young parts, and I had to play a middle-aged American producer. I must, in fact, have made the others look even more ancient than they were, but working with martinets like Marie Tempest was quite extraordinary. She had to make a grand entrance, even at rehearsal, and during performances, at the end of any speech of hers, she led her own applause as soon as she got into the wings. Her curtain calls were mini masterpieces. She would get her maid to push her little white Sealyham on stage, and her sentimental reunion with the dog would guarantee there was never a dry eye in the house, and regularly won her at least two extra curtain calls.

A.E. Matthews was something of a comic figure off stage as well as on. He used to arrive at rehearsals on his bicycle, which he rode right into the theatre, and propped up on the back wall of the stage, and he always wore riding breeches, and a Norfolk jacket. But in performance, he kept a straight face at all times, and had everyone in stitches. Such fine comic actors never laugh themselves. And that's the point. By playing it straight, they convey a marvellous dry humour. In high comedy you're paying the audience the compliment of thinking they're intelligent enough to derive the humour from your performance themselves.

The funniest off-stage performance I remember A.E. giving was once when we'd all spent some time between trains drinking in the Railway Hotel somewhere on tour, and half-way through the evening A.E. turned to the assembled company and asked impatiently: "What time does this bloody hotel get to London?"

50

For my part of the middle-aged American producer in *Short Story*, I put on a terrible American accent made up from some remote idea of how Americans speak. I can't think what it sounded like, but somehow, in spite of it, Tyrone Guthrie, who was considered an important director even then, liked what I did enough to offer me another job. I'll never forget how it happened. We were trying the play out in Glasgow, and he came over to me in the bar of the Central Hotel there and said: "How'd you like to go to New York? We're going to do a play there called *Sweet Aloes* written by an actress, Joyce Carey. There's a good part in it for you and I'd like you to do it."

I'd never thought of going to New York, and I was thrilled. Meanwhile, however, *Short Story* did rather well, and we settled down to a nice little run in London, with the glittering prospect of New York at the end of it. In those days you couldn't fly, so it was always a question of going by sea, and when the show closed, I got myself on to one of the great transatlantic liners as soon as I possibly could. I was terribly excited, but completely unprepared for the New York winter, and as soon as we had all met up and begun rehearsals, I realized that I hadn't got any of the right clothes and was getting frozen stiff. I didn't have enough money to kit myself out properly for the cold, so I bought some underclothes, and I ran everywhere. I ran from bar to bar and stuffed myself with spirits so I could get to the theatre and rehearse without freezing to death.

The female lead in *Sweet Aloes*, which had been played in London by Diana Wynyard, was to be played in America by Evelyn Laye. She was a popular singing star who had been the toast of New York since she'd starred in Noel Coward's *Bittersweet* on Broadway in 1929, but she'd never done a straight play before. She was married to Frank Lawton, who had made a number of films in

51

Hollywood, and they were very nice to me, letting me fall asleep on the floor of their luxurious apartment whenever Evelyn had – rather too successfully – taught me her own special theories of relaxation. But what I remember best from that first visit to New York was the cold, and the wonderful jazz.

This was 1934, and jazz had just moved up from New Orleans to Harlem, from where it was rocking the town. There was Paul Whiteman and Benny Goodman and Count Basie and Fats Waller and Jack Teagarden and Louis Armstrong all playing. It was the period of the night clubs and the big bands were in full swing. Prohibition had just been lifted, and most of the restaurants and bars had been speak-easies. There was a club I used to go to quite a lot called Jack and Charlie's on West 52nd Street. It's still in existence now, and I still go to it, but now it's called Twenty One and is a famous restaurant. The kind of smart people who go to it now are probably quite unaware that in the bad old prohibition days it was a place where you knocked and gave a password to get in and have a drink.

We were well into rehearsal when, suddenly, the stage-hands went on strike, and as we weren't allowed to handle the props ourselves, and we weren't allowed to rehearse on stage with the props while the strike was on, we were in trouble. Then it was that Tyrone Guthrie came to the rescue. He found a rehearsal room where he *was* allowed to use props and where we weren't obliged to have stage-hands to hand them out. I can vividly remember seeing Tyrone Guthrie, this marvellous tall lanky Irishman, pushing a handcart with all the props in it, followed by the entire company, all trudging their way up Fifth Avenue behind him to the rehearsal room. It was quite an amusing and extraordinary sight, and it was thanks to his energy and enterprise that we were able to continue rehearsing.

When *Sweet Aloes* opened, however, we did not have the success we'd hoped for. "This might be alright for a foggy London morning," wrote Robert Benchley, in the *New Yorker*, "but it doesn't suit the bright sparkling Manhattan weather." And to add insult to injury, he dubbed the play "*Sweet Alousy*". We ran for about three weeks, and off we came, and though my performance had been well-reviewed enough to get me some "nibbles" of interest from the Hollywood studios, I came back to England immediately. Things didn't look too good at that time – I was out of work for a little while after I came back – but after two or three months I somehow managed to get hold of a copy of a play called *Heroes Don't Care*, and this marked the beginning of a good run of luck for me.

Heroes Don't Care was a comedy sending up the Polar Expedition, of all things. It had been written by two ladies living in Australia, who had thought up a very funny and original idea. I played a man who developed frostbite early on in the expedition, so he literally got cold feet! He'd plodded as far as Narvik, decided that he couldn't face struggling on to the North Pole, and reckoned that the only way he could leave the expedition was to do something so dreadful he'd be expelled. And the only way he could figure out to get expelled was to have an affair with the leader of the expedition's wife. The leader was played by Felix Aylmer, who gave a very funny performance, aided by a huge white bristling moustache, and raged about in a suitably blimp and mock heroic manner. His wife was played by Carol Goodner, and I had no trouble seducing her – she was a very attractive girl. We had a hilarious seduction scene together, the leader/husband found out, and I was drummed out.

53

I was, of course, delighted, but the interesting thing was
– so was the audience. They were actually *on my side* in
the whole affair, instead of on Felix Aylmer's, and when
I left Narvik and went home and the Polar expedition
continued without me, they were happy for me, instead
of being outraged by my bad behaviour. The audience
rooted for the cad, rather than the genuine hero, and I
suppose it was only possible to extract comedy out of such
a situation because the time was ripe for the introduction
of the anti-hero into the theatre. *Heroes Don't Care* was
one of the first anti-hero comedies to be done in England,
and helped to create a long and successful vogue in this
genre. People were ready, in the mid-Thirties, to laugh
at established heroic values. The government and a large
proportion of the governing classes were busy appeasing
Hitler. At the Oxford Union, the undergraduates had
voted against fighting for King and Country, and there
was definitely a moral decline in English public life. From
the beginning of 1936 people were roaring with laughter at
our antics in *Heroes Don't Care*, and three and a half
years later, the Second World War was declared.

Historical hindsight apart, *Heroes Don't Care* was a
big success, and led me on to the biggest success I'd
had yet.

A young man called Terence Rattigan had written a play
titled *French Without Tears*, based on his own experiences
when he'd been sent to learn French at a crammers'
establishment in south-west France. It was to go on at
The Criterion Theatre in Piccadilly Circus, and because
he had seen and liked *Heroes Don't Care*, he asked me
to play the lead in it. I was offered the top West End
salary of twenty-five pounds a week, but in spite of this,
I deliberated a bit – I usually do. There was no way of

telling that this modest production, cast almost entirely with young hopefuls – Kay Hammond, Trevor Howard, Guy Middleton, Roland Culver, Robert Flemyng, Jessica Tandy and myself – was destined to become the biggest comedy hit of the Thirties. It had originally been seen as a stop-gap at the Criterion, and no-one seemed to expect anything special of it. Of course, the script was always very funny, but it was regarded, at the beginning, as just a nice cheerful little play.

I played one of the sex-starved students, the Hon. Alan Howard, and I was in love with the sex-pot, Diana Lake (Kay Hammond), who played havoc with our concentration on our studies. Trevor Howard was her brother – the only one of the students free from her potent allure – and the central joke of the play was the absolutely terrible French spoken, or attempted, by the English students. Terry was very funny about how clueless the average Englishman is both at foreign languages, and at love. He'd spotted this, and pinned it down hilariously, giving us ridiculous dialogue in which we had to speak the most utter drivel in French. In the first few minutes of the play, Guy Middleton set the tone by delivering what was probably the funniest line. He was desperately trying to translate the phrase: "She has ideas above her station", and he translated it as: "Elle a des idées au dessus de sa gare", which is the wrong sort of station, of course.

Jokes like that made everybody roar with laughter, but nevertheless, rehearsals were fairly low key, and the mood just before we opened, on 6 November 1936, was so gloomy that three of the backers were desperate to get out. I remember them sitting around after the dress rehearsal moaning about it. How I wished I could have laid my hands on a hundred pounds. With that princely sum, I could, at that moment, have bought a third share of that play, and become rich. For somehow, with only fair reviews and little advertising, *French Without Tears* hit gold. It ran for 1,039 performances, became a thundering success, and occupied my evenings happily for the next two years.

Everything about that show was a happy experience. Both the writer and the director became lifelong friends of mine as a result of it. Terry Rattigan was a suave character, and very good company, and I remember how I enjoyed golfing with him at Sunningdale during that period. The director, Harold French, was such a good friend that he used to risk driving to France with me for weekend breaks, sometimes, in whatever unreliable motorcar I was running then. Soon after *French Without Tears*, he directed me in two very successful plays at the Haymarket in 1939 and 1941 respectively, Noel Coward's *Design for Living*, and S.N. Behrman's *No Time for Comedy*, and he and I still lunch together at the Garrick Club in London.

Fortunately, by the time I did *French Without Tears*, I knew enough to recognize it as the upswing of my career which had started with the Van Druten play *After All*. And because I realized I'd got lucky at last, I was therefore able to enjoy myself properly – and hugely. We were all young, our play was not only the toast of the town, it was actually fun, as well as very hard work, and we ourselves were a riotous success at the height of the glamorous pre-war period. Everybody came to see us, and I remember seeing the audience from the stage of the Criterion one evening at the end of 1936 or the beginning of 1937, and there was a sea of white ties! In those days everybody came to the theatre in evening dress, the men in tails, the women in long dresses, long gloves, and tiaras, if they'd got them. They'd probably all been out for drinks before the show, and they were all going out to supper afterwards. The Criterion Theatre was – and is – right bang in the centre of

Piccadilly Circus, so you saw people wandering around the nearby streets in full evening dress and all their jewellery, as a matter of course, and they travelled by bus, some of them – no-one thought of pinching anything in those days. The cockneys just gaped in awe and admiration. They expected the Toffs to be dressed like that.

We became a vogue, a household word, and everybody, from royalty to aristocracy to café-society dropped in to see us – if they could get seats! – before going on to some night club like Ciro's, or out to supper. We'd become a favourite stopping-off place, almost like Cochrane's legendary but more sophisticated intimate reviews which were so fashionable at that period, and which I loved. These were little after-dinner shows with music and sketches, often starring a particularly debonair hero of mine, Jack Buchanan, and Gertie Lawrence, whom I adored. Very few entertainments have ever been as enjoyable as those little late night shows were, and nothing sums up the whole mood of the Thirties as well as the memory of the Cochrane reviews. After the show, I too, would dress up, go out to dine, see an after-dinner review, and, probably, go dancing. And, of course, this world of privilege, both on and off the stage, was taken utterly for granted.

It was not to last very much longer.

CHAPTER 4

LIVE WIRES

*I*t was during the period, after *Heroes Don't Care* and before *French Without Tears*, that I was put under contract by Alexander Korda at London Films and started to make films during the day at Denham Studios and come back to the theatre at night. This meant I was working a twelve-hour day, first all day at the studio and then after a snack, performing at the theatre, eight times a week. I was working terribly hard and making quite a decent amount of money. I remembered it as being something like £5,000 a year, but when I checked the records, I found I was actually getting £2,500 a year, which only goes to show what has happened to the value of money! Anyway, £2,500 a year was quite a lot in those days, and was certainly a fortune for me! And the great thing was that, although this arrangement gave me the security of a long-term contract, it did not prevent me from continuing with my stage career.

There was a price for this security, however. There always is. And the price in this case was that any salary I got for my stage work went straight into Korda's pocket, not mine. Under the terms of the contract, any extra money I earned outside my film work went to the studio and became part of the annual salary they paid me. At the time, this seemed perfectly fair, it was standard practice, and nobody complained. Altogether, I managed, I've no idea how, to make five films during the run of *French Without Tears*, some of them quite interesting. You never work so hard as when you are the flavour of the month!

The first film I made for Korda was *Men are not Gods* with Miriam Hopkins, Gertrude Lawrence, A.E. Matthews and Sebastian Shaw, written and directed by Walter Reisch. A.E. Matthews played the influential drama critic of a newspaper, Miriam Hopkins played his secretary and Sebastian Shaw played a celebrated actor starring in *Othello*, and caught between the two women. As Desdemona, Gertrude Lawrence almost got killed for real on stage by her real life husband – it was a melodrama. I was a writer of obituaries on the newspaper, and always trying to get more space for myself, which was good for a laugh. I was also supposed to be wildly in love with Miriam Hopkins. This shouldn't have been difficult – she was very beautiful – but, though some reviewers seemed to think I draped myself round doorways rather humorously, and used my long, lanky body quite effectively, I didn't think I was much good in this film. I gave an interview to the film critic Freda Bruce Lockhart a year or so later, and told her: "I thought I was foul in *Men are not Gods*. Of course, I knew nothing about film acting. I'd done nothing but some quota quickies. The director wanted pace from my part. So I gabbled my head off, and really hardly knew what I was doing."

This was hardly surprising, because acting in films, in front of the camera, is an entirely different kettle of fish from the kind of stage acting I'd become used to. At first it is absolutely terrifying. Your whole body goes rigid, none of the things you have learned in the theatre seem to apply, and you don't know what to do. Apart from a few film naturals, like Cary Grant, or Marilyn Monroe, who seem to love the camera, and probably wouldn't know what to do with themselves on a stage, I don't think anyone relaxes enough to be good for their first few films. I'd done a few tiny bit parts in unimportant movies very early on in my career, and I knew that, at first, I wasn't very good at it. I had all the usual beginner's problems. I felt hideous and unphotogenic, and a lot of this was to do with being self-conscious, or camera-conscious, and not *thinking* what I was saying. On film, the thinking process shows in your eyes and on your face, which it doesn't have to do so much on stage. You can often get by with good clear diction and an intelligent use of body movement on the stage, because theatre is more a speaking medium than a thinking medium. But good film-acting means thinking right. Film-acting is an eye-job, a head-job. If you think of the screen, you only really remember faces.

In 1937, the same year as *Men are not Gods* and while I was on stage every night in *French Without Tears*, I did a film called *Storm in a Teacup* with Vivien Leigh, a witty, social comedy based on a play by the Scottish playwright James Bridie, which had Vivien and I sparring about everything from love to politics. It is, perhaps, not sufficiently known that Vivien was a talented comedienne, with a very special and endearing quality hard to define. It wasn't just the kind of pertness someone so ravishingly pretty would be expected to have, it was a very special sense of gaiety perhaps best described as insouciance, and it fitted her very well for the kind of barbed dialogue of the Bridie piece. It is a great pity she didn't do more comedy, I think. Once again, I was a newspaper reporter, this time

61

dedicated to puncturing the pompousness of a man who wants to be the first Prime Minister of Scotland, played by old friend and champion laugher from Liverpool Rep., Cecil Parker.

I liked *Storm in a Teacup*, which took about six weeks to make, partly because I liked Victor Savile, the director. He was a man who could make me relax in front of the camera, in spite of my initial fear of it, without stopping me being funny. Directors are more important in films than they are in the theatre, and a good film director can help an actor a lot, especially if he knows the particular problems the actor has, and chooses the easier bits for him to start with. A chap who's experienced with actors won't give you terribly exacting things to do in the first few days, but will ease you in gently by letting you do some little scenes. He won't bang you on for a big scene the first or second day, he'll let you get gradually into the mood of a part. The fact that films are shot out of sequence also means that the director has to be more cogent with the script. He has to hold it all together, and has to give actors more direction than they would need on stage.

The main reason, however, why I liked making *Storm in a Teacup* was Vivien Leigh. Vivien was an old friend of mine, and I was enormously fond of her. She was then with Larry Olivier, though I don't think they were married yet, and they were both friends of mine, though I can remember driving her back from the studios and casting adoring glances at her all the way – as everyone knows, she was irresistibly beautiful – while she waxed lyrical non-stop about Larry. Much of the spirit of the immediate pre-war period with all its fun and glamour comes back to me when I think of our weekends together at Larry and Vivien's lovely country retreat, Notley Abbey, or at their house in Chelsea. At Notley Abbey Vivien was for ever holding house parties at which her energy never dimmed, though the guests were frequently sagging with tiredness. Besides myself, other guests frequently included Noel Coward, Tyrone Guthrie, the Ralph Richardsons, the David Nivens, John and Mary Mills, Godfrey Winn, Bea Lillie, Robert Helpman and Gertie Lawrence. Orson Welles was often there, constantly tapping away at his typewriter, writing some new screenplay or other (probably, at that time, an early draft of *Citizen Kane*, which was made in 1941).

We specialized in pranks and practical jokes at Notley. Larry was a ball of fire when he was with Vivien, and Vivien was just a ball of fire! She never slept. I suppose none of us did very much, in those days. It was nothing for us all to drive off into the night after our respective shows, and reach Notley Abbey at about 1 a.m. to find the house blazing with lights, the drinks prepared, and a candlelit dinner served at two in the morning. After dinner, Orson Welles would be telling fascinating stories about the Emperor Maximilian or someone else suitably unlikely, over the port, while some of us were nodding off, and others creeping surreptitiously up to bed. Vivien never let anyone go to bed if she could help it. At other times we'd have bacon and eggs in the kitchen at 2 a.m. – and still Vivien, with her manic energy, would be up and about her gardening soon after dawn. There's no doubt that she and Larry adored each other. He doted on her, and she on him. But there was a great temperamental difference between them which both found hard to take.

It was a wonderful time for them, they were doing good work, and were madly in love, and Vivien, in particular, was on the crest of a wave when she landed the part of Scarlett O'Hara in *Gone with the Wind* in 1939. But there was a black and puritanical side to Larry – his

63

personality gained from being with her, he got lighter when she was around – whereas Vivien was wittier and much more lively and on to the next thing than Larry was. She was a real live-wire, and she kept him going and refused to let him give way to his dark side, and get depressed or down. The sadness was that all this energy was manic, and meant that she stayed awake endlessly, exhausted everyone, exhausted herself, and then collapsed. When this happened, everyone got very worried about her, because she really collapsed, she would sometimes even go into comas, and though we all knew that she was highly strung and unbalanced, and not at all well, there wasn't much any of us could do about it.

Naturally, all this was very hard on Larry, and he found life with Vivien very difficult, not only because of the worry of looking after her, but because he could never have any sleep and he had somehow to find the energy for his work. He was always sitting there with his mouth a thin line waiting to go to bed, and he used to plead with her to let him sleep, but she was often so funny when she was up late, and had been drinking too much, which we all did, I suppose, that it always seemed churlish not to go along with her.

Godfrey Winn actually complained in print once that after these customary late nights, Vivien would always send a manservant to tap on his door at some uncouth hour in the morning to ask his help in dead-heading her pinks or her roses, or to join her for a game of bowls. Poor Godfrey! He was probably more exhausted than any of us, having played several sets of Wimbledon-standard tennis that afternoon – he was a tennis champion as well as a columnist – and he noted, in one of his auto-biographical books, that I was a total flop at tennis, running towards the ball as if I thought my racquet

64

was a butterfly net, and getting extremely exasperated with myself at my inadequacy in this department. He added that I compensated later for my shortcomings on the tennis court with my repartee off it. And as he wrote of our weekends at Notley Abbey that they were "like being part of an exquisite charade, performed by an all-star cast, whose gaiety and wit and charm carried the whole improvisation", I think I'll have to forgive him his condescension.

The following year I did another film with Vivien, *St Martin's Lane*, known in America as *Sidewalks of London*, about street entertainers, or buskers as they were called, people who spent their lives acting on the street, instead of on the stage, and entertaining the queues who were going into the big London theatres or cinemas. It was an interesting idea, though rather theatrical, I'd have thought. Stories of this kind were popular in the Thirties, but somehow, I don't think they'd have much appeal today. Strangely enough, Tyrone Guthrie was in *St Martin's Lane*, and as there were musicians in it, so was a man called Larry Adler who played the mouth organ – a long way from his harmonica recitals in Carnegie Hall or Symphony Hall in Boston! The most interesting actor in this film, however, was definitely Charles Laughton, who was naturally cast as a rather larger than life character who went about doing bits of poetic recitation in the street. Laughton was a really extraordinary man, and perhaps the most extraordinary thing about him was his size. He was a very large and very extrovert actor, and everybody thought he was a genius. I didn't. I thought he was more of a show-off, really. He was also very difficult to act with because of the sheer size of him. If you were doing a two-shot with Charles it was almost impossible to get into the shot. The frame was quite simply full of him. You'd

65

be looking over his shoulder, or under his arm, or between his legs, but you couldn't share a shot with Charles, there was no room. It was very irritating.

He also behaved in a very eccentric way, which some people thought meant for certain he was a genius. He was living up a tree during the time we were making that film. And as he was married to Elsa Lanchester, I think she may have lived in the trunk somewhere, or in the root, maybe. One of the things I shall always remember about Charles was that he used to come into the theatre clutching tiny little wild flowers in his huge hand, flowers he'd picked in the woods on his way to the studio from his tree house. It was touching, really. He was like some giant in a fairy tale trying not to crush something delicate in his enormous paw. He was an interesting actor, though, with a magic all his own, and he chose some fascinating parts, though he belonged to the wildly extroverted school of acting, half conceit and half real talent. His eccentricity could be genuinely touching, but I was never sure whether Laughton was a talented actor or just a show-off.

An even more star-studded film I did was *The Citadel*, based on A.J. Cronin's best-selling novel, in which Robert Donat played the dedicated doctor and I played the unscrupulous one. Robert Donat was a lovely actor with a beautiful voice, a genuinely talented man whose tragically early death was a great loss to the profession. In the cast with us were Rosalind Russell, Ralph Richardson, Emlyn Williams, Nora Swinburne, Athene Seyler, Felix Aylmer, and Cecil Parker – again! There was one scene in *The Citadel* which gave me a great deal of trouble in my off-screen life. I'm asked by a fellow doctor how my patient's chest is doing, and I reply, gleefully, "It's a treasure chest!" After making that film I couldn't go to see a doctor without him bringing that up. Ironically,

I was still a terrible hypochondriac at the time, and was always going to specialists and having ridiculous, fashionable tests of one kind or another which made me something of a treasure chest to the medicos myself.

There couldn't have been anything much the matter with me, considering my daily twelve-hour work schedule. It was crazy – and I did this for two solid years. We all did it, and looking back on that time, I don't know how we did it, except that we were all young. It was absurd the amount of energy you needed. I used to get up at six o'clock in the morning, drive down to Denham Studios, work there until about five thirty, go back to my flat in Sloane Street for a quick meal, then go to the Criterion, and do a show which finished at around eleven at night. Unsurprisingly, I became thoroughly exhausted, and eventually asked to be released when *French Without Tears* transferred to the Piccadilly Theatre. I need hardly add that this kind of schedule did nothing to enhance the quality of my private life, and I had, in fact, become separated from my first wife.

I had a month's much-needed rest then because after two years of playing to packed houses at the Criterion, and five films, I felt I was doing all right and while I might not deserve a holiday, I could just about afford to take the risk. As it worked out, I came back and went straight into the Theatre Royal, Haymarket, in January 1939 to do Noel Coward's sparkling *Design for Living*. Binkie Beaumont was producing, and he had become a great friend and staunch ally of mine since the day he had insisted on getting me as a very young actor into *Short Story* to lower the overall age of the cast. *Design for Living* was a three-hander, about a ménage à trois, and starred Diana Wynyard and Anton Walbrook and myself. I loved working with Diana, we were already old friends, and she

67

was very professional, but Anton Walbrook was another story. He hated me playing loud New Orleans jazz on the gramophone in my dressing room, and used to retaliate – ever more loudly – with the German and Austrian classics. For a while it was total war, musically speaking, that is, and we must have had the noisiest backstage anywhere in London.

We were courting disaster, actually, because the play had been first put on in New York with Coward himself playing my part, and the Lunts, Alfred Lunt and Lynne Fontanne as the others, but on the whole we had splendid reviews and much praise all round. Only the most austere critic of them all, James Agate, neglected to add to the general chorus of approval, and found that we fell short of the scintillating performances he had seen on Broadway. "Rex Harrison tries hard, but not hard enough," was the burden of his review, a pretty damning thing to say when I was out to convey easy, relaxed charm. We played, in spite of this, to packed and enthusiastic audiences throughout the tense period of the Phoney Peace, until, on 3 September 1939, the show was temporarily closed by the outbreak of the Second World War.

I tried to volunteer immediately, but at first they wouldn't have me. This was because Churchill was very keen on keeping the theatres going during the Blitz – he thought it was good for morale – and he'd issued an order stating that "key actors" should be exempt from the Armed Services. If we were doing a show, we had to play at extraordinary hours because the Blackout was of the utmost importance, and the Blitz was much too serious to risk having people in such exposed places as theatres after dark. So we used to play matinées every day, before the bombs came over, and then go off to hide in shelters, and I spent quite a lot of my time at the Haymarket firewatching with the firemen, and sleeping at the theatre. Incendiary bombs would come down, which we had to extinguish with sand, or hastily kick off the roof before they set fire to everything. So some nights I would be firewatching and putting out incendiaries, and some nights I'd spend in shelters, and this went on throughout the rest of 1939 and 1940.

While I was frustratedly waiting to find out who these wretched "key actors" were supposed to be, I went round the provinces with the West End production of *Design for Living*, playing to wildly appreciative audiences everywhere, and it was while we were appearing at The Prince of Wales Theatre in Birmingham (bombed soon after, in 1941), that I met an enchantingly pretty and unusual girl called Lilli Palmer. She was apt to be a bit snooty at first, perhaps because she saw me scrutinizing her through my monocle across the hotel dining room, but she was acting in a play with Leslie Banks, of bandage fame, and Leslie introduced us. Lilli turned out to be much more than a very pretty face. She was an uncompromisingly honest and straightforward girl who had already, at twenty or twenty-one, known great hardship when she had to leave her devoted family and promising acting career in Berlin and start again in England, because she was Jewish. It transpired that the next touring venue for both of us was Liverpool, and I agreed to drive her up there. She had a particularly jealous and evil-tempered Scots terrier who was touring with her, and throughout that journey he did his best to scare me off. I need hardly say that he failed dismally in this attempt.

Still waiting to enlist when the tour ended, I made two more films, *The Silent Battle* with Valerie Hobson, directed by her then husband Anthony Havelock-Allen, and *Over the Moon* in which Herbert Lomas and Wilfrid Hyde White also appeared, and my co-star was Merle

Oberon. But the best film I made in this period was undoubtedly *Night Train to Munich* (American title simply *Night Train*).

Although this was early days for him as director, *Night Train* was Carol Reed at his best, and I found him excellent to work with. Apart from being a technical perfectionist as a film-maker, Carol was wonderfully considerate to actors – and always managed, somehow, to make you relax. The film was a comedy thriller about the war, and only the ironically humorous and particularly British spirit of the script writers, Frank Launder and Sidney Gilliat, who had already written Hitchcock's famous *The Lady Vanishes*, could have managed to make a comedy thriller out of a story in which British Intelligence is pitted against the Nazi menace at the very moment (1941) when we might well have lost the war. And only because of the sang-froid of everyone in the cast, did we get away with it. This included Paul Henreid, who played chief Nazi, Margaret Lockwood, that marvellously unflappable pair, Basil Rathbone and Naunton Wayne, James Harcourt, Felix Aylmer, Roland Culver and Irene Handl, who played a station mistress.

Feeling against the Germans ran pretty high just then, and not only had I to spend a great deal of the film disguised as a German Army officer, making proper use, at last, of my famous adolescent monocle, and trying for a high-pitched German accent, but when we transformed Lime Grove studios briefly into German headquarters and flew the swastika flag for just one shot, there was uproar in the streets round Shepherd's Bush – and some very useful publicity

The film was much liked, both in England and America, (where it was distributed by Twentieth Century-Fox) but apart from some terrific action scenes and chases, in one of which I had to leap from one Swiss mountain cable car to another in mid-air in order to escape, what I liked about the film was the way it suggested that British indomitability is based on impudence. I'd always known that our secret weapon was our humour.

At this time, I was also playing in S.N. Behrman's aptly named *No Time for Comedy* at the Haymarket, with Diana Wynyard and Lilli Palmer, where we gave matinées only, to packed houses, as the evenings were under the strictest Blackout rules. The wartime audiences were fantastic. They'd been up all night coping with the Blitz – London was a scene of devastation, buildings on the ground, scaffolding everywhere, piles of dust and bricks – but the cockney spirit remained cheerful and resilient throughout. Your average Londoner is a gutsy sort of creature, who, though he may be a damned nuisance during peace time when his natural belligerence has to manifest itself at football matches, is magnificent in national crises such as war, when the same rogue spirit keeps him going. These audiences were more than happy to be able to sit in the theatre and laugh – laughter was the safety valve they needed to keep sane. Churchill knew what he was talking about.

It was a strange old time, a million light years from the safe and privileged world of *French Without Tears*. Throughout the thick of the Blitz, I was living at Claridge's, which was considered to be a very solid building, particularly the hall under the stairs. I was acting during the afternoon, and firewatching at night, or sitting up drinking and smoking with chums as the bombs rained down. You couldn't sleep in the Blitz until the all-clear went at dawn. Every morning I'd stagger out through rubble to see if the Haymarket was still standing. By some miracle, it always was, though the hotel outside

71

the stage door was hit, and the roof of the theatre itself was irreparably damaged. The roof has leaked ever since, so that to this day, you can be standing in the wings at the Haymarket (as I was last year in *The Admirable Crichton*), with your feet in a puddle of water. One day they'll have to do something about that roof.

In the midst of all this, I somehow managed to film Shaw's *Major Barbara*, with Wendy Hiller, Robert Morley, Sybil Thorndike, and Deborah Kerr among others, directed, if that's the word, by the amusing but rascally Gabriel Pascal, who had managed to buy the film rights to all of Shaw's plays for a few shillings, but who had to be guided through the production by his editor, David Lean, his cameramen Ronald Neame and Freddie Young, and my friend, the stage director, Harold French, who was acting as dialogue director on the film. According to Alan Jay Lerner, Pascal was a Romanian who claimed to be Hungarian and looked like a Himalayan. He was circular in shape, his voice had the timbre of a 78 record played at 33 r.p.m., and his English would have foxed even Henry Higgins. There are many versions of how Pascal acquired the rights to Shaw's plays but the one I heard goes as follows:

One day he appeared at the door of Shaw's cottage in Ayot St Lawrence and rang the doorbell. A maid answered it, and Pascal asked to see Mr Shaw. "May I ask who sent you?" asked the maid. "Yes," he said. "Fate sent me." Shaw, who was on the stairs, heard this announcement and came to the door himself. "Who are you?" he asked. Pascal answered, "I am Gabriel Pascal. I am motion picture producer and I wish to bring your works of genius to screen." "How much money do you have?" asked Shaw. Pascal reached in his pocket and took out a few shillings. "Twelve shillings," he replied. "Come in," said Shaw. "You're the first honest film producer I've ever met."

During the production of *Major Barbara*, I met Shaw, and although he was no help whatsoever with my part of Cusins, or with a particular non-love scene Wendy Hiller and I had been trying to play, this experience started me on my life-long affinity with the work of Shaw, who – as some people have said – became my Shakespeare.

At that point, however, Wendy and I had got stuck over a terribly high-flown love scene, and Pascal said: "GBS is coming down to the studio, why don't you ask him about it?" So Wendy and I sat one on each side of the elderly Shaw, a splendid, but formidable figure, with his long white beard, tweed bicycling trousers, and walking stick, and we said: "Could you illuminate this scene a little bit for us, so we'll find it easier to act?" Shaw read through the scene very solemnly, looked rather doleful, and didn't say anything for rather a long time. Then he said: "Ach, what a terrible scene! WHAT a terrible scene!" It was clear he hadn't looked at the play since 1913. Naturally, we were totally disarmed by his candour, but it wasn't much help to us. He didn't give us a clue as to how we should play it.

He was a very funny fellow in some respects, was Shaw. In *Major Barbara*, all the other relationships in the play are fine, including that between Barbara and her father, the millionaire arms manufacturer, Undershaft, and that between Undershaft and Cusins. But the love affair between Barbara and Cusins is undeveloped. Relating opposing ideas was something Shaw did brilliantly, but the relationships between men and women – those got him really stuck.

I was very much involved, also, in a real-life tragedy, during the making of *Major Barbara*, when Harold French's first wife, Phyllis, a very attractive girl, was killed in an air raid over London. He used to come into my dressing room in the mornings to ring her up and see if she was all right. We were all staying out at Denham for the film, and she was living in their house in London right through the Blitz. One morning he telephoned, as usual, and there was that awful unobtainable noise on the line which often meant that a building had been knocked down. Harold went absolutely white, jumped into his car and drove to London. But when he arrived he found the house in ruins and his wife dead. It was awful, the worst thing in the world, really, and there is so little you can do to comfort people in such extremity, though all of his friends tried to do our best.

By this time (1941) both Laurence Olivier and Ralph Richardson had got themselves into the Fleet Air Arm, and the powers that be still wouldn't come out and say who the "key actors" were. So I thought, to hell with this, I'm fed up with feeling embarrassed wandering around in civilian clothes, and, unbeknown to the management, I went in front of an RAF Board to try to get into the Air Force. The Board was composed mostly of air-marshals and air-vice-marshals, and one of them looked down a list and said: "You realize, Harrison, you're exempt?" And I said: "Yes, sir, but I don't want to be. I want to go into the Services. You won't publish who should be exempt and who is a key actor, so I'd rather not be exempt." And one old boy said to me: "You'll never regret this, Harrison. You'll never regret it."

Well, I never did regret it because I went into the Air Force and in the end I was given a good and extremely interesting job as Flying Control Liaison Officer in the RAF Voluntary Reserve, which meant learning something completely new, and certainly new to me, to do with radar, and getting our bombers in at night. I had different means of getting our aircraft down when they were in distress, or

coming back shot-up, and guiding them into different aero-
dromes. I also had means of putting up flares, organizing
air-sea rescue, and all that. It was done mostly on the tele-
phone. I was in radio-telephone contact with the ground
flight control or air-sea rescue, and I could talk directly to
them. I worked in the underground War Rooms in 10 Group
in the West Country, then they moved me to 11 Group at
Uxbridge, which was the control room for the coast from
the Wash down to Southampton. I was in the Service for
most of the war, from 1942–1945, and became so absorbed
in what I was doing that I never missed acting once.

In January 1943 I had some leave, and married Lilli
Palmer at Caxton Hall in London, my divorce from
Collette having gone through the previous July. Arthur
Barbosa was my best man. The first part of our marriage
was full of narrow escapes from German bombs. Once the
control tower at a Fighter Command aerodrome where I
was working was nearly blown to bits, and when we got
the planes down, we had to go down to the airfield through
a barrage of anti-personnel bombs which looked like large
jam jars and were guaranteed to take your leg off, and
pull the men, both dead and alive, out of the planes. And
once, when Lilli and I were at the house we'd rented near
the Denham film studios, with Deborah Kerr and Harold
French, the house was bombed, and fell, literally, round
our ears. Luckily, it had been raining, and the ground
the bomb fell in was soft, otherwise we'd have all been
killed. As it was Lilli had a cut wrist, and Deborah's
hair was covered in grey/white plaster which had mixed
with the drink she'd spilled and formed a solid halo which
wouldn't come off. I had a cut on my forehead, and a week
later, went black and blue all over as a result of the blast,
which had knocked me clear across the room.

I was still in the Air Force when my second son, Carey

Alfred, decided to be born during one of the worst air raids over London. We were lucky that the London Clinic was not hit, and as soon as I could, I got Lilli and the baby out of London, where they were safer, but not safe. Yet another quiet country house we'd taken was bombed, and only a vast rhododendron tree in the drive prevented Carey being blown up in his pram. In 1945, somewhat against my will, I was taken out of the Service, and honourably discharged, with medals, because Noel Coward wanted me to do *Blythe Spirit*, and he was so insistent that Mountbatten intervened.

Blythe Spirit was not a play I liked, and I certainly didn't think much of the film we made of it. David Lean directed it, but the shooting was unimaginative and flat, a filmed stage play. He didn't direct me too well, either – he hasn't a great sense of humour – and I think even Noel, who had wanted him very much, was disappointed. David Lean may be a great director for drama, but he's not great at comedy, so *Blythe Spirit* was very stiffly done. By that time it was over three years since I'd done any acting, and I can remember feeling a bit shaky about it, and almost, but not quite, as strange as when I'd first started, but Lean did something to me on that film which I shall never forget, and which was unforgivable in any circumstances. I was trying to make one of those difficult Noel Coward scenes work – I've never thought *Blythe Spirit* was one of his better plays – and I was doing my best, such as it is, when David said: "I don't think that's very funny." And he turned round to the cameraman, Ronnie Neame, and said: "Did you think that was funny, Ronnie?" Ronnie said: "Oh, no, I didn't think it was funny." So what do you do next, if it isn't funny?

I admit I was fairly insecure at that time, having just come out of the Air Force, and I didn't need to be told

76

that what I was doing wasn't funny. But even if it wasn't funny, and I hadn't just come out of the Air Force, I didn't want to be told. It was a terrible thing to do to an actor. Anyway, that's a story against David, who is, as I say, a great director, but not for comedy.

In 1945 I also made the interminable *I Live in Grosvenor Square*, with Anna Neagle, produced and directed by her husband Herbert Wilcox, but then I was lucky enough to get an excellent Launder and Gilliatt comedy *The Rake's Progress* (American title *Notorious Gentleman*) with Lilli Palmer, Godfrey Tearle, and Margaret Johnston, among others, in which I played a man who, although a total cad in peace time becomes a hero in the war.

Until then, my parts had, I suppose, been very much products of the Thirties. Some dialogue from an unremarkable film I'd made with Diana Churchill, *School for Husbands*, gives the flavour of the period, and the kind of parts I got, quite well:

SOMEBODY'S WIFE: I hear you've made love to women on the slightest provocation.

ME: That's quite untrue. I seldom need any provocation at all.

Now, at the end of the war, came a film which tried to say something about the irresponsible types I'd been making my living by portraying, and what it said was, the war had killed them off. At the end of *The Rake's Progress* I'm made to say something which did not augur well for my career:

My type's becoming obsolete. The thirties produced us and the champagne's gone flat and we're going out with the Thirties . . .

77

The film was considered controversial, since the cad is an upper-class sort of chap, who, it seems, in spite of his general immorality, or amorality, is just the type we needed to win the war. And in spite of the controversy, or perhaps because of it, *The Rake's Progress* was my most successful film to date.

CHAPTER 5

HOLLYWOOD FANFARE I

Nothing was further from my mind when I came out of the Air Force at the end of the war than that there would be a fat Hollywood contract waiting for me, but it seemed that two of my films, *Night Train* and *The Rake's Progress*, had been shown in America, and much liked, and Twentieth Century-Fox were offering me a long-term contract with – and this was rare – the first film named. The first film they wanted me to make for them was a very tempting one; it was *Anna and the King of Siam*, based on the best-selling novel by Margaret Landon, and I had to play an oriental potentate – the King of Siam. Irene Dunne had agreed to play the heroine, Anna, and Lee J. Cobb was going to play my Prime Minister. It was all very exciting, and though I didn't have a clue how I could play an oriental potentate, I booked myself on the first transatlantic liner out of Southampton I could find.

The first part of that journey to America was the most extraordinary voyage of my life. I crossed the Atlantic on the *Queen Elizabeth*, which was packed to the gills with

American soldiers going home at the end of the war. Lilli and I were about the only civilians on board, and we fell over GIs everywhere, eating in shifts, and sleeping mattress to mattress on the decks. It was a situation full of drama – some of the boys were longing to get home, others had left girls behind in England, all of them had experienced the grimness of war – and I'll never forget the amazing reception the soldiers had as we steamed up the Hudson River. The ha-ha boats, little river tugs dressed up, came out to welcome the troops, with bands playing on them, girls singing and dancing, streamers, balloons, loud hailers. There were even welcome-home parties families had organized for their beloveds on the docks. It was a thrilling, and deeply moving experience – an absolutely miraculous arrival in New York.

From New York, we travelled three nights and two days on the Super Chief train across the American continent through the mid-West prairies, crossing the Rockies, going through the wonderful West, and then through miles of orange and grapefruit groves, arriving, eventually, at Pasadena. It was a world so different from shell-shocked Britain, so colourful and lush, I could see it was going to take a lot of growing used to. Stuffed full of immediate post-wartime British attitudes, I felt sure that life in Los Angeles would be bad for me, simply because it was so luxurious, and I'd been brought up, as we all were, to mistrust such easy things. This made me pretty wary of this sunny, moneyed world and in some ways, I never grew used to Hollywood at all.

In spite of my misgivings, however, I discovered that there's a lot to be said for California, precisely because it is so relaxed. The sun shines, and you get into your car, you can keep the top open, and you don't have to wear a tie. And, of course, you can drift along very pleasantly

like that. But once I'd pulled myself together, and reported
to the studio, and started learning the script, I found I was
working so damned hard, I might have been anywhere. I
was back to my normal routine during filming, getting up
at six o'clock in the morning, and coming home at half
past seven at night, so I didn't really see a great deal of the
Californian sun. It's true there were times when I played
a lot of golf at Bel Air, and the other clubs round there,
but on the whole I didn't spend much time in Hollywood
when I wasn't working.

The part of the King of Siam posed tremendous problems from the start. I'd done lots of homework about
the Siamese background before leaving England, but I'd
never played an oriental before, and I simply didn't know
how to tackle it. I wanted to do justice to the subject –
King Mongkut is a very strong character, and Margaret
Landon's novel was based on the true life story of a young
British widow, Anna Leonowens, who became governess to
the king's sixty or seventy children in 1862, and managed
to teach English ways to his harem of wives and some
English values to the king himself. A stirring story. I felt
sure that as soon as I reached Hollywood, the Mecca of
the movies, where they knew everything about making
films, they would know how to help me, and I would get
expert help from the director and the studios. Little did
I know Hollywood. Nobody had given it a thought. The
director was a nice man called John Cromwell, but I soon
saw that he was not intending to give me any particular
rehearsal or direction of any kind. In fact, nobody told me
how to do anything, and the only thing they seemed to be
interested in at the studios was the problem with my eyes,
and that was quite fascinating, because oriental eyes are
very different from occidental eyes.

Oriental eyes look narrow, or slit, because their tear

ducts don't show, so the studio spent most of their time covering up my tear ducts with little bits of rubber which they made and inserted, one each side of my nose, and this did close my eyes up considerably, I must say. Apart from that, they managed to find the weirdest clothes to put me in, but that was all they did, so I had to continue my researches and try to be as oriental as I could. It seemed a bit much to me, getting a young man from Huyton, outside Liverpool, to play an oriental potentate, without any expert help or guidance from anyone, and as I needed some instruction from somewhere, I found myself a coach, a woman who had helped Lilli with the problems of acting in English when she first came over from Germany, and she coached me, privately, in voice and movements, based on the research I'd done myself on oriental behaviour, until eventually I got some of the strangeness I wanted into the part.

I studied a lot about speech patterns, which are very different from ours, and I felt it was very important to get the movements exactly right, especially the hand movements, which are rather controlled in orientals, so my whole performance had to be rather still and precise. When we started shooting, however, the director, John Cromwell, was horrified to hear the authentic high-pitched laughs and strange guttural noises I made, and asked me to please speak in my normal, Rex Harrison, voice. After all, that was what they were paying for. I had to enlist the producer, Darryl Zanuck, who, amazingly enough, took my part against the director, something unheard of in Hollywood. From then on, I did my part as I wanted to, but John Cromwell never spoke another word to me.

I have to admit that this did not stop me from enjoying the part enormously. It was quite a challenge, and I had a marvellous death scene at the end. There was also the great good fortune to be acting with Irene Dunne and Lee J. Cobb. Irene Dunne was a delight to work with, a dear woman and tremendously accomplished actress, and Lee J. Cobb one of the strongest American actors of his generation, and one I have always admired.

Anna and the King of Siam was much liked, by the studio, and the audiences, and won Academy Awards for Cinematography, Art Direction and Set Decoration.

I needed a rest when I finished *Anna and the King of Siam*, but it is very difficult to rest from the business of acting in Hollywood. Everything there is linked to the film industry, and it's hard to escape from your career. The trick with Los Angeles is not to stay there too long – it's a great place to go to and then to get out of – especially when you're not working, because it's too lush, and draws you into bad habits. There are endless parties being given in the stars' houses, and you've no excuse not to go to them if you're not filming the next day. The English set were always giving Saturday night soirées in their houses, so I began to do the usual rounds, and I saw a lot of David Niven – a lovely man, very amusing, and great fun to be with, and of Ronald Coleman and his wife Benita, who were both very nice. The English set centred round the Colemans – Ronnie was sort of captain of the English team, in spite of the fact that he used to keep himself rather apart from the crowd. I admired him as an actor – he had a lovely voice, and was one of those rare people who was marvellously successful in his profession, and in his life, too. So, although I never considered myself part of the Hollywood high-life, I gradually became one of their group, and gave my own soirées.

It was a very exciting time in Hollywood in 1946 because most of the American stars had been in the Forces, and were coming back from their war service eager to work, so there was great activity, with the studios going full-tilt. Clark Gable had just been demobbed, and so had Tyrone Power, so I made a lot of new friends. Ty Power, in particular, became a great friend of mine. He was married to a very charming French actress, Annabella, and I saw a great deal of them, and of the Charles Boyers, too. It was really a very jolly period, but all the time I was enjoying their company, and enjoying the parties and the drinks, I was thinking – I shouldn't be doing this! It was all so luxurious and so tempting I thought I'd be swallowed up by it and nobody in the real world would ever hear of me again. The theatre was my real world and I missed the theatre, it was in my blood and I'd been brought up in it, and although filming was very exciting out there in Hollywood in those days, it didn't seem to use my energies. I had a lot of energy in those days, it astounds me to think how much energy I had, so making films and going to all those parties was lovely, but it wasn't enough.

One party which I attended wasn't at all lovely; it was one given by Tyrone Power and Annabella, when that awful accident happened to David Niven's young wife, Primrose. It sounds ridiculous, but a lot of Hollywod houses have these winding spiral staircases, and we were playing hide-and-seek. Primrose opened a cupboard door to hide in it, and it wasn't a cupboard door, it was the door to the cellar stairs. She fell down the whole flight of steep stone steps, and knocked herself out. I can still remember her lying with her head in Lilli's lap before we got her to hospital. Nobody thought she would die, but a few days later, she did. Oh, it was awful, and of course, it was terrible for David. A tragedy.

The second film I did in Hollywood was *The Ghost and Mrs Muir*, with Gene Tierney, directed by the immensely talented Joseph Mankiewicz. This was a delicate and unusual love story taken from a book by R.A. Dick, and written for the screen by Philip Dunne, and in it Gene Tierney played a beautiful widow, and I played the ghost of a sea captain who falls in love with her.

The picture had an idea which was somewhat out of the ordinary, the mood of it was genuinely romantic but not cloying, and I particularly enjoyed making it because I knew and liked Gene Tierney, who was, herself, very far from ordinary. The widow's young daughter was played by Natalie Wood, who started her career as a child film-star. At the time of its release, I don't think it was a great success, but recently it's been shown on television and seems, with age, to have become a favourite. I've always been rather fond of it myself because it began my association with Joe Mankiewicz, with whom I subsequently made *Escape* (1948), *Cleopatra* (1963), and *The Honey Pot* (1967).

I think perhaps the Hollywood moguls were testing me, or something, because after playing an oriental potentate, and a ghost who falls in love, they decided I was ready to play a real, red-blooded man, a sort of Rhett Butler type, a lusty rake of the deep South, to Maureen O'Hara's Scarlett in *The Foxes of Harrow* based on a popular novel by Frank Yerby. This was obviously set to be a winner, for like *Gone with the Wind*, it was a southern American saga set in a big house called Harrow, and the Foxes were supposed to be an Irish American family. They dressed me up in all sorts of elaborate clothes, and, for the first and only time I can remember, gave me a moustache. This did not do for me what it had done for David Niven or Ronald Coleman, and I was becoming fed up with all this Hollywood codswallop. Their attitudes towards me, and the kind of parts they were offering me were getting tiresome.

The truth was that they didn't really know what to do with me, in Hollywood. They didn't understand what I could do. They thought I was what is known as a "character man". You always have to be in some category out there, you're either a baddy or a goody, or a character man. I don't know why they wanted me, really. They didn't know anything about the acting tradition I'd come from. They didn't know anything about high comedy.

They did know of Cary Grant, they'd heard of him, they knew what he did, and they'd sort of heard of Fred Astaire, and they'd realized that he could dance, as well as play comedy, but beyond that their imaginations didn't go very far. We're talking about the mid-Forties, when they were making a lot of movies, including sophisticated comedies, but nothing in quite my style of polished high comedy. The tone was – somehow – different. Cary Grant comedies were awfully good, and he was marvellous at them, but they weren't quite the same. I suppose the Hollywood moguls thought I was very English, and rather ugly and strange looking, and didn't look enough like Cary Grant, so whenever they got their hands on a witty or stylish script they instantly thought of Cary Grant for it, and he played it in his own mid-Atlantic style, only more on the American side than the English. This is odd, really, when you think that Cary Grant was once an Englishman called Archie Leach, yet the way he played comedy, he could easily have been American. His manner was forceful and direct, he was extremely handsome, in an even-featured American kind of way, and he had trained himself to speak in a curious mid-Atlantic accent, the advantage of which was that he could be understood both sides of the pond. It was something to do with the vowel sounds in the AAAA's, so that he sounded a bit East Coast.

Twentieth Century-Fox may not have had a clue how

to use their contract artists, but nevertheless they required them to be always on call. In those days you were not allowed to be choosy over scripts, and as they presented me with a lot of scripts that I didn't like very much, I was constantly being reprimanded, sent for by the front office to go and see them, and hauled over the coals. They had the perfect right to lay me off, in other words not pay me anything, until I'd accepted one of the scripts they wanted me to do, but they didn't lay me off, they were very good about that, they kept on forking out the dough, and I kept turning down the scripts. But it didn't make me the most popular boy in the school.

My judgement about scripts is not bad, but I have a reputation for being choosy. It has been said that I'm as fastidious about scripts as I am about tailoring. I tend to know, in both cases, exactly what suits me. I therefore also know what doesn't. Anyone who had seen the scripts I'd been given wouldn't have been surprised I turned them down. You didn't need terribly good judgement to say No.

None of that quite explains my own Hollywood troubles, though, because I don't think David Niven had to turn down a lot of scripts. He did very well, and obtained quite a lot of good parts, and I think it was because they could categorize him more easily with that moustache – he was a British military type. Everybody grew little moustaches then, inspired by the leader of the Brit-pack, Ronald Coleman, and I began to think that perhaps my troubles stemmed from the fact that I didn't have a Ronnie Coleman moustache. But as I've said, when I did grow one, for *The Foxes of Harrow*, it didn't do me any good at all.

It was a pity, really, because by this time I was beginning to enjoy working with the camera. There's a lot of talk about the camera loving certain actors, but it only loves you if you love it back, and, as in life, you need a little time to fall in love. You have to become used to the camera's character, its little foibles, its own quaint little ways. The camera always gives a little whirr when the film starts to go round inside those large reels, and at the beginning that whirr used to petrify me. Now I love the whirr, and I don't really start to act until I hear it. Once I got used to it, I grew to like the noise of it because I knew what it meant. It tells you that the film is turning round inside the camera and is recording what I'm trying to do – for good or bad.

One of the most fascinating differences between stage and screen acting is that the camera actually catches what you are thinking, whereas on the stage you could think until you were blue in the face and no-one would notice. The audience would simply think you'd forgotten your lines. With a camera in front of you, every single nuance shows up, and for this reason, I found it rather an intriguing acting form to master, or try to master, because it was so different from stage acting. On stage, there are many different levels to your performance, but screen acting is all naturalism.

All in all, though, I never really felt at home in Hollywood. When I first went to parties with the stars I felt like a film-fan. Here were the famous faces I'd previously watched, with awe-struck admiration, like everybody else, from my seat at the Empire, Leicester Square. Now here they were, in the same room as I was, and not merely in the same room, but – since Hollywood parties followed some antique provincial custom whereby the women stay at one end of the room and the men at the other – I was generally at the same end of the same room. Yet when I dared to enter into conversation with these legendary heroes, their conversation seemed very strange to me. Gary Cooper, Clark Gable, James Stewart, Spencer Tracy all talked about huntin', shootin' and fishin' like so many squires or sportsmen. They never talked about acting, never about the film they were currently in. Later on, I understood why they did not. These people were film stars, not actors of the kind I'd known in the theatre, and as such, they were busy being Gary Cooper, Clark Gable, James Stewart, and Spencer Tracy, on screen as well as off.

One weekend, when I'd gone golfing and fishing with David Niven and Nigel Bruce, I spent some time alone with Clark Gable. At first he was completely non-communicative, and fished from his canoe in silence, but later on, he started grumbling to me, and warming to his grumbles in a way I instantly recognized. He grumbled about the studio, the scripts, the parts they gave him, and I was pleased – and relieved – to hear these grumbles.

You can always recognize the real actors, the best actors – they always grumble. Ask anyone who worked with Humphrey Bogart and they'll tell you he was a real pain to be around on a film-set with, always making trouble, always complaining that everybody else had the good lines, and his were utter rubbish. Grumbling and grousing and bitching the whole picture through. Ask anyone who worked with Cary Grant. An actor who worked with him at the peak of his career once told me: "I did two pictures with Cary Grant and both times it was the same fight: he was convinced he had no charm and couldn't do a lot of scenes because the audiences wouldn't buy him. It was madness – here he was, maybe the most charming actor ever, and it was like pulling teeth. He was absolutely certain that his charm had gone."

I always remember Alan Jay Lerner telling me that once

when he was doing a film with Fred Astaire, and he was walking across the deserted MGM set late at night, a weary figure appeared with a towel around his neck, came over, and threw his arm heavily around Alan's neck. It was Fred, who thought nothing of working for three or four days on two bars of music, because something else which is characteristic of the best actors, and indeed of the best artists in all areas of the theatre, is that they quite simply work harder than anyone else, and care more about their work than anyone else. It is their sense of perfection which makes them bad-tempered and bitchy, and quite often – but not always, as I know to my cost – when the people they have been bitchy to see the end-result, all is forgiven. Anyway, Fred Astaire threw his arm round Alan's neck and he said: "Oh Alan, why doesn't someone tell me I cannot dance?"

It was nice to know that Clark Gable had joined this fretful, bad-tempered, genuine – and exclusive – company.

In the end I think that, socially, being English in Hollywood was like walking a bit of a tightrope. There were so many unwritten rules and regulations which didn't make much sense to me. One was the necessity of kowtowing to the gossip columnists, for this was the period when the two Dragon Ladies, Hedda Hopper and Louella Parsons, held sway. I fell foul of these two fiends from the beginning, and once, when I saw and heard Hedda Hopper being nasty to Gene Tierney because Gene had had the temerity to withhold the information that she was newly pregnant, I lost my temper. I think it must have been after that I was quoted as saying: "Hollywood and I have no future in common – and I doubt if Hollywood has a future at all."

Anyway, after *The Foxes of Harrow*, I went to Darryl Zanuck – Zanuck ran Twentieth Century-Fox – and I said,

"Listen, Mr Zanuck, I really would like to do something different next year. I'm enjoying Hollywood, but I'm getting very restless here." I told him there was a play by John Galsworthy which I'd loved when I'd seen my favourite Gerald Du Maurier do it in 1926, and I wondered if there was any possibility of making it into a film. It was called *Escape*, and it all took place on Dartmoor and in London, which meant that the studio would have to let me return to England for a bit. "Is there any chance of your getting hold of it?" I asked Mr Zanuck. "Well, I don't know, Rex," he said. "We'll try."

This was very nice of him, in the circumstances, as I didn't see that much of him, except when he walked from his office to his lunch room across the lot, surrounded by aides and waving a Polo mallet. I mean, he could very well have suspended me, which would have been the normal thing to do in those days if a contract player repeatedly turned down scripts and wouldn't work, but they were always very agreeable to me, at Fox, even though I had turned down a lot of stuff there, and the following year I did, in fact, go home to England and make *Escape* with Joseph Mankiewicz directing. I was lucky enough to have become a great favourite of the studio after *Anna and the King of Siam*, and *The Ghost and Mrs Muir*, and I think they were trying to please me.

Whether they had any inkling of my own attitudes towards work and money, and whether this influenced them at all, I shall never know, but after I first started to make enough money to live decently, which was at the time of *French Without Tears* and my first film contract with Korda, I had made a decision that money would never be the important side of my life. I love making money, and I like having money, but I don't work for the money. I do it because I like what I'm doing. It is very important for an actor to be able to afford that decision, for if he's just going round money-grubbing, choosing parts to make himself a lot of money, it will show in his work, and it isn't worth it. I never accepted parts just for the money because I'm intrinsically interested in the subject matter, and not what they're going to pay me. It is desperately important for an actor to think out his attitude to this side of life in the theatre and in films, and particularly in films.

Meanwhile, through my agent, Leland Hayward, later a successful producer, I had met a lot of people in Hollywood who were in the theatre, and among them was Maxwell Anderson, who was a playwright of considerable power and skill. He was the founder member of the Playwright's Company, a very strong body of men, who formed themselves into a production company in 1938 in order to produce their own plays. They were all playwrights, all producing a play a year, and all living on the Eastern seaboard. Apart from Anderson, the other members were S.N. Behrman, whose play *No Time for Comedy* I'd done in London in 1941, Sidney Howard, Elmer Rice, and Robert E. Sherwood. Later on they were joined by some producers, and by the distinguished German composer Kurt Weill, who had previously worked with Brecht, and was now doing wonderful work in America – his haunting number, "September Song" was composed in the USA.

Maxwell Anderson had an idea for a play which rather intrigued me, and though he knew I was under contract to Fox, he suggested it to me. It was an unusual part for me. He had written a verse play about Henry VIII of England and Anne Boleyn, called *Anne of the Thousand Days*. The reason for the title was that the time from the day Anne Boleyn met Henry VIII until the time she was beheaded was actually a thousand days – the romance lasted a

92

thousand days. It was an enormously attractive play, I thought. I didn't have the least idea, at that stage, how I was going to manage being Henry VIII, because he was a vast man, bigger even than Charles Laughton – he was enormous, but he wasn't all fat, he was a great athlete, he used to joust a lot, so he was muscle, as well. One way or another, though, Henry was a man of gigantic proportions, and as I am so long and thin, and could hardly be a more opposite physical type, it puzzled and challenged me how I was going to be able to convey his size. When Maxwell Anderson first came round to see me with the play, however, I hadn't really thought about those problems, let alone started to tackle them. I just liked the play, and Max was awfully keen for me to do it.

I explained to him that as I'd just got back to California from having made *Escape* in England, it might be difficult just then to find a way out of my contract, leave Fox, and go back into the theatre. Sure enough when I went to talk to Zanuck about the release to do the play on Broadway, he demurred, because he said he had another film ready for me to go straight into, and it was a film called *Unfaithfully Yours* which was going to be written and directed by Preston Sturges. Well, I rather wanted to do that because Preston was a unique and very funny man. I'd met him several times. So I said: "If I do *Unfaithfully Yours* can I leave and go back to the theatre?" And he said: "Well, let's think about it."

Anyway, I proceeded to do *Unfaithfully Yours*, which has now become something of a classic, and is shown in New York because all Preston's films have become classics. He was the most extraordinary man to work with. First of all, he used to direct in a fez, and the reason he wore a fez was he wanted everybody to know where he was all the time. He didn't want people to come on the set and say where's Preston, they would know where Preston was because they'd look for the red fez. And he ran the film-set rather like a circus. It wasn't that he didn't want anyone to see what he was doing; on the contrary, he would open the doors of the sound stage and call out: "Come and have a look at this – it's wonderful, come and have a look!" And he used to sit under the camera roaring with laughter, stuffing handkerchiefs into his mouth to stop himself laughing at his own jokes which he'd written.

Sometimes I thought why the hell is Preston running this scene so long? I'd be sitting doing something with a tape machine, for instance, and I'd think: my God he's running this too long! And I'd sit there playing with it, and he'd be stuffing handkerchiefs into his mouth and roaring with laughter. He always had his dog – a Doberman pinscher – on the set with him, who always barked at the wrong time. Nobody could stop the dog behaving like that, because Preston loved his dog and he loved his fez and he was going to have a ball, which he did. Working with him was really an extraordinary experience. I loved making that film with Preston, and became very fond of him. He was an understanding, very sophisticated, very Europeanized man, and the story he'd written which he wanted me to do was about a world-wide conductor who got into trouble.

The problem with this was that I had to learn how to conduct an orchestra, and though I am reasonably musical, I had no idea how to set about such a task. Fortunately I had a marvellous young English conductor, Robin Sanders-Clark, as my coach, and he must have done wonders with me, for, at the end of filming, the orchestra revealed that, though rightly sceptical about my musicianship to begin with, they had actually followed my beat as the film went on, as if I were their real conductor!

I was immensely touched, especially when they ganged up and wrote a "Harrison Fanfare" for me, to commemorate their "amazement and delight" in what they called my "histrionic feat".

Preston Sturges was a true original, a man who wrote, directed and produced his movies, and had his own quirky ideas about what he wanted to say in them. I suppose it says something about the Hollywood of the time that he was allowed to. He was a stickler, a hard task-master, who, besides making me into an amateur conductor, made his actors learn elaborate dialogue, as well as fall about constantly, at risk to life and limb, in a series of elaborate slapstick routines which only he could have devised. But it was all great fun, and I grew very fond of Preston. I consider myself lucky to have had the experience of working with him, for that, too, meant constant amazement and delight.

When *Unfaithfully Yours* finally finished I felt I was free to go back to my first love, the theatre, in *Anne of the Thousand Days*, and to give my undivided attention to the problem of attaining Henry VIII's great girth.

Putting on physical girth round the waist and chest is not all that difficult. You can put cages on underneath your clothes, and your clothes can be cut in such a way that padding will do everything. It is getting your head and your legs into proportion which poses the real problem.

I had to have a plaster cast made of my head, which was an extremely unpleasant experience. It is rather like being buried alive. A nightmare! You are completely encased in cement, your only survival kit is two straws up your nose which you breathe through violently, or not violently, as the case may be, while the clay sets, and is – eventually – cracked open. I'd no idea how gruesome it was going to be. They never tell you these things in advance. You sit there, breathing painfully through the straws while the plaster hardens, and you wonder if you'll ever get out alive, and what possible profession you could take up instead of the idiotic one of acting, in the unlikely event that you survive in a fit state to do anything. Eventually, they present you with a death mask of yourself, which is very cheering.

And I went through all this before I knew for certain whether Fox would let me do the play! I must have been mad. And then there were the legs – the legs are very uncomfortable, because of the plaster casts, because when the plaster casts are taken off your legs, a lot of your hair comes off as well, so it was enormously painful doing the plaster casts on my legs. In fact it was like a particularly refined kind of Chinese torture. I did both legs up to the thighs and right down to the ankles. Then once they have a plaster cast of your rather thin leg, they pour layers of some material over it – I'm not sure what the material is, but what you finish up with are like large socks which you pull on and which completely encase your own legs, with muscles and knees all defined, so it's like putting on a pair of tights, only they're big. It does the trick for the legs. This was wonderful, I thought, and was all done in California, where they are expert, I must say, at that sort of job.

That wasn't the end of my transformation into Henry VIII, however. There remained the problem of my face and head. After all, one's head, face, beard, whatever, has to match the size of one's body. You can't have a small head on top of a large body. Henry's head was rather a square-shaped head, and I did that with the hat, so at least I didn't have to wear a wig, as well! I had one of those Henry VIII hats – the ones he wears in the famous Holbein painting – and I don't think I ever took it off. The beard was also very important – it squared me off – but before I put the beard on I had to

96

put small pieces of foam rubber on my cheeks separately every night, to get the face right.

Being successfully bulked out for the part, was not, however, the end of the story. To be convincing as Henry VIII I had to study movement. When you play a large, stout man, your body behaviour, your timing, and your walk, all have to match your size, so I rehearsed in full foam rubber and costume, and managed to develop a heavy man's lumbering gait. I studied Holbein's painting of Henry quite a lot, and tried to strike his stance and attitude, and the way he held his body. A very large man with a very large physique emerged. And, as I have said, Henry was a very athletic man, he wasn't fat, he was just big, and very tough. He was a giant of a man. And very sexy.

It was a complex business, because some very large men have very agile minds, and I don't remember that I slowed down much, because I didn't think the play warranted it. The play presented a very quick-witted man, so I kept my mind alert, although I was large, and it seemed to work. The ladies like me in it. They thought I was marvellous. Another very important aspect of the role was voice. I dropped my voice an octave or so, and used only the lower registers, so that my voice would also fit the size of the man. I didn't think you could have a high voice coming out of such a large body, so I played it all in the lower registers to portray the weight of the man.

It is a strange fact that, throughout my career, I have played some roles which might have been better played by someone short and fat. Henry VIII is one obvious example, but there have been other short, powerful types, like Julius Caesar, who was brilliantly played by Claude Rains, an actor who was short, though not, as I remember, fat, in the film of *Caesar and Cleopatra*; and Lord Loam in

The Admirable Crichton, who was originally played by a short fat man, and is really, I think, a short man's part. Lord Loam is an enormously ineffectual peer, and this would be easier to convey if you were dumpy and fat and physically funny. Doctor Dolittle was also supposed to be small and tubby, but I identified so much with his character and with his love for animals that I didn't have a problem with him.

It's a funny business, being an actor. In the beginning, you are presented with yourself as your instrument, and you have to come to terms with what that is, and what you can usefully do with it. If you have any sense, you should be able to take advantage of your physical type in the parts you play, so that if you are short, your shortness can be used to suggest the kind of aggression or assertiveness short powerful men often have. On the whole, though, and taking into consideration a huge range of parts, it is probably always better to be tall on stage, than short. It is always a slight handicap to be towered over by all the other men in the cast, and it does limit you as to the parts you can play. And of course, I have often been able to use being tall to advantage, managing to look gangling and uncertain, and draping myself in doorways, for example, in early films like *Men are not Gods*, or being dominating, as Higgins, or intimidating, as Caesar.

A lot of awful things happened while we were rehearsing *Anne of the Thousand Days*. There were very many tricky changes of costume and scenery, and, at first, many of the technical ideas didn't work. At one point we had to change costumes in one small section of a revolving stage while it was going round, so we all became dizzy. Another time, Joyce Redman, who was giving a beautiful performance as Anne Boleyn, got her skirt caught in the revolving stage, and was glimpsed from the front in her petticoat. My intestines got themselves into such a twist that I believe the x-rays of them are still being shown to medical students in Philadelphia as a hideous example of extreme stress. We opened in Philadelphia, while Maxwell Anderson, distinguished Pulitzer prize-winning author and member of the excellent Playwright's Company that he was, was still locked up in his hotel room feverishly rewriting and writing new scenes which we would read during the day and go on and play that night. We opened out of town with the play in November 1948, and I remember that we had all kinds of different troubles with the production before we eventually got it right. The famous award-winning designer Jo Mielziner did the sets – over that period he won Tony Awards for *Sleepy Hollow*, *Summer and Smoke*, *Death of a Salesman*, *South Pacific*, *The Innocents*, and *The King and I*. Naturally, he won one, too, for the design of *Anne of the Thousand Days*. His sets were beautiful, but full of difficulties, and because there were a lot of soliloquies in the play, we sat in chairs, and the chairs were put forward into the audience, rather like a close-up in films, so that one sat in this chair and it was supposed to go forward into the audience, and you would do your soliloquy and fade back into the scene. It sounded brilliant, but it didn't work, and we had terrible trouble with those chairs on the road.

Apart from the fact that my costumes worked – Motley was an excellent costume designer – and my padding worked brilliantly, things couldn't have looked worse for coming into Broadway. But, in the event, the play was a great success, and was acclaimed by all the critics as a masterpiece. We opened on 8 December 1948 at the Shubert Theatre, New York, and didn't close until October 1949, after 288 performances – by popular demand, we re-opened again after the usual summer break. At the end of the New York run we toured the Midwest and Canada with the show and it was elected the Best Play of the Year. I won the Best Actor of the Year Award for it in 1949 for my portrayal of Henry VIII – my first Tony.

The Tony is really the Antoinette Perry Award, but is known in the business as the Tony Award. I have three Tonys, one for *Anne*, in 1949, one for *My Fair Lady*, in 1956, and one for "Contributions to the Theatre", which I won in 1969. They were, therefore, spread out over my career, and I'm very proud of my Tonys. There's a lot of competition for them, and in those days, especially, there was very strong competition indeed because acting performances in the New York theatre were very fine at that time. In fact, I think Lee J. Cobb was up for one that same year – 1949 – for his extraordinarily powerful performance in Arthur Miller's *Death of a Salesman*. That play won the Tony Award for Best Play that year, its director Elia Kazan, won the director's Tony, and Arthur Kennedy won the Tony for Best Supporting role, but I won the Best Actor Tony for *Anne of the Thousand Days*.

Perhaps the best way of giving you an idea of the calibre of the acting at that time is to point out that in 1947 the Best Actor/Dramatic Star Tony was shared by José Ferrer, for *Cyrano de Bergerac*, and Frederic March, for *Years Ago*. In 1948, it was shared by three actors, Henry Fonda, for *Mister Roberts*, Paul Kelly, for *Commando Decision*, and Basil Rathbone for *The Heiress*. In 1949, it was only me. I was naturally very pleased, Max Anderson was very pleased, and, in the end, that difficult verse play turned out to be a triumph. Not only did it take me back to the theatre – and I was immensely relieved to be back on the stage again – but it established me on Broadway as an English actor of note, a reputation which, I'm happy to say, I still retain.

CHAPTER 6

PLEASURES
OF PORTOFINO

*I*n mid-career, actors must find
ways of relaxing and escaping all the pressures, and I was
very lucky in this respect because it was during this period
that I fell in love with the ancient Italian seaside town of
Portofino. I was once more in my natural element, out of
Hollywood and back in the theatre, but I was working
very hard, and the house I built bit by bit on the hill
above Portofino was to become very important indeed to
me, and to provide much peace and tranquillity in times
of need. To pay for a plot of land there, with a fabulous
view, and to pay for the gradual building of my house, I
made one or two uninspired films, about which the less
said the better – except that it was worth it. The house
was a constant source of joy to me and all those close to
me, because it allowed me to recharge my batteries. It was
a glorious place to go, and I used it a great deal, as an
escape.

I found I could relax there because it was a different
life altogether, miles away from any theatre. There was
no one you *had* to see, nothing you *had* to do. I did a

101

lot of sailing and made a few good friends among fellow sailors in the port. It was wonderful. You were completely removed from city life. I used to go for long walks across the hills, and drop down into a little port called San Fruttuoso. I'd lunch there – it was really just a monastery and a few fishing boats – and then I'd go back in a boat I'd had sent round, along the coast to Portofino. I swam a lot, and I had a motor boat which got me from A to B rather quicker than sailing, and I had my jeep to get me up the extremely steep and rocky incline to the house.

I've never had a place, before or since, where I could relax so totally. Life there was so slow and so sweet, and we had our own wine, which the gardener made from our own vineyards, and darling old Maria Lanfranconi looked after me, and would cook us a spaghetti with tomatoes and fresh basil in the house. We ate very well, and we drank very well and there were absolutely no pressures of any kind. It certainly helped me to do that all important thing: conserve my inner feelings.

Sometimes, when I was mulling over whether to do a play or a script, or how to play a part, I would go there in order to disappear. People might have known where I was, but they couldn't reach me. I could make up my own mind while fiddling around in my vineyard, without any producers to hassle me. Looking back, I can see now that I was at a crossroads. Rodgers and Hammerstein auditioned me for their musical version of *Anna and the King of Siam*, which was to be called *The King and I*. I sang some songs for them, but they didn't like me, and I didn't get it. Instead, I did something very different – T.S. Eliot's austere verse play *The Cocktail Party*. I had seen Alec Guinness in it in New York, and it seemed both interesting and prestigious, so I agreed to do it on the London stage, but in the event, I hated doing so.

I believed very strongly in *The Cocktail Party*'s central theme – that when people are undergoing great mental anguish, they will seek out "guardians", people who have already been through the fire and endured, to help them through. But going on in the part of a dessicated psychiatrist who thinks he is God, in a play which shows no human warmth whatsoever, was like stepping under a cold shower.

The Cocktail Party is a strange play of Eliot's, and I never quite understood it. I played the psychiatrist, the "Unknown Stranger", and the director was a man called E. Martin Browne, who directed most of Eliot's plays. I got on with Martin Browne quite well, and while we were rehearsing I used to take him out to lunch and say to him: "Martin, what does all this mean? I don't understand a lot of it. Can you explain it to me?" And he would say: "No, I don't like to do that. I don't think it should be explained. I think it should just be said. Just say the verse clearly and it'll carry you, don't worry. The audience may not know what it means either, but it has a great quality to it, that play." He was damn right, it did, and I shouldn't really have worried a damn about what things meant because it really didn't matter what things meant. It *was* a very fine play. It was just that doing it still meant stepping under a cold shower every night.

I had an excellent cast with me in *The Cocktail Party*: Ian Hunter – a very good actor, I was very fond of Ian – Margaret Leighton, Donald Houston and Alison Leggat, and we had a very good season indeed in London. But there were certain ironies to our success, for while I was having this rather chilly intellectual experience at The New Theatre, Yul Brynner was getting the warmest praise in *The King and I*. He deserved it. He was quite magnificent, and there is no doubt that his performance helped to make the

production a record-breaking success, so when he opened I
sent him a telegram saying: The King is dead, long live the
King! But it's quite a thought that if I had done *The King
and I*, I would never have been able to do *My Fair Lady*.
I simply wouldn't have been free. And that, I suppose, is
destiny of some kind – or at least, show business!

In 1950, came the delightful *Bell, Book and Candle* by
John Van Druten, a genuinely witty and light-hearted
piece about a beautiful witch who casts her spells in
modern Manhattan. Lilli Palmer played the witch, who
loses her power to bewitch men if she falls genuinely in
love, as ordinary mortals do. John Van Druten directed
us himself, and the play was produced on Broadway by
Irene Selznick. *Bell, Book and Candle* was an extremely
well-made comedy, and was a great success, running at the
Ethel Barrymore Theatre, New York for 233 performances,
or six months, and only coming off then because it was
still the custom, pre air-conditioning, to come off for the
stifling summer months in the city.

Variety paid Lilli and I what I suppose was their ultimate compliment in describing us as a kind of junior Alfred
Lunt and Lynne Fontanne, and was of the opinion that:
"The play provides the Harrisons with several captivating
love scenes, which are played with diverting realism, and
which staid suburban matrons can comfortably relish, since
the stars are married in private life." Even that eminent
critic George Jean Nathan said the play had charm, whatever that is, and, as J.M. Barrie once noted, "If you have
charm, you don't really need to have anything else; and if
you don't have it, it doesn't matter what else you have."

Bell, Book and Candle took the public imagination to
such an extent that, four years later, we brought it to
the Phoenix Theatre, London, where I directed it myself,

and had Wilfrid Lawson, with his wonderful demoniacal laugh, in it as the male witch, the warlock, and Athene Seyler as the older, female witch. We did quite a bit of laughing together during that production, and it ran so long that both Lilli and I had, eventually, to be replaced. At first, Joan Greenwood took over from Lilli, then after she and I had met, but by coincidence, the part was offered to Kay Kendall, and the play became known in certain circles as *Bell, Book and Kendall*. When the play was filmed, however, the starring roles went to James Stewart, Jack Lemmon and Kim Novak.

While I was playing in the first stage production of *Bell, Book and Candle* on Broadway, Laurence Olivier had been starring in London in *Venus Observed*, another difficult verse play – this time by Christopher Fry. It is hard to remember now, that during that period, the beginning of the second Elizabethan Age in England, we were all firmly convinced that a revival of the great verse drama of Elizabeth I was taking place, and that Eliot and Fry were its two most important writers. Naturally enough, a great many actors wanted to be part of so historical a happening in the theatre, but I didn't. I knew that verse drama – the ancient or the modern variety – was not my style, but because of the success of the Maxwell Anderson play, and then the Eliot play, I seemed to have got into it, all the same, and so when Larry asked me if I'd like to play the part he'd played in *Venus Observed* on Broadway, with him directing, I accepted. I should really have known better!

The production was considered a fair success, but not by me. This was partly because the producers insisted that we do the play in a huge, barn-like theatre, completely unsuited to the delicate verbal fireworks of the piece, but, whatever the size of the theatre, or the conditions,

I couldn't enjoy doing the modern verse plays because
they didn't suit my style of acting. The metre was modern
– it bore no comparison to Shakespeare's – but it had
something about it, nevertheless, which constipated you
a little bit. You had to stay within the rhythms of the
author, and I like breaking up rhythms in modern plays.
I like to be able to make my own rhythms, and make my
own timing out of comedy, so that my pauses don't always
come where the author intended them. I've always found
you could get a great many marvellous effects like that,
so I was really after plays by the modern prose writers,
rather than the modern verse writers.

It was, of course, rather pleasant being directed by
Larry, though I can't remember one single thing he said
to me. Maybe we were a little shy of each other, and he
didn't want to disturb me. He was quiet and respectful and
very nice, and we put the play on and it ran, but I don't
remember that he enlightened me in any way as to how to
deal with modern verse. I don't think actors should direct,
anyway, especially if they are in the production as well.
Not that Larry did try to direct *Venus Observed* and act in
it himself, but he had done so plenty of times before, on the
stage, and in his famous Shakespeare films. I think that
directors should be apart from actors. The director should
be a separate individual who understands the actor, and
who has a bird's eye view of a production, which he can't
have if he tries to be in the production as well.

Having said that, however, I made the very same mistake myself the following year (1953) when I did a play of
Peter Ustinov's, *The Love of Four Colonels* in New York,
and for some reason decided I wanted to direct it, as well
as act in it. I didn't enjoy the experience for the simple
reason that it's very difficult to be in two places at the
same time. As director you've got to be in the auditorium

watching the play, and as actor, you've got to be on the stage. If you're on the stage playing a lead, you're unable to view the play properly because you're on stage most of the time, so you get no perspective – no bird's eye view – and that's very important for a director, for without it you don't get the correct balance on the play, so you can't give the actors any advice. When you're acting with somebody else on stage, you are a little bit like a horse with blinkers on, you see them but you don't really see what their values are from the front of the house. Only when you get out there, can you tell an actor that he's not projecting enough, that he's going down his shirt front, that he has to have more energy – all the things that are necessary in acting, but which you can't see when you're on the stage. So it's not a good thing to do both at the same time.

The Love of Four Colonels was my first stab at directing, and part of the reason for wanting to do it – a large part – was that Ustinov, the author/actor/comic and entertainer for all seasons, had been so marvellously funny in it in London. I put it on for the Theatre Guild of New York at the Shubert Theatre, and, despite the difficulties of directing as well as acting in a production, which I've described above, I found it fascinating to do. The play consisted of four plays within the play, which were parodies of Shakespeare, Restoration Comedy, Chekhov and Modern American Drama, each with their appropriate costumes, wigs, and even, in the case of one of my own parts, a plaster cast on one leg. It was an elaborate production, because, apart from satirizing the four types of drama I've just mentioned, Ustinov was also sending up four distinct national types, the four Colonels of the title, English, French, Russian and American. We had a good run, and I was particularly pleased when Peter Ustinov won the Best Foreign Play Award for it. So was Peter Ustinov!

It was when we were doing *The Love of Four Colonels* in Boston in 1953 that I gave up smoking. I positively had to, because I was feeling so odd that I couldn't feel the nerve endings in my finger tips, and the doctor said I had an advanced case of nicotine poisoning. I switched to cigars at first, then slowly gave up the cigars, and the whole process took about six months. It was just as well I did, because I went into a couple of films then, one of which was the most energetic piece of work, involving a great deal of riding, fencing, swordplay, duels on horseback, and general swashbuckling, and I certainly wouldn't have been able to do any of it if I'd been unfit.

The first of these two films occurred when Lilli and I were asked by the brilliant but "difficult" film director Stanley Kramer to make a film of Jan de Hartog's play *The Fourposter* which Hume Cronyn and Jessica Tandy had made a success on Broadway. The story centred round the fourposter bed of the title, and described forty-five years of a marriage, beginning with the couple's wedding night in 1897. We were, of course, called upon to age forty-five years during the production, and at times, it felt like it!

The second film was *King Richard and the Crusaders*, a Hollywood epic, based on Sir Walter Scott's novel *The Talisman*, which, although it had George Sanders as King Richard, myself as Saladin, King of the Saracens, Laurence Harvey as the juvenile lead, and Virginia Mayo as the blonde heroine, is now remembered chiefly for a priceless bit of dialogue, spoken – or rather shrilled – by Virginia Mayo:

War, war, that's all you think of, Dick Plantagenet!

King Richard was my first experience of Hollywood devices like the Falling Down Horse, and the Getting

Up Horse, horses trained to help actors in this kind of action picture. They also had special Rearing Horses, and Bucking Horses, as well as spectacular stunt men for all the jousting feats. This was the Hollywood, in all its glorious absurdity, that I had never known, and although I tried to enjoy the bizarre madness of the place, I couldn't wait to get out of the place again.

I don't know what I'd have done without my holidays in Portofino during this period of ups and downs in my career. I could always relax there, go off sailing for the day and forget about work completely. I was completely relaxed socially, too, and never did any of the boring or conventional entertaining or being entertained some people go in for. The Contessa Besozzi, from whom I had bought the land in the first place, was tickled to death at the idea that I was coming to live there because she thought I'd bring some new blood to the place, but I had no intention of mixing with the stuffy Italian bourgeoisie. When I did, occasionally, have them to dinner, it was never a sparkling success, and they bored my chums silly.

I generally only invited my best and oldest friends to stay – Bob Coote and Jack Merivale were there quite often – and we were fairly riotous in our own particular way. We led very much our own lives, went out for picnics, came back for dinner, had a fairly regulated day, but not at all regulated in the formal Italian way. For a start we didn't have an indoor dining room – we ate entirely on the terrace – and they all have those over-stuffed interior dining rooms, and think only peasants eat outside.

I once had the Duke and Duchess of Windsor to lunch, but I did it in my own way, told no-one, and made absolutely no fuss about it. Nor did I invite special guests to meet them, there were just the chums who were staying in the house at the time. In any case, one couldn't have invited any of one's English friends – that would not have been at all the thing to do. They were a very strange couple, I thought, and I remember that I picked them up in the jeep at the bottom of the hill as I did with all my visitors, and brought them up to the house, but it was not a relaxed or jolly occasion. He was still being terribly grand, and even though he'd abdicated the throne some fifteen years before, he behaved as if he was still the King of England. I had to give him the top of my table, he expected it. And then I had to spend the whole time being polite and calling him Sir. Conversation was stilted and difficult, to say the least, and there were no jokes or fun of any kind. My chums took a pretty dim view of the proceedings, Jack Merivale, in particular.

During all this, I was staring hard at the Duchess, but however hard I stared, I couldn't make out what could possibly have attracted him to her. I thought she was awful, and totally unfeminine, and he was excessively stupid, so, all in all, it was not my idea of an amusing luncheon party.

Things were incomparably better when Larry and Vivien Olivier came to stay, or John and Mary Mills, or the French actor Jean-Pierre Aumont. John Mills amused us all by making little 8-millimetre films in which he always played the comic. The weather was always warm, the sea unpolluted, and the port, because it was almost land-locked, was utterly unspoiled. Life in the piazza and the little restaurants and shops around the piazza still goes on as it ever did. I went there recently and had dinner in the Castelletto at the top of the hill, and I saw that nothing there had changed – only myself. The Castelletto is a minute castle with an incredible view, and there's a lift which goes up through the rocks to the Castello, and from there you have to climb steps to the Castelletto – the two little turrets like hats at the top. I never used to think anything of it – I used to have immensely strong legs – but now I see it's an absolutely fearsome climb!

Isaiah Berlin, who's been a friend of mine since I first met him and his nice wife Aline in Portofino, and discussed the problems of the atomic bomb, is an amazing man. He's older than me, and he can still climb up giant hills. He has to, since he and Aline live at the top of one near Portofino. Nowadays, I tend to see Isaiah more in London than in Italy, often at the Garrick Club. I also had some very nice friends of Welsh and English aristocratic extraction, whom I used to visit at their castle in Portofino. They were the Hon. Auberon Herbert, and his mother, Lady Mary Herbert, and you would turn up at their place and you'd never know what interesting people you were going to meet. Once I met Evelyn Waugh there, but despite his reputation for being rude to everyone, he was quite polite and nice.

Most of the time, however, I wasn't socializing at all, I was out sailing or walking on the hills, or helping our gardener to make our own white wine from our own vineyard. And storing up the all-important inner energy for the next round.

Sidney Gilliat, who with Frank Launder had written *The Rake's Progress*, which had been such a success during the last days of the war in 1945, wrote to tell me that he had written a new comedy film with me in mind, a sort of companion piece to *The Rake's Progress*, to be shot at Shepperton Studios in England. Just as the first film had been named after one of Hogarth's great series of paintings, the second one was to be called after its companion series, *Marriage à la Mode*. The American distributors, however, didn't understand that, so the film came out in 1955 under the title *The Constant Husband*, and has provided a constant source of amusement ever since. In fact, it was shown on television in England in the summer of 1989, and still made people laugh a lot, which is very pleasant to hear.

The Constant Husband has a very funny idea, though it's a bit broader in concept than the scripts written by Launder and Gilliat as a team. It is about a man who keeps losing his memory when it comes to women, and finds, to his horror, that he has married no less than seven wives, all of whom are determined to stay married to him. His very attractive defence counsel is played by Margaret Leighton, but when she gets him off, he pleads to be allowed to go back to prison, the only place he's out of the clutches of all his wives. Needless to say, the lawyer springs him from the back door of the prison, into her car, and into her arms! No-one could have had a more delectable collection of female co-stars than I had in this film: apart from Margaret Leighton, there was a young French actress, Nicole Maury, and the irresistible young English actress, Kay Kendall, who had made her film début to great acclaim in the wildly hilarious, and wildly successful *Geneviève*.

Very quickly, Kay's delightfully whacky sense of humour began to exercise an extraordinary fascination over me, and we started to have enormous fun together. It was impossible to avoid having fun with Kay. She showed me bits of London I didn't know – she and her mother and sister had lived right through the Blitz over a famous pub in St Martin's Lane, The Salisbury, and she knew every market stall and every café in Covent Garden. She was young – 26 to my 46 – and full of mischief, and with her, life seemed to open up anew, and become full of promise.

But what could I do about it? At the end of *The Constant Husband*, I was booked to do the London production of *Bell, Book and Candle* with my wife playing a witch, and sometime during the run of that, to direct no less a personage than Edith Evans in *Nina* by the French playwright, André Roussin.

I tried, really tried, to forget about Kay, but though she was not playing a witch, she had put a spell on me, and life without her didn't seem worth the candle. At one point we ran away together into the hills above Portofino, and the enchanted streets of the ancient town of Genoa, but real life claimed us back, and it was while I was playing in *Bell, Book and Candle* in London, that Alan Jay Lerner and Frederick Loewe came to see me and asked if I would do a musical they were writing based on Shaw's *Pygmalion*.

CHAPTER 7

MY FAIR LADY

PART I
How It Happened

*I'*ve always been fascinated by the musical field, perhaps because it's so different from other forms of theatre. I love all the different, colourful theatrical expressions they use, which you don't get in the so-called legitimate theatre, and I've always loved going to musicals and shows with musical sketches in them, like intimate reviews. But although I am quite musical, and I know that at least I have got a good sense of rhythm, I'd never done a musical show myself – so when Alan Jay Lerner and Frederick (known as Fritz) Loewe came and asked me if I would like to do a musical of, of all things, Shaw's *Pygmalion*, I didn't think I could do it. I didn't think I was in any way equipped to do it. And, on top of that, I was worried about turning one of Shaw's best plays into a musical. A lot of my friends said: Oh my God, you can't do that, you're supposed to be a loyal interpreter of Shaw, practically a guardian of Shaw. Poor old GBS'll turn in his grave! You can't make *Pygmalion* into a *musical*! It's disgraceful.

Besides, the show wasn't anything like so promising then. In fact, all Lerner and Loewe had got when they first came round to see me – only I didn't discover this until much, much later – were the rights to turn the play into a musical, and all they'd got to offer me were a few numbers, a very few numbers – hardly any of the ones which turned up finally in the show – and they were mostly the girl's numbers. They had written very little, at that stage, for Higgins, and though I knew *Pygmalion* was a very fine play, I was very much in two minds about whether I should do it or not. So as usual with me, I dithered.

At the beginning the show wasn't called *My Fair Lady* at all, it was called *Lady Liza*, and I learned something from the titling of it which was really rather fascinating: in the musical comedy field there are female titles and male titles, and they'd given it a female title in the shape of *Lady Liza* because in the initial stages they wanted to centre it round a female star, so they'd designed it as a female vehicle. Later on, when they got me, they decided to change the title to a masculine title, and so, after considering lots of perfectly awful ones it became *My Fair Lady* – the purpose of the possessive *My* being to stress the dominating masculine angle – and also to be a pun, in the cockney accent, on Mayfair Lady, which Eliza wasn't, and Higgins made her seem.

Well, this kind of thing was all new to me. I'd never heard of such things as male or female titles before, and I began to discover that putting a musical together is rivetting. It's not at all like accepting a play and saying: Yes, I'll do that, and you know what you're referring to because the play exists. Musicals are done very much catch as catch can. They are made while you're

Centre stage
at an
early age

Little brother Rex
on holiday
with his two sisters,
Sylvia *(left)*
and Marjorie

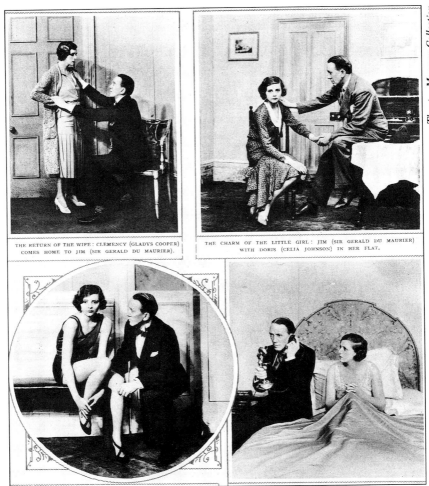

THE RETURN OF THE WIFE: CLEMENCY (GLADYS COOPER)
COMES HOME TO JIM (SIR GERALD DU MAURIER).

THE CHARM OF THE LITTLE GIRL: JIM (SIR GERALD DU MAURIER)
WITH DORIS (CELIA JOHNSON) IN HER FLAT.

The inimitable Gerald Du Maurier, whose
naturalism so inspired Rex Harrison's acting

Ralph Lynne and
Tom Walls in *Turkey
Time*, one of their
famous Aldwych farces

Rex, Marie Tempest
and Rex's hero,
A.E.Matthews, in a
scene from *Short Story*

In *Heroes Don't Care*,
with Coral Browne. 'I
haven't much of a nose,
but I seem to smell
something distinctly
dirty in that remark.'

French Without Tears -
Terence Rattigan's
comedy classic
at the Criterion

With Diana Wynyard in
Noel Coward's
Design for Living
at the Theatre Royal,
Haymarket

Thomas Newbiggin Stapleton in *Men Are Not Gods*

Harley Prentiss in *St Martin's Lane,* with Vivien Leigh

Dickie Randall in
Carol Reed's
Night Train to Munich

Twentieth Century Fox

Cusins in Shaw's *Major Barbara*, with Wendy Hiller

Janus Films

Vivian
Kenway in
The Rake's
Progress

Off to Hollywood with
Lilli Palmer

King Mongkut in *Anna
and the King of Siam*

Four Musketeers in Hollywood: *(left to right)*
Douglas Fairbanks Jr, David Niven, Rex and Robert Coote

The Ghost of Captain Daniel Gregg in
The Ghost and Mrs Muir, with Gene Tierney

Charles Hathaway in
The Constant Husband

Professor Higgins in the
Drury Lane Production
of *My Fair Lady*,
with Julie Andrews

My Fair Lady
at Drury Lane

With Kay Kendall, enjoying a well-earned cuppa

(bottom left) Mikail Platonov in *Platonov*

(bottom right) Julius Caesar in *Cleopatra*,
with Elizabeth Taylor

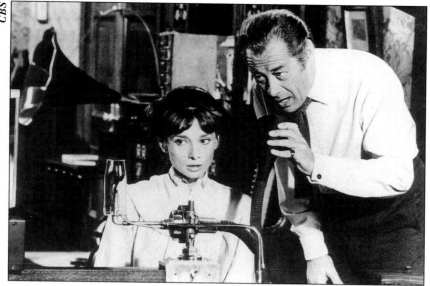

Professor Higgins in the film of *My Fair Lady*,
with Audrey Hepburn

(bottom left) High Style

(bottom right) With his two sons Carey *(left)* and Noel,
relaxing in Portofino

Off stage with dog
Homer in Portofino

Dr Dolittle in
Doctor Dolittle

Douglas H. Jeffery

Zoe Dominic

(top left) Pirandello's *Enrico Quattro*

(top right) Captain Shotover in Shaw's *Heartbreak House*

As the Earl of Loam in *The Admirable Crichton,* with Edward Fox

Zoë Dominic

Sir Rex and Lady Harrison
at Buckingham Palace, 25 July 1989

rehearsing, or while you're on the road, but I didn't know that at the time.

What I did know was that when Lerner and Loewe came and played me the first songs they'd written I hated them, and when they asked me what I thought, I told them immediately. I said: "I hate them." It's difficult enough, anyway, to understand the value of a song when it's first played to you, out of context, and on an old piano, with the composer, who isn't a pianist, playing the tune, and the lyricist, who isn't a singer, singing the words. Moss Hart, the wonderful director of *My Fair Lady*, about whom more anon, used to tell a story about when he was writing a satirical revue with Irving Berlin, called *As Thousands Cheer*, and Irving, who was totally self-taught as a musician and as a pianist, rushed round to his apartment in a state of excitement, and played him a little number called "Easter Parade" which was meant to be the grand finale. It sounded so terrible, Moss didn't know what to do, and then he remembered something. "Irving," he said, "play 'Blue Skies' for me." Irving played "Blue Skies" and that sounded just as terrible. "Okay," said Moss, "I think 'Easter Parade' must be a terrific song."

What Fritz and Alan played me on that occasion were the first two songs they'd written for Higgins – "Please Don't Marry Me", which was their first attempt to write a song about Higgins's attitude to women, and "Lady Liza", in which Higgins reassures Eliza before she goes to the ball. Apart from that, they'd written another song which also bit the dust pretty quickly called "Say a Prayer for Me Tonight", which was supposed to be Eliza worrying about going to the ball. It says something for the professionalism, and I suppose also the characters of Fritz and Alan, that when I said I hated their two songs they immediately agreed with me, and both of them said that as soon as they'd got to know me and begun reacting to my personality they knew that the two songs they'd written were merely slick and clever and superficial, and didn't reflect the character I was to play.

Once they turned their attention to the combined personalities of Henry Higgins and myself, and Alan told me that pretty soon Higgins and I became interchangeable in his mind, they began to realize that instead of the fact that I am an actor and not a singer being a drawback, it gave them an opportunity to develop a new style for me, and that the secret lay in writing lyrics and music which would coincide exactly with the way I would speak that line. A good example comes in "I'm an Ordinary Man":

> But let a woman in your life
> And your sabbatical is through!
> In a line that never ends
> Come an army of her friends;
> Come to jabber and to chatter
> And to tell her what the matter
> Is with you.

This is composed so that it can be spoken or sung without altering the music, and has nothing at all to do with vocal range. Slowly, Fritz and Alan began to realize that the songs they wrote for me, which could be described as comedy songs, had to be written to be spoken. They also began to realize that my songs had to be built on a strong foundation of emotion. The first one they tried was "Why can't the English teach their children how to speak?" and it didn't work very well because at the beginning it was just a statement of Higgins's intellectual position – until they injected into it all the anger and frustration he would feel:

118

An Englishman's way of speaking absolutely
classifies him.
The moment he talks he makes some other
Englishman despise him.

And:

Arabians learn Arabian with the speed of summer
lightning.
The Hebrews learn it backwards, which is
absolutely frightening.
But use proper English, you're regarded as a freak.
Why can't the English
Why can't the English
Learn to speak?!

Once they'd cottoned on to the idea that I had to speak
rather than sing, things improved at a great rate, though I
continued to give Alan trouble for a bit over "Why Can't the
English?" and kept telling him that I didn't want to sound
like an inferior Noel Coward. But when Alan recovered
from this fit of rudeness, he saw the point, and changed
the rhyme scheme so it became less Cowardly. Originally
he had written:

Why can't the English teach their children how to
speak?
In Norway there are legions
Of literate Norwegians.

After our conversation, this became:

Why can't the English teach their children how to
speak?

This verbal class distinction by now should be antique.

Which also made the line a great deal easier to act.

They followed "Why Can't the English?" with "An Ordinary Man", which replaced one of the songs I'd hated, "Please Don't Marry Me", and began to get Higgins off to the races. I must admit it is a song I never warmed to, but I supposed that, with hindsight there is something fairly hilarious in the fact that a song which goes:

> Oh, let a woman in your life
> And you invite eternal strife!
> Let them buy their wedding bands
> For those anxious little hands;
> I'd be equally as willing
> For a dentist to be drilling
> Than to ever let a woman in my life.

was written by a man who liked women so much he had been married six times (by then), to be sung by a man who likes women so much he has been married six times (by now)!

But before we get on to how I learned a technique with which to do these songs, it is worth recording that Lerner and Loewe had had an earlier try, around 1952, at making *Pygmalion* into a musical, and had found it impossible. The story didn't provide them with any of the then prerequisites of a musical comedy show: there was no obvious ensemble, or chorus line, which was thought to be essential in any musical, there was no sub-plot to parallel the main plot, and it was not a love story, it was more a non-love story. Neither Alan, who had done the screenplay for Minnelli's famous film musical

120

An American in Paris, or Fritz and Alan together, who had written the brilliant and successful stage musicals *Brigadoon* and *Paint Your Wagon* by that time, had the slightest idea how to set about writing a non-love song. And then, as if to plunge them further into gloom, they bumped into Oscar Hammerstein at Madison Square Garden in New York City during the famous Presidential elections when the Democratic candidate, Adlai Stevenson, was up against Eisenhower, and Oscar Hammerstein asked them how they were getting on with *Pygmalion*, and Alan answered "Slowly". "Dick Rodgers and I worked on it for over a year," Hammerstein told them, "and we gave it up. It can't be done," he said.

What with that and the election results, Alan and Fritz considered themselves defeated in good company that evening, and the idea didn't surface again for another couple of years, by which time, a lot of things had happened. For one thing, that old rogue, Gabriel Pascal, had kicked the bucket, and though, in the end, that made the question of the rights to Shaw's play even more complicated, it made Lerner and Loewe start thinking about the project again. Meanwhile, musical comedy itself had begun to change, and certain things, like sub-plots and chorus lines no longer seemed essential. Most important of all, attitudes to love and the love story element in shows were becoming subtler and more sophisticated. Of course, things don't change in the theatre overnight. It may seem like that, when, all of a sudden you feel a major change, but you know that a great deal of work, and a great many things have been leading up to it. However, it seemed that maybe, now, you could even make a musical from a non-love story!

Poor Fritz and Alan also had to overcome another of my misgivings: at the very beginning I had flatly refused to play Higgins because I believed that Leslie Howard,

121

who had played him in the 1938 film *Pygmalion* with Wendy Hiller as Eliza, was completely brilliant, and no other actor could compete with him in the part. I made them watch the film with me, and Alan pointed out to me that when, after the ball, Eliza cries out: "What is to become of me?" and Leslie Howard delivers the line: "Oh, that's what's worrying you, is it?" he does it in such a way that you saw that he understood her feelings very well. Leslie Howard's reaction was too sympathetic and not in Higgins's character. It was not until then that I began to see what I could do with the part. Alan said he didn't believe that Higgins had the slightest idea what was worrying Eliza, and I agreed with him. I had to convey the genuine amazement of the man when he discovers that the girl has any feelings of any kind at all.

Anyway, Fritz and Alan started working on *Pygmalion* again, and gradually they lined up some brilliant people. Alan had already arranged for Herman Levin to be his producer for whatever show he, Alan, did next. They got Oliver Smith to do the sets, and it was unanimously agreed that Cecil Beaton was the best possible person to do the costumes. I think it was Alan who said about Beaton that when you looked at him, it was difficult to know whether he designed the Edwardian era or the Edwardian era designed him. It was equally difficult to ask Beaton to design costumes alone, for he usually liked to design an entire show, and somehow, eventually he did manage to do most of it – in Drury Lane, and later, in the film.

Alan always said that the first person he'd thought of for Higgins was me. He and I had met while I was appearing in Maxwell Anderson's play *Anne of the Thousand Days* on Broadway, and we used to go out to Maxwell Anderson's house after the Saturday night performance where there was generally a penny poker game. The composer Kurt

Weill was often a guest there, and Kurt was thinking of doing a new English version of *The Threepenny Opera* for me, and Alan asked him if I could sing, to which Kurt replied: "Enough." This monosyllabic reply apparently stuck firmly in Alan's head – I must say he had an extraordinary memory for such things. He also had a remarkable persistence in pursuing, and achieving, what he wanted, which in this case, was for me to stop dithering about whether I'd do the show and make up my mind. To this end, he and Fritz hung about London for weeks while I was acting in *Bell, Book and Candle*, using their time to learn exactly how cockney rhyming slang works (a rude noise became a "raspberry" because the full rhyming slang for it is raspberry tart, and the rhyming word – which I leave you to work out for yourself – is dropped). They were writing Eliza's number "Wouldn't It Be Luverly?" with its clever cockney touches, such as "absobloominlutely" – and waiting for me.

Alan described what happened next in his book *The Street Where I Live*. "On the Sunday of our fifth week, Rex called and suggested that he, Fritz and I, take a walk in Hyde Park. Rex is over six feet tall, and Fritz and I, as I have mentioned, are over five feet tall. Rex also takes long strides which he executes briskly, his head high and pointing in the direction he wishes to go. The walk through Hyde Park consisted of Rex walking and Fritz and I jogging along next to him.

"We 'walked' for almost three hours, Rex chatting away, Fritz and I panting away. Then all at once he stopped. He turned to us and said, almost out of nowhere: 'All right. I'll do it.' Fritz and I were almost too exhausted to register any joy, but it did not matter because I do not think he would have noticed it. We exited out of Hyde Park and Fritz said he thought he would go back to the hotel and take a little nap before dinner. He woke up two days later. I, however, was going on a bit farther and so Rex and I continued on together. When we parted he turned to me, looked at me for a long moment, and then said: 'I don't know why, but I have faith in you.' "

Alan goes on to say how moved etc. he was by my saying this, but all I can say now is, thank God Lerner and Loewe were so persuasive and such a talented team, and thank God I did decide to do it, because having a success of that magnitude at that period of one's life was a great boost to my career. It took up a great number of years – I did it on stage for two years in New York, and a year in London at Drury Lane, and then, later on, made the film of it, so altogether it was four years' work. But wonderful work. There's something about the magnitude of a big success in a musical which in many ways is infinitely bigger than a straight play. The elements in it are so great. Of course, we didn't get it right for a long time, and I don't blame myself for wondering, at the beginning, whether I should do it or not. It's a big step, and a big risk to take on a musical when you've never done one, and you can't sing. I was risking the whole of my serious reputation for a certain, very particular kind of comedy acting, to do something I didn't know I could do. And, as I've said, there were hardly any Higgins songs in it at the beginning.

We didn't even have the numbers when we went into rehearsal, and I didn't have "I've Grown Accustomed to Her Face" when I said I'd do the show. That was written while I was still in London doing *Bell, Book and Candle* in the theatre, and Alan and Fritzi greeted me with a rendering of it on the piano when I got to New York, just before Christmas 1955. They'd finished it three days before I arrived, and I thought it was wonderful right from the start, a beautiful piece, which became, and still is, my personal favourite. They could not have given me a better Christmas present:

> I've grown accustomed to her face!
> She almost makes the day begin.
> I've grown accustomed to the tune
> She whistles night and noon.
> Her smiles. Her frowns.
> Her ups, her downs,
> Are second nature to me now;
> Like breathing out and breathing in.

The refrains and everything were already in it, it was very well conceived.

Some of my best songs were not put in until we were on the road, however. "Why Can't a Woman Be More Like a Man", in the second half of the play, wasn't there until we got to Philadelphia. In a musical, the show is built on the road, it is *made* into a success. And Lerner and Loewe and the director, Moss Hart, and I must say, myself, forced that show into being the success it was.

PART 2

Getting it Together

Moss Hart was an extraordinarily talented man, and immensely respected, and we were very lucky to have him on the show. Alan Lerner described Moss as "in every sense of the word a man of the theatre, a gentleman of the theatre, and the last of his breed", and I agree with him. By the time he came to direct *My Fair Lady*, Moss Hart was already a legend on Broadway.

His first success, *Once in a Lifetime*, had been written with George Kaufman, and his book *Act One* tells the story of the difficulties of his life up until he struck gold. George Kaufman was a man who continually cracked jokes like "A satire is a play that closes Saturday", or "A success d'estime is a play that runs out of steam" – and Moss wrote six plays with him. One of them, *You Can't Take It With You*, won the Pulitzer Prize in 1937. Moss also wrote books for musicals with scores by Rodgers and Hart, Cole Porter, Irving Berlin, Kurt Weill and Ira Gershwin, and in 1946 wrote the screenplay for *Gentleman's Agreement* which won the Academy Award for the Best Picture of the Year.

It follows that when Moss decided to become a director, he knew all the aspects of the thing, and understood, perhaps better than anyone, how important the preparation period is – casting, planning, working with the author, and working with the actors. He even, and this is rare, understood the problems of the producer, and the economics of a show. He was witty, salty, and terrific company. He had remained a confirmed bachelor until his early forties, but then he married a lively, attractive singer called Kitty Carlisle, and they lived the life of a golden couple, entertaining in great style on Park Avenue, the centre of a brilliantly funny, talented group of people who knew above all how to have fun, as well as work hard. All this was cut off tragically when Moss died of a heart attack at the early age of fifty-seven. He is still mourned.

Like most people who are very good at their jobs, Moss couldn't suffer fools gladly, and Alan told me of one occasion when he showed great anger, in Alan and

126

Fritz's defence. They were playing the songs through to a choreographer, who was being auditioned for the show, and when they came to the song "You Did It", where Higgins and Pickering (I had brought in my old friend Robert Coote to play this role), tell the servants what happened at the ball, the choreographer in question piped up that the song was "wrong" because it described off-stage action. Moss's face flushed with anger. He turned to the offending choreographer and hissed through his teeth: "Wrong? Two very talented men have spent a great deal of time and effort creating that number and after one hearing you pass judgement and say it's wrong?" Nothing could have induced Moss to hire that choreographer after that.

Perhaps the best example I can remember of Moss in action, was the following exhibition of his technique in persuading actors or actresses to work for him, as reported in Alan's book *The Street Where I Live*. We had all decided that Cathleen Nesbit was absolutely the right person to play the part of my mother, Mrs Higgins, but we all knew that it was much too small a role for Cathleen, who was used to playing leads, to much acclaim. Moss telephoned her and asked her to come to his office to see him. Then he said to her: "Cathleen, the role of Mrs Higgins was never a great role in *Pygmalion* and it is even smaller in the musical version. Furthermore, I want you to know it will not get any bigger and might even become smaller on the road. But we want you very much. Cecil (Beaton) has designed some ravishing clothes, you will look beautiful, and you will receive your usual salary." Then he leaned forward: "Also, Cathleen, I beg you to consider this. For years now you have been appearing in very large roles in very bad plays, to which all your friends have come out of loyalty and suffered through the evening. I believe they will have a very good time at this play and

I think you owe it to them to give them a nice evening in the theatre."

It was the most infernal cheek, of course, but according to Alan, Cathleen was "completely bewitched" by this approach, and accepted the part the following day. Moss then switched his efforts over to Alan himself, because he and Fritzi had written six numbers in succession which had all been discarded, and though they had been working steadily for sixteen months, were still short of three important songs. Moss telephoned Alan and commanded him to cancel all his plans that weekend, they were going to Atlantic City. This was about the most unlikely place for them to work that anyone could have thought of, especially in winter – it was mid-November – but naturally, Moss had his reasons. At that period Atlantic City was a run-down seaside resort, full of decaying grand hotels and no-one in them. Moss reserved the entire penthouse of one of them, and saw to it that Alan was stationed at his typewriter by seven-thirty next morning. He himself arose at around eleven, they went for long walks and talks on the boardwalk which Alan describes as some of the most delightful he has ever had.

They discussed every single aspect of the show, and at the end of the weekend the lyrics of the show were almost finished, though they were still working on "Get Me to the Church on Time", on "I Could Have Danced All Night", and on the song which was eventually to become "I've Grown Accustomed to Her Face". I believe that Moss also gave the same sort of treatment to Julie Andrews when she was having trouble in mastering the cockney accent. Americans may believe that all English people know how to speak Cockney, but Julie had been gently reared in a middle-class suburb called Walton-on-Thames, and was finding it very difficult indeed. It was rather funny, really,

128

though not for her, because there was I, as Higgins, trying to get her to speak proper on stage, while off stage she had to get an American phoneticist (what would Shaw have said to that, I wonder?) to teach her to speak cockney! Anyway, I remember that Moss closed down rehearsals for two days, barred us all from the stage, and spent them rehearsing Julie, who emerged at the end of it a lot more like Eliza Doolittle.

At the beginning of rehearsals, when Moss realized how much confidence I needed to tackle the new (to me) form of the musical, he rearranged everything so that for the first week, evening rehearsals were devoted entirely to me and the staging of my numbers, and I am eternally grateful to him for it. He understood the importance of the unexpected in the theatre, the fact that anything can happen, in that most volatile of situations, when you are making the show as you go along, and he knew how to use the unexpected, sometimes magical things, and incorporate them into the finished production. Only a real professional like Moss would have the grace to walk up on the stage at rehearsal and say to the actors: "I haven't a clue what to do with this scene. Does anyone have an idea?" "Every show," he used to say, "at the end of it, makes you feel like an amateur."

Meanwhile, with all this attention being paid by Moss to Alan and Fritz and Julie and myself, Stanley Holloway, who was playing the important role of Eliza's father, the dustman, Alfred Doolittle, and had two of the most popular numbers in the show, "Wiv a Little Bit o'Luck", and "Get Me to the Church on Time", was getting a little bit miffed, and feeling somewhat neglected, and had apparently told his agent he wanted out. Moss's way of tackling him was entirely typical. "Look Stanley," he said, taking him off into a corner of the stage, "I am rehearsing a girl who has never played a major role in her life, and an actor who has never sung on the stage in his life. You have done both. If you feel neglected, it is a compliment." Stanley roared with laughter, and there was no more talk from him of his leaving the show.

Looking back on how it all began, I see now why Lerner and Loewe were so anxious for me to commit myself before they could begin writing the show. It is true that they'd said: "Listen, Rex, we can't write this musical for you unless we know you're going to do it," but it was only later, when we'd started work, that I began to understand *why* they'd said it. I didn't realize at the time that musicals are adjusted to personalities, and the people who write them can't write their numbers for somebody, and then that somebody decide not to do it. Also, I was in doubts at the beginning about how to handle the songs, and when they came to me in the first place and all my friends said "Don't you *dare* do it, Rex, it's a disgraceful idea", I didn't know what to do. In the end, however, I think people being shocked at the idea probably made me more interested rather than less, but I had no idea what was going to happen. It could have been a disaster.

My chief worry, at the beginning of the enterprise, was, of course, that perhaps the lyrics wouldn't match Shaw's dialogue in *Pygmalion*. But I had reckoned without the brilliance of Alan Jay Lerner, who, I think, succeeded admirably in getting the lyrics to match Shaw in both style and feeling.

Even so, I believe I irritated everybody at rehearsals by going round with my Penguin edition of *Pygmalion* in my pocket, referring to it constantly, and interrupting Moss Hart while he was directing us, to argue out every point.

According to Lerner, I'd adopted the attitude of Shaw's

130

defender against "the barbaric Americans", and referred to my precious Penguin "at least four times a day". If a speech didn't seem right to me, he says, I'd cry out "Where's my Penguin?" and check the book to see what damage he had done to Shaw. Eventually, after putting up with this for a bit, Lerner went off to a taxidermist and purchased a stuffed penguin. And the next time I yelled, "Where's my Penguin?" he rolled the stuffed bird out on to the stage, whereupon everybody, including me, howled with laughter. After that, Alan says that I never again referred to my Penguin book, but actually, I think that by that time I had come to believe that he was keeping faith with Shaw as much as I was. One day they presented me – on stage – with the famous stuffed Penguin as an additional birthday present when I happened to have a birthday somewhere on the road, and I kept the stuffed Penguin as a mascot in my dressing room throughout the entire run of the production.

Naturally, Alan did write some lines of his own, but most of the time he used to fool me that he had found them in one of Shaw's essays or letters. In his defence he says that he did this because on one occasion, after rehearsing the speech which comes just before "The Rain in Spain" where Higgins says to Eliza: "Oh, Eliza, I know you're tired. I know your nerves are as raw as meat in the butcher's window, but think what you are trying to accomplish. The majesty and grandeur of the English language . . . " etc. I said to him: "That's a damn fine speech. Where in Shaw did you find it?" And he said: "I wrote it." Alan insisted that once he'd confessed, I lost respect for the speech, and kept getting it wrong, so after that, he never confessed again. In the end, though, I was so satisfied we were getting Shaw right that two weeks before the English opening at Drury Lane I gave an interview to

The Times in which I said that in the entire play there were only six lines not written by Bernard Shaw.

My next major worry, or perhaps it was my first, was that I couldn't sing.

PART 3

How the Higgins Sing/Speak was Evolved

Evolving the musical style of the now famous sing/speak was certainly very hard work for me. Right from the beginning, as soon as they'd asked me to do it, I'd said, "Well I don't know that I can sing." And they suggested that I go to a voice trainer, or somebody who teaches singing, and see what the result would be. So I did. I went solemnly, every day to a man in Wigmore Street in London who was a voice trainer, but I mean a real one, who taught people to sing. Very quickly, after two or three lessons, I realized I was never going to be a very good singer, that even to become a very indifferent tenor or baritone would take me ten years, and even then, I'd be fairly indifferent as a singer. So I thought, well to hell with this, I can't do it, and there's no point in going on with it.

I rang up Lerner in New York and said: "Listen, Alan, I don't think it's any good. I can't do it. I'm never going to be able to sing like this man wants me to sing. He's a teacher of *bel canto*, and he wants me to become an Italian and roar through the window,

132

and try to hit that house across the street with my voice."
"Wait a minute," said Alan, "perhaps you've got the wrong
man." And I said, "Perhaps I have." "There's a man I
know," continued Alan, "who's a conductor in the pit at
the London Coliseum, and he's called Bill Low. I think
he might be able to help you."

I was living in a hotel at the time, and I had permission
to have a piano in my suite, so Bill Low came up and all
I had was "I'm an Ordinary Man", which I was working
on at that time, and I did it for him. He listened for a
bit, and then he said that in music halls they often have
musical numbers which they talk on pitch. "You mean,
they don't hit the notes?" I asked him. And he said,
"Well, they don't hit the notes in the ordinary singers'
way . . ."

Then Bill Low went through "I'm an Ordinary Man"
with me and just gave me a rough idea of how to talk on
pitch. When you say talking on pitch, it sounds terribly
easy, but it's not. You've got to be very musical and have
a great sense of rhythm to be able to do it at all, because
you're not singing, but you must always be true on the note.
If you talk flat or talk sharp it's just as bad as singing flat
or singing sharp. You've got to sing right bang in the middle
of the note, you've got to talk in the middle of the note.

That's what Louis Armstrong said to me, months later,
when he came round to see me at the Mark Hellinger
Theatre. "You're hitting every note right down the middle,"
he said. And that's, apparently, just what I was doing! But
I wouldn't have been hitting every note right in the middle
if I hadn't been vaguely musical in the first place. This
is where I found the sense of timing I had learned so
painfully in the theatre enormously important, because
to come into a vocal number without singing, you have to
have a tremendous feeling of rhythm. You don't come into

a song as a singer would, with a note, you come in with the spoken word. And then you either let the orchestra start and you chase them, or you let the orchestra chase you.

As I'd never worked with an orchestra before, I had never had the experience of thirty-six men pounding away at my feet like an express train and not being able to stop them. It was bloody frightening. In fact, I was so frightened of the orchestra at the beginning that I used to pretend they weren't there. It became a principle of mine never to look at the conductor for a signal to start. He had to look at me. For Franz Allers, who was an experienced Austrian conductor of operettas in the Viennese tradition, this was a complete reversal of anything *he*'d experienced. I don't think he'd ever come across anyone like me before. But I wouldn't give him any signals, I would just start, and he would have to bring the orchestra in underneath me.

My determination not to look at the orchestra led to an incident which became known as "The Famous White Coat Incident". One summer's day, Franz came in dressed in a white coat, and I sent him a note asking him to take it off as I could see him!

It goes without saying that, to do a show like this, you have to have a great rapport with the conductor of the orchestra. In *My Fair Lady* we were lucky to have Franz Allers, all the way through the show, and he used to come and see me every night after the performance. He was terribly important to me, because he knew what I was up to, and he was able to control a huge orchestra to accommodate my style, my particular kind of work. When Julie Andrews vocalized a number, for instance, he probably conducted the orchestra in a totally different manner, a manner dictated by the fact that Julie Andrews is a singer, and I am not. Franz Allers was enjoying himself hugely, in the same way I was, because it was a great challenge to him, as well. It was something new to him, having such a big orchestra and doing such unusual work, and he was loving every moment of it.

People often ask me if I invented a new form of the German *Sprechgesang* in my performance as Higgins, but I don't think I invented anything. What I was doing in *My Fair Lady* was not so much derived from the German, as from the music halls, as I've said. They had patter songs, in which people spoke to the rhythm of a tune. It's an old and evocative form, and you get much more meaning into words when you use the music as underscoring than singers can do when they sing them. This is because you can give full weight and true expression to them. With ordinary singing, especially opera singing, you're thinking much more of the noise you're making. You can't give words and music equal weight, you see, that's the trouble. You're generally thinking of the noise, the notes you're hitting, or are meant to be hitting, and it's impossible to think the meaning of a song through.

Perhaps some opera singers – if they're very brilliant – can feel a song, emotionally, while they're singing it, but then those songs were created totally differently. They were much more about what my *bel canto* teacher wanted me to do, bouncing the voice across the street, and hitting something. In *My Fair Lady*, with those brilliant lyrics, you had to be terribly aware that you were audible, and I think that Franz Allers had to keep the orchestra down for me in certain places. We evolved a method whereby I had one instrument in the orchestra which carried my melody for me, because somebody had to carry the melody of my songs. I wasn't. I was just thinking and talking my song through. In this case, the instrument happened to be a clarinet, an instrument I love, so I learned to rely on the fact that the clarinet in the pit would always play my melodies. He helped me enormously, that clarinet player, because I was able to pitch at that one instrument, you see, and it gave me a feeling of security to know I could always hear the clarinet when I was on stage.

My part as Higgins called for me to go in and out of song, and in and out of a Shaw scene without appearing to do anything very much. The orchestra would start, and I would go into a song which was an extension of the scene. This was very difficult for me, as I'd never done anything remotely like it before. I'd never sung with an orchestra, and all the time we'd been rehearsing on the road, I'd just done it with a piano. Kitty Carlisle Hart, Moss's wife, is herself a singer, and she'd warned me not to panic at the first orchestra rehearsal when I found I couldn't hear my melody. And Julie Andrews told me not to worry about the orchestra. "You'll find it like a glorious eiderdown on which you sit," she said.

Well, I never found it an eiderdown, and in spite of all this good advice, I did panic. I panicked at the first night with orchestra in New Haven, about which more later, but gradually I learned all sorts of very interesting things about singing with an orchestra, and I discovered that it was nicer than just having a piano, it was more support, and the more I used the orchestra, the more I liked it. Most of the time, however, I wasn't singing, I was acting, and talking the numbers, so I can't say the featherbed effect was the same for me as it was for a real singer, like Julie. I also learned a lot about the technique of doing a musical, such as how to be able to go out of a Shaw scene and into a number without apparently changing gear.

You had to be prepared for a very considerable energy level to maintain the control you needed. And to get over a large orchestra, which was in the pit, you had to bring up your energy level and your voice levels very considerably from the dialogue scenes to the songs. These were all things I had to learn, and I found them very fascinating to learn, and enjoyed doing it enormously. And the more I did it, the more clearly I realized how much the show had managed to retain the original spirit of Shaw's play. In fact, it was quite extraordinary the way the songs did pick up the spirit of the dialogue scenes that went before them.

The traumas continued, however, well after the first official rehearsal. I remember that occasion very well. Chairs had been arranged on stage for the company, and Moss had arranged an exhibition of sketches of the scenery and costumes round the edges of the stage. The production team faced the actors, sitting at long desks to take notes, and Fritz and Alan were, of course, at the piano. The cast read the script aloud, Moss read the stage directions, and when we came to a song, Fritz and Alan played and "sang" it at the piano.

In his autobiography, *Act One*, Moss Hart says that he learned to expect, as director, that all plays would sound frightful at first reading, and that there is almost an unwritten code among actors to mumble and twitch and make the poor author quake in his shoes at the time he has wasted writing such an appalling piece of utter rubbish. He goes on to say that only twice had he "listened to a first reading in which the stars gave as brilliant a performance at the first reading as they subsequently gave on the stage, and I have never ceased to be grateful to them for it.

"Gertrude Lawrence, at the first reading of *Lady in the Dark*, and Rex Harrison, at the first reading of *My Fair Lady*, plunged into their parts with an electric excitement, from the first line onward, that was contagious enough to make their own excitement spread through the rest of the cast like a forest fire; it made this usually dispiriting experience a thing to be set apart and remembered with gratitude."

Well, that was particularly gracious of him, and I have to record that the reading of the first act went very well, and so did the second – for everyone but me! My face apparently got longer and longer, and my voice softer and softer, and eventually Alan noticed, and, being Alan, knew exactly why. Higgins had somehow got lost in the second act. Well, they went into a little huddle, and evidently Moss agreed, and they concurred. They decided that Higgins was missing something called "musical expression" in the second act. I'd never heard of "musical expression" – it was one of those musical comedy terms quite new to me – but it seemed to mean they were going to have to give me more songs.

The song they wrote to fill that gap arrived in Alan's head, he told me, after we had been strolling down Fifth Avenue one day not long before reviewing our respective problems, past and present, with the fairer sex. It was characteristic of Alan that he had just remarked that between us we had supported more women than Playtex, when he says I stopped him, and the crowds around us, by saying in a loud voice: "Wouldn't it be marvellous if we were homosexuals?!" Alan said he didn't think so, and we walked on, but the idea must have stuck in his mind. We walked back to the Hotel Pierre, still discussing women, to find Alan's then wife, Nancy Olson, waiting for him in a hell of a bad temper. She was a pretty but earnest girl, and she was having difficulties with Alan at the time, accusing him of being a workaholic, who preferred to spend his evenings working with the boys rather than being with her. Alan, for his part, was doing his best to shut her up and prevent her from interrupting our conversation when suddenly she said bitterly: "What you really mean, Alan, is why can't a woman be more like a man?"

Alan raced to his desk and penned the immortal lines, using "Why can't a woman be more like a man" as the refrain, and deciding to call the finished song "A Hymn to Him". Quite why I was also in trouble with women at that point, I can't remember, but Alan swore that when he and Fritzi played the number through to me, I took it home to learn without a smile, saying simply: "Quite right! You're absolutely right!"

Another tricky moment during rehearsals was when I realized that I was expected to stand up on stage like an idiot doing nothing while Julie Andrews sang the whole of her "Without You" song at me. I made it very clear immediately that this was *not on*, and that I would not stand up there and be made a fool of. I had no objection to Julie singing the song. I simply refused to be there while she did so. As the point of this scene in the play is that she is finally triumphing over Higgins –

> Without your pulling it, the tide comes in
> Without your twirling it, the earth can spin
> Without your pushing them, the clouds roll by
> If they can do without you, ducky, so can I!

I can see that my objection to being there posed difficulties. Fritz and Alan and Moss went away to sort it out, but I had no idea what they'd decided, and in the train to New Haven Moss told me that it was his opinion that I would look more of an idiot – or a "horse's ass" as he put it – doing that number if I didn't turn up on stage than if I did, and that I should trust him to show me how it would work.

Well, much to the general surprise, I think, I turned up – probably because I did trust Mossie, and discovered that

139

the boys had written in two verses to be done by me at the end of Julie's song, in which Higgins reacts to Eliza's new independence with delight:

> By George, I really did it
> I did it. I did it.
> I said I'd make a woman
> And indeed I did.
>
> I knew that I could do it!
> I knew it! I knew it!
> I said I'd make a woman
> And succeed I did!

It was very hard work on the road, doing eight shows a week of the original version, and putting in new numbers all the time. We were on the road for ten or twelve weeks before we got it right. Moss knew the musical was much too long and he knew where he wanted to cut it, but he wanted to see it in front of an audience to check whether they agreed with the places he wanted to make cuts. In New Haven the curtain came down at twenty minutes past midnight! When we opened in New Haven, I was still doing numbers which I had only done in public once. One of these was called "Come to the Ball", and consisted of a whole ballet sequence where Liza was coached how to behave at the ball, and a Higgins song called "Come to the Ball" which was meant to be part of the ballet. Then they decided the whole thing was cumbersome and unnecessary, and cut it out entirely. Then there was the number called "Lady Liza", which was skilfully turned into "The Ascot Gavotte", until, all in all, the show was stripped down to a pretty good line. It's amazing the things they do with musicals. A great deal of very clever fudging goes on.

In view of all this, it is not surprising that I was in such a panic the night we opened in New Haven.

In Alan's book, he says: "Far and away the most exciting event for any company in any musical is the moment it hears the orchestra for the first time. Eyes beam and pop, delight is squealed, cheers ricochet from wall to wall . . ." Well, this may be the case for most people, but in *My Fair Lady* it was certainly not the case for me. I had rehearsed my numbers in a hall standing next to Franz Allers with everyone on the same level as myself. Now, suddenly, I found myself on stage with thirty strange people making strange noises directly below me, and no idea at all where the melody could be found. Seeing my panic, Moss promised me I could rehearse alone with the orchestra in front of the house curtain for as long as I needed.

Well, I did that, and of course it helped, and I learned something else very important about musicals and working with an orchestra. I learned that you can't pause, as you do in the theatre, for the laugh, because the orchestra goes straight on without you and it cannot stop, and you are absolutely lost. At first I was appalled by this, and in even more terror of the orchestra than usual. It happened when we were rehearsing "A Hymn for Him", and I said: "What do you expect me to do? Sing through the laugh?" And they said yes, that's what you have to do. Anyway, I panicked that first night in New Haven and I got cold feet and I actually shut myself in my dressing room and said: "I can't open, I just cannot open," and I refused to go on. I believed that the show, and in particular, my own performance, were not ready for the public eye, and the agents were scurrying about, and the PR people, trying to persuade me to go on, and they said: "Listen, the house is full and it's snowing outside, it'll be a scandal if you don't go on," and I said, "Listen, I'm not ready. I will

141

go on if I have to, but I'm not ready to do it, *I am not ready to do it!*"

It was in the dead of winter, in fact, I think there was a blizzard going on outside, and the manager of the theatre, and my agent, and all manner of people kept rapping at my door and saying: "People are already struggling through the snow on their way to the theatre. We cannot disappoint them. The house is filling up. There's a tremendous atmosphere of expectation." And then their threats became more and more desperate, and they said: "You can't do this, it's unprofessional. We'll be letting down a regular audience, an audience that keeps this theatre going, year after year, when you are not here to care, and it's they and us who'll suffer long after you've moved on. At seven thirty we'll have to make an announcement that there'll be no show, and it'll be your fault and there will be a riot in the lobby. The folks'll demand to know why, and we'll have no option but to tell them it's because Rex Harrison refuses to go on!"

Well, I went on. But I'd caused such chaos, that Kitty Hart remembers Moss's brother, Bernie, who was one of the stage managers on the show, having to round up the cast and stage hands by going round all the local cinemas, interrupting the films by getting the house lights put on, and yelling: "Everybody from the *My Fair Lady* company back to the theatre, we *are* opening tonight!" He had to do the same in gyms and health clubs, and people were leaping off massage tables and running for the theatre in their towels. I still can't believe that I was much good that opening night in New Haven, but to my immense surprise, everybody, even Moss's wife, Kitty Hart, said: "Rex gave a performance that made theatrical history."

This began to look as if it were true, because once we opened in New York tickets became so scarce that I'm told that a new, more sophisticated kind of blackmarket grew up – burglars were bribing people out of their houses, by sending them pairs of tickets through the post, so they could rob their apartments while they were out at the show!

Despite our success in New Haven, tension certainly mounted the evening of our opening in New York, and this time, it was not I who was the most terrified. After the final curtain I went to my dressing room, which was full of enthusiastic friends and had the atmosphere of a good party. The producer Leland Hayward who had once been my agent and his wife Nancy, known as Slim, were there, and Slim took one look at Alan Jay's face, grabbed him by the arm and led him outside. "Alan," she said, "listen to me, and listen to me well. What is happening in this theatre is incredible. It is something that has happened to very few people and will never happen to you again. So for Christ's sake, stop worrying and enjoy it. Do you hear me? Enjoy it!" She gave Alan a great bear hug and came back to my dressing room, but Alan told me afterwards that until that opening night was over he could not relax.

Even Moss cracked, for at the end of the first scene, the audience listened attentively, and applauded enthusiastically, but didn't laugh a lot. This was, of course, because there aren't many laughs in the opening scene, but Moss didn't think of that. He rushed frantically over to Fritz and Alan, who were standing staring at the stage, Alan tense, and Fritz completely nerveless and happy. "I knew it," Moss told them. "It's just a New Haven hit. That's all. Just a New Haven hit." Fritz looked at him with an amused but sympathetic smile on his face. "My darling Mossie," he said, "if you don't know this is the biggest hit that has ever come to New York you had better come with me and get a drink." He led Moss from the theatre to the nearest bar. When they returned about five minutes later, "With a Little Bit O'Luck" was stopping the show, and at the end of "The Rain in Spain" the applause was thunderous and deafening.

At the end of the show there was curtain call after curtain call, and even from the stage you could see that the audience were surging down the aisles, crying "Bravo" and applauding with their hands over their heads. Alan said that he was so overwhelmed he felt lonely, so he rushed backstage to my dressing room. But *en route* there he bumped, literally, into Marlene Dietrich who was all in white from top to toe, including her face, which was thickly covered with white powder. She embraced Alan so hard that he spent the rest of the evening white-faced, despite the passionate congratulations rained down on him.

PART 4
Doing the Show

There were constant queues, and standing room only, every night for *My Fair Lady* in New York, and the audiences were wonderfully enthusiastic. There's something special about New York in this respect. It does have an electrical climate, and enthusiasm is in the air. And then New Yorkers adore success and want to be part of it, to let it rub off on them, or at least to share in it for an evening.

Naturally, when one provokes a great deal of public excitement, one is also exposing oneself to danger, and I remembered an occasion when someone threatened my life when I was doing *My Fair Lady* there. In that production, one of the things I had to do every night, before I went on the stage to do "I've Grown Accustomed to Her Face", was I had to run round the back past the stage manager and go on with my "Damn, damn, damn." Well, at that particular time there was a man called the Mad Bomber in New York, who used to go around planting bombs anywhere they could make a scene or a scandal.

The Mad Bomber seemed to like to leave bombs, and though I knew about the Mad Bomber's existence, I didn't know anything about the Mad Bomber and myself. Just as I passed the Stage Manager, a dear friend of mine called Biff Liff, who is now a very successful agent, said to me: "Don't worry, Rex, if you hear a noise." I said: "What do you mean, hear a noise?" – and went on the stage and did the number, and when I came off I said to Biff: "What the hell did you mean, if I hear a noise?" He said: "Well, we had a letter from the Mad Bomber saying he'd put a bomb under the front row of the stalls and it was timed to explode while you were doing that number."

"Well, thank you very much," I said. "I'm expendable, then, am I?" He could at least have said: "Don't go on." But he was hoping that it was a leg-pull, which it turned out to be, because no sound was heard. I suppose it would have been a good feather in the Mad Bomber's cap if he'd been able to exterminate me at that time, because by this stage, the very title of *My Fair Lady* was a synonym for success. Many years later I was told that it had become the longest-running show in Broadway history, passing the 10 million dollar mark for gross receipts by December 1958, and earning more than $20 million by 1978. But when we opened in 1956 I remember all of us thinking that it would be wonderful if we could sell 50,000 copies of the record album! Record sales were generally very much smaller then than the runaway figures of the 60's and 70's, but by 1978 I believe we had sold 18 million copies of that record album, while the film we made of it in 1964 grossed something like £400 million in the first year. It was even called the greatest showbiz success of the century. And the title, which we had such doubts about, is a perfect example of a title which became good because the show was a success. If *My Fair Lady* had been a failure, or a flop, as a show, it would have been a lousy title.

Oh, it was a wonderful time! And what was so marvellous was that everybody enjoyed it so much, not only the actors, but Fritz and Alan, too. Fritz used to come and watch it every single night, and he used to finish up in my dressing room talking to all my guests. He had an absolute ball during the run of *My Fair Lady*! There was always a queue, prepared for a long wait, and equipped with flasks and rugs and things, every night, right through Manhattan's fierce midwinter. It was standing room only, so the poor things wouldn't even get a proper seat when they did eventually get inside. And more often than not, Fritzi used to finish up talking to the stalwarts in the queue, as well. He used to come back to the theatre after supper and introduce himself to them, and sit half the night chatting them up. He had a wonderful time.

All the great and the good, the rich and the famous and the talented, presidents and kings came to see the show, and congratulate one or other of us afterwards, but naturally enough the ones that mattered most to us were the members of our own professions whom we admired. One of the greatest thrills we had was learning of Cole Porter's enthusiasm for the show, and for Alan and Fritz, especially, it was magic.

For the composer and the lyricist to find that the great Cole Porter took a seat every week to listen to *their* songs, was the ultimate accolade. And what a thrill for all of us! He was such a clever man, Cole Porter, an absolutely

146

brilliant lyricist, and he was very charming, too. He used really to dress up, and put a carnation in the buttonhole of his dinner jacket. As far as I know, he came by himself, and always sat in the same seat. It was enormously flattering, but how he could bear to see the show so many times, I don't know. I suppose he saw something fresh in it every time. Or perhaps he just had a passion for it. But, then, someone like Cole Porter, with his sense of style, his understanding of good and bad, and his recognition of excellence, would naturally like a show as perfect in all its parts as *My Fair Lady*, and would no doubt have seen what an extraordinary coming together of talents it was, a fusion, in which everybody was giving their most excellent work.

It was this kind of recognition which made it matter to me that Louis Armstrong came round to see me after he'd seen the show, to tell me I had perfect pitch, and that I'd hit the note right down the middle every time! It wasn't just that it was lovely to see him, because I've always admired him so much, and love jazz, and think Satchmo was a great musician, but the compliment was that much greater because, in 1957, during the run of *My Fair Lady* in New York, but before he had seen me in it, I'd done a TV film with him, *Crescendo*, a sort of potted history of American music, in which he and I did a number called "That's Jazz" together. Louis didn't know then if I had any sense of rhythm, so he kept a firm clutch on my knee throughout the number, and kept pushing it to the rhythm. He didn't really need to, but it was so sweet of him, I didn't like to stop him. So when he came round to see me after *My Fair Lady*, and congratulated me, I knew I had a sense of rhythm, after all!

Another little accolade I received for the musical and which mattered to me a lot – because it showed that I had somehow managed to cope with the musical form – happened when Spencer Tracy came to see the show. He came round to see me in my dressing room afterwards, and he brought Frank Sinatra with him. They'd had a marvellous time, and they were being very effusive and very complimentary to me, and Spence said: "When you did that last number (I suppose he meant "Accustomed to Her Face"), you made the little Wop cry." It was a strange way to put it, and an odd way to describe Sinatra, but I thought it was rather sweet.

The more public accolades weren't lacking either. We won the Best Musical Award for that year, and I won the Best Acting Award for my part as Higgins, the Antoinette Perry Award, or Tony – my second Tony. Later on, the film of *My Fair Lady* won the Oscar, and I won the Oscar, too, and I went to Hollywood for the Oscar ceremony. But that's another story which I shall tell a little later on.

I had another extraordinary experience in New York, while doing the show, which stands out in my memory from all the other extraordinary experiences we had. We'd been playing it for about a year on Broadway, and I was near the end of the show, in the middle of "I've Grown Accustomed to Her Face" which I did in front of a drop cloth of the street. Behind the drop cloth was the study, which was flown in, in the blackout, and then I went out of "Accustomed to Her Face" into the study and finished the play with "Where the devil are my slippers?"

So there I was in the middle of "Accustomed" and suddenly there was a tremendous explosion, a terrible crash behind me, and the drop cloth was blown out and through the drop cloth came showers of little bits of wood. There was a commotion, and in the commotion Franz Allers must have dropped his hands, so the orchestra stopped, and when I came to from the shock, wondering what the hell had happened, I had no orchestra. Nothing was happening, everything was silent, and I couldn't go on without it.

I suppose one's reactions are heightened when one is on the stage, you're ready for anything, so I called out to Franz for the clarinet, which was carrying my melody, and I was able to go on with the number and finish it. But as I was finishing the number I realized that what had happened was that the ropes carrying the scenery over the months we'd been playing must have got frayed, and the whole of that heavy set had fallen behind me, and crashed and broken. I thought, well, I can't finish the play now, so I had to explain to the audience what it was had happened, and I had to bring Julie on and say: "What should happen now is that the curtain would go up, we'd be in the study scene, she comes on, and I say where the devil are my slippers." And so we finished that way, and the audience loved it.

Audiences love strange impromptu things to happen on stage. It makes them feel involved in the glamour of live theatre. For actors, however, there's more danger than glamour to this kind of thing, though what this experience showed me was just how terribly alert you are when you're on stage. You're able to think very fast. And you may have to. That set collapsing and crashing down on the stage like that was really dangerous. We were all damned lucky we escaped. If I'd been inside the set, I could have been killed. A heavy spiral staircase made of wood had smashed to pieces. Naturally, I made enquiries afterwards, to find out what had happened, and was told that the ropes had, indeed, frayed. They were very sorry. Sorry! Meanwhile they got a mock up set, a canvas job, so we could go on next night, because to have a replica of the set built was going to take several weeks.

On these occasions, you feel you have to be cool, you just have to be, but what amazed me was that Franz Allers stopped conducting the orchestra. And I had to have the clarinet to get started again. I was dependent on that clarinet. It's odd really. He was so important to me, and yet I never got to know that clarinettist. Musicians come in, do the job, and then they probably go off somewhere else and do another job. So, somehow, in these big musicals, you never really meet the members of the orchestra – there are vast numbers of them. It's a big pit and there's a lot of chaps down there.

Doing a part as demanding as Higgins for three solid years, two in New York, and one in London, is asking for trouble, really. Any actor will tell you that after a long run the part becomes so automatic that if you falter you forget everything, and you simply can't go on. This is especially true in a musical play. I don't think anybody realizes the agony actors go through if they play a thing for a long time. It becomes meaningless after a while. If you've done it eight times a week for a year, or two years, your mind is apt to wander a little bit, and if it wanders for a second and you think: what am I going to have for supper? in the middle of it all, you don't know where you are for a minute, then you catch it again. But it gives you such a mental shock that for a week you're terrified it's going to happen again. It's not fun.

This did start happening to me at the Mark Hellinger Theatre in New York after I'd been doing the show eight times a week for about a year and a half, and I can tell you that there is nothing more terrifying in an actor's life. It also happened towards the end of my run at Drury Lane – don't forget that this was my third year of the show –

150

and I used to have to have the lyrics at the side of the stage before I went on, because I knew them too well and they made no sense to me any more.

Long runs are always hard on actors, but I think the problem was exacerbated, too, by the nature of the words in *My Fair Lady*, and also the nature of the sing/speak technique. Both the lyrics and the music were so clever and so intricate that if you forgot one line, you could not go back, especially as the damned orchestra wouldn't stop. It just went on inexorably without you, and pushed you forward.

The lyrics had always given me a hard time. Moss Hart remembered that there were tremendous rages from me, and stalkings off during rehearsals, but he forgave me when he discovered that I "was not a frivolous man, and that what I achieved I got from digging, digging" – he meant working extremely hard. But late in the run it was my discovery that, with such a finely tuned musical, there's no way you can find your way back when you blow a line, that really frightened me. This kind of thing is the worst nightmare imaginable, and is the reason a lot of the time, why actors won't accept long runs.

In most ways, the New York run was a lucky time for me. I had an enviable style of life and was lent some pretty glamorous homes to stay in. But on the other hand, Henry Higgins was an exceptionally hard and demanding part. The curtain at the Mark Hellinger Theatre didn't come down until 11.20 each night, and I was always aware that every other actor in New York was able to start relaxing a good twenty minutes earlier than I was.

This meant that a day in the life of Professor Higgins followed a certain predictable pattern. After the show I was able to wind down with a drink, but I still had to entertain, I had to entertain my guests, and as the

151

show was so popular my dressing room was always full of people. I couldn't even start getting out of my clothes for half an hour. It was usually well after midnight when I left the theatre and drove back to wherever I was staying. At home, there would be something left out for me to eat, and I'd be able to relax at last. This was, in some ways, the best moment of the day. I was getting unwound by now, was glad the show was over without mishap for one more night, and safe in the knowledge that the tension would not begin again until tomorrow.

At that point, I used to feel absolutely splendid – both fit and elated at the same time. Part of that was because I'd done a lot of exercise, both on and off the stage, which made me sleep well, and I'd have eight or nine hours in bed, then the next day the tension about the next performance would begin.

Matinée days are always a long haul, and two shows a day of *My Fair Lady* were particularly exhausting. On matinée days I'd try to snatch some sleep between performances, and on other days I'd walk a lot to keep fit. On stage a lot of energy comes through the legs, and I've always found that walking is good for restoring them. I played a lot of golf, too, but usually only on Mondays, which was the only day of the week we had off. Whatever you do to keep yourself in form, however, there are always days when you know you're not on top, and that can be pretty depressing. You have somehow to pull yourself together and get on with it. That's one of the trials of our profession. You're always trying to give a top standard of performance however you feel, even if the nerves of your stomach play up, as mine do. It's not surprising that nervous stomach is known as the actor's disease.

I always banish people from my dressing room half an hour before the performance, so I can concentrate. I don't have any particular rituals, but I try to pull myself together, and compose myself. If there is anything you're particularly nervous about you may go through it. In *My Fair Lady*, I was never worried about the dialogue scenes, but I always had those difficult lyrics on the dressing table.

After two years of packed houses in New York, we brought the show to The Drury Lane Theatre, London, where *My Fair Lady* opened on 30 April 1958. There was immense press coverage, and most of the reviews were pretty good raves. Naturally, some of the English critics felt they ought not to like the show, since the Americans had made such a ballyhoo over a British play by an Irish author starring English actors, and a lot of other English talent, but most of them were forced to agree that, actually, it was as good as they'd been led to expect it would be. From the New York opening in 1956 onwards, there had been a huge smuggling trade in the original gramophone record album of the show from the USA since it was not officially available in Britain before we opened at Drury Lane. This may have lessened the excitement of the event, because a lot of people knew what to expect, but in most cases it worked for us rather than against, and seemed to mean they could hardly wait to see the songs performed live. *Variety*'s London reviewer "Myro" opined that the London production was actually better than the New York one because of the slightly larger dimensions of the stage!

Three days after the opening, we did a Royal Command Performance for the Queen and Prince Philip, which got even more press coverage than the opening had done, and though some people were worried when it was observed that Prince Philip laughed all the way through and Her Majesty did not, I had the satisfaction, afterwards, of the Queen telling me personally that she loved the show.

*

It's strange, really, what will make a good musical. I mean, it's a very good play of Shaw's, *Pygmalion*, but you wouldn't have thought of it as a musical. Yet what a subject for a musical it turned out to be! Just to have Shaw's "book" was a godsend, something that never could happen again. You don't get "books" of that quality in musicals, as a general rule. There was so much to work on, the material was so rich, and the lyrics so haunting. They really were so clever, Fritz and Alan. It was a joyous meeting of the minds. They were both tremendous admirers of Shaw, and I think they really did have an affinity with him. Alan certainly did, and I think Fritz must have had, too – his music was so enchanting.

I suppose that out of all the songs, "Accustomed to Her Face" remains my favourite. They got it dead right, and it was marvellously, brilliantly done. It seemed to touch something profoundly personal in every member of the audience and provided me with the perfect vehicle with which to show the bewilderment of the average Englishman of Higgins's time and class when confronted with anything at all to do with the life of the emotions. Because there are traces of pain, or at least genuine feeling behind the bewilderment, the audience, especially the hard-boiled ones who have had their emotions similarly repressed, were often moved to tears. Shaw knew all about the repression, if not the feelings, and made Higgins the epitome of this very recognizable kind of Englishman, and the addition of the music and the lyric took it straight into people's hearts.

What people don't realize, however, is that *Pygmalion* still works like a dream as a straight play, and it's a shame that it should be considered difficult to put on nowadays, with the success of the musical looming over it. This is particularly sad as there are lots of beautiful

154

things in the play which weren't in the musical, as well as the other way round.

It's a shame, too, that actors find it as difficult, now, to take on the part of Higgins after seeing me, as I did after seeing Leslie Howard. I've become almost too closely identified with the part. Of course, the part of Higgins has been played by lots of other people – Peter O'Toole played him in a straight production of the play on Broadway, quite a while after *My Fair Lady*, and I managed to overcome my initial reluctance, and went to see him. He had a lovely cast with him, and he made a marvellous Higgins. He was very funny in it, really awfully good, and I went round to see him afterwards and told him so. But for years I could never bear to see anyone else do it – the part was so much in my head, and Higgins had become so much a part of me, and I of him.

PART 5
Filming My Fair Lady

It is hard to remember, now, but Warner Brothers dithered about for ages deciding whether or not I should play Higgins in the film of *My Fair Lady*. Jack Warner of Warner Brothers wanted to produce the film as his last production at Warner Brothers. The trouble was that he wanted all the main parts to be played by Hollywood film stars. He wanted Cary Grant to play Higgins, he wanted James Cagney to play Doolittle, and he wanted Audrey Hepburn to play Eliza – the only one of the three he got.

I played Higgins and Stanley Holloway played Doolittle, and Gladys Cooper played my mother, Mrs Higgins. (I can't remember who he'd wanted to play her!)

I retreated to Portofino, and pottered around among my vines, having fun building a garden house and a sunken Roman bath designed by Arthur Barbosa. Meanwhile, George Cukor, who was to direct the picture, flew out to the desert to interview Peter O'Toole, who was playing Lawrence of Arabia at the time. Then he asked Cary Grant, who said: "Not only will I not play Higgins, if you don't put Rex Harrison in it, I won't go and see it." I sat tight. One evening George Cukor telephoned on a crackly line from California and asked me to make a photographic test for the part. I laughed. "I'm not making any tests," I told him. "If you want me to play the part, then I'll come." As a joke, I then sent him some polaroid photos which had been taken while we'd been fooling about on my boat, in which I appeared stark naked, holding, in one picture, a Chianti bottle in front of me, and in another, a strategically placed copy of the *New Statesman*. "You wanted a test," I told him. I'll never know what happened, but this piece of bare-faced effrontery seemed to do the trick. I think they had probably thought I looked as old as Caesar (I'd made *Caesar and Cleopatra* in the interim), and of course, I did – as Caesar! I had needed to look lined and careworn for the part. Now they saw that I was not as decrepit as they feared. Such is Hollywood! They returned the photos to me intact – and I got the part.

Filming *My Fair Lady* was not at all a piece of cake. For one thing, it was five years since I'd played the part, and for another, I had to re-think my whole performance in film terms.

Luckily for me, George Cukor was directing, and he's a very experienced director, so I went to George and I said:

"For God's sake, if you see me giving a stagey performance of Higgins, please stop me, because I want to play the part correctly for the camera." George Cukor still works in front of the camera, rather than looking through it all the time, which means that his technique is more like the technique of stage directing. Because of this, and the fact that I knew the show so well, I was able to insist on doing my musical numbers live, a practice unheard of in Hollywood musicals.

When musicals are filmed, they don't want the expense or the inconvenience of a large orchestra on the set in the studio, so they pre-record the music and play it back to the actors through loudspeakers. Most actors prefer to pre-record their songs, too, so that when they're on set they don't have to sing to the orchestral accompaniment, they can just get on with acting the part, though they do have to be very careful to get their lip movements perfectly synchronized. I didn't want to pre-record my songs – I wanted to sing them live, as I'd done on stage, so that the only part of my numbers which was canned was the orchestral backing.

Anything unusual naturally causes a certain amount of consternation in the studio, but George Cukor loved the idea, and thought that was the right way to do it. So I did every one of my numbers live, and the only number I had any trouble with was "Accustomed to Her Face" because, to get the poignancy of that song, which comes right at the end of the show, I needed the weight of the whole show to go before it, and for the film I had to do it out of context. But when Cukor saw my difficulty, he just arranged things technically so that I could do whatever I liked and the cameras would follow me and pick up everything I did!

We had a good company on the film, and the only

snag, really, was Audrey not being able to sing. I'd done the show for so long in the theatre with Julie that *any* new leading lady was going to be a problem. Julie Andrews and I had grown into a completely easy working relationship during the long run of the stage show (I reckoned up once that I'd played Higgins in the theatre 1,006 times!), and before we even get to the problem of Audrey's singing, poor Audrey had the unenviable task of taking over Julie's part, through no fault of her own. Like most things in Hollywood, it had happened entirely for commercial reasons – the studio thought they needed a big film star to carry the costs of the thing, as they were already taking a great risk on having a stage actor like me to play the leading male role, and they couldn't have a young unknown – unknown in film terms, that is – playing opposite me. Such are the exigencies of Hollywood! Audrey also had to weather a great deal of adverse press publicity about how much she was being paid, for most of the press had sided with Julie, and had wanted Julie to get the part.

Audrey is a very sensitive person, and could not fail to feel all this. And on top of that, she was not allowed to sing her own part, which she badly wanted to do. It quickly leaked to the press that she was being dubbed, so wasn't "really" singing the part she'd wrested from Julie and for which she was being so highly, and publicly, paid. She had to be dubbed, and she mouthed the words while somebody else sang it, and I found it quite difficult to make the film with her like this, because I'd grown used to Julie singing her numbers at me every night on stage for three whole years.

Actually, I think that in the end, Audrey gave an enchanting performance on film, and there's no doubt that she contributed greatly to the film's enormous success and lasting popularity. And in the end, the fact that Julie won an Oscar for her performance as *Mary Poppins* on the very same occasion I won mine for Higgins, seemed like some kind of rough justice, Hollywood style. Actually, some aspects of that Oscar ceremony were very embarrassing, because the Warner Brothers PR people spent a lot of time and effort trying to keep Julie and myself apart – at least in front of the press photographers. The one thing they didn't want the papers to get was a picture of Julie and myself together, because she'd won her Oscar for a different picture made for a different studio. Poor Gladys Cooper was thrown into the fray because she'd won an Oscar for her performance as my mother, Mrs Higgins, and she was found somewhere and dragged in and I was made to pose for pictures with her, instead of with Audrey/Eliza, who hadn't won anything. It was awful, even though I was only an onlooker in a make-believe scandal created entirely by the press and the PR.

I remained perfectly friendly with both Julie and Audrey throughout all this, and Julie and I were both happy as clams with our respective Oscars, and I was, of course, delighted that Julie had won an Oscar. It was only right and proper, and she deserved it. The only thing I was not delighted with was that she didn't do the film with me, and that was only partly because it would have been much easier for me if she had. There was a certain irony, too, about Jack Warner's position at that Oscar ceremony, because there he was, having wanted to recast the whole thing for the film, watching me, whom he hadn't wanted, collect my Oscar, and not Audrey, whom he had wanted, while the girl he'd turned down for Eliza, Julie Andrews, won one for another studio.

Apart from my own Oscar, which I was lucky enough to win over stiff competition that year – Richard Burton and Peter O'Toole for *Becket*, Anthony Quinn for *Zorba the Greek*, and Peter Sellers for *Dr Strangelove* – the film triumphed in several categories. George Cukor won Best Director, Harry Stradling for Best Colour Cinematography, Gene Allen, Cecil Beaton and George James for Best Colour Art Direction and Set Decoration, the Warner Bros Sound Dept and André Previn for Best Music Adaptation, and Cecil Beaton again (on his own) for Best Colour Costume Design. Even Kenneth Tynan, the Angries' own critic, reviewing the film in the *Observer*, said, "Rex Harrison is incomparable. Give him a simple, helpless line like: 'Damn Mrs Pearce, and damn the coffee, and damn you!' and he will make it sound as elegantly yet majestically final as a trio of crashing chords at the end of a symphony. His eyes are mere slits and his stance is preposterously angular; but he exudes that combination of the aggressor and the injured, the schoolmaster and the truant, which adds up in Britain (and elsewhere) to erotic infallibility. From the opening words of a number such as 'A Hymn to Him' ('What in all of heaven can have prompted her to go?') you know that you are in absolutely safe hands; a supreme performer is in charge, steering you as a master helmsman steers his yacht."

CHAPTER 8

GRUMBLE AND GRUNT

*E*ven if my off-stage life had been perfectly normal, I suppose that the phenomenal success I had had in *My Fair Lady* would have affected it, and I would have been in a somewhat odd state after three years' playing Higgins every night, two on Broadway and one in London. But as it was, things were as far from normal as they could be. The three years of my triumph in *My Fair Lady* were the best – and the worst – years of my life, because I lived them with Kay Kendall, whom I loved very much, and during them I had learned that Kay was going to die.

Soon after *My Fair Lady* had opened on Broadway, Kay and I had enjoyed a fabulous summer together, the summer of 1956, full of love and fun, and the silly practical jokes Kay loved to play, in a house we'd taken on Long Island. She'd been bursting with life and *joie de vivre*, but towards the end of the summer she seemed very tired – we both were – so we both went into New York and had routine check-ups. After that Kay went off to Hollywood to make a film, *Les Girls*, with George Cukor, and for some reason – perhaps I suspected something – I didn't speak to the doctor about her until January 1957, when he rang me and asked me to come and see him. I remember it was a matinée day and I went between shows.

This was when he gave me the appalling, the terrible news. The tests had shown that Kay had a kind of leu-kaemia which was incurable and had only two years, at most, to live. The shock was unbelievable, especially as he told me quite categorically that there was nothing – medically – they could do. It was clear to me, as soon as the numbness caused by shock wore off, however, what I – as a non-doctor – had to do. I had to keep the information from Katie at all costs. I had to protect her and look after her without seeming obviously to do so, and in order to do this properly, I had to marry her.

Lilli had previously promised to divorce me, and I mar-ried Kay at an after-midnight ceremony on 23 June 1957 during the New York run of *My Fair Lady* at a strange little church in New York called the Universalist Church of the Divine Paternity, and then I married her again in the garden of my old friend Leland Hayward. The first time Kay had been terribly nervous, and had alternated between fits of giggles and fits of weeping. The second time was great fun, and we both enjoyed it enormously. It's the supreme irony, I suppose, that just when I should have been so happy, doing the show I loved, and married to the woman I loved, I spent most of the time in despair with the strain of keeping the truth from Kay, and trying to find any way possible to prolong her life.

The doctors and I had decided to tell her that her tiredness was caused by anaemia, which we were treating with some pills available only in Switzerland. I'd discov-ered, through a wonderful doctor I'd found in London, Dr Goldman, that the only thing the medical profession could attempt to do for Kay was to try to slow down the progress of the disease with some Swiss medicines, so every so often I would take her to a Swiss clinic, in St Moritz, where they would look after her for a bit. In fact, I think that treatment, and those Swiss pills did prolong her life by about a year.

Naturally, Kay – or Katie, as we all called her – who had made such an impact as a comedienne in *Geneviève* in 1953, with her irresistibly crazy trumpet-blowing scene, wanted to go on working as much as possible, and we managed to find something we could work together in. This seemed like a very good idea. I'd always missed her tremendously whenever we'd had to be apart, and at one point I'd apparently told Alan Lerner that I couldn't work unless she was around. "It's not how much I'll miss her that bothers me," he reported me as saying, "but what will I do for fun?" Anyway, after she made *Les Girls*, and though she was feeling increasingly frail, she was keen for us to do a film together, and to be directed by the great Vincente Minnelli, who among many other things, had directed Alan Jay Lerner's screenplay for the famous film musical of George Gershwin's *An American in Paris*. The film was called *The Reluctant Debutante*, based on a comedy written by William Douglas Home, and ideally suited to Kay, who was a glorious, natural, funny, and beautiful girl, and a great comedienne.

We played a couple called Lord and Lady Broadbent, and I was supposed to be presenting my American daughter by an earlier marriage, played by Sandra Dee, at Court. The film was actually a sly look at the quaint old-fashioned custom of presenting débutantes to the Queen, which was about to be demolished as undemocratic. Minnelli described the film as being about parents who behave like teenagers, and teenagers who behave like adults, and we had a lovely time behaving mostly like teenagers while doing it. Minnelli had, of course, made a lot of *An American in Paris* on location in Paris, and as part of *The Reluctant Debutante* had to be shot in that city, it was great fun being there with him, especially as, at that time, Minnelli was married to Judy Garland, whom I had met in Hollywood and admired very much – a very great star and a great performer. Their daughter, Liza Minnelli, was, at that time, still a little girl. The film was shot in early 1958, and had to be finished before I started rehearsals at The Theatre Royal, Drury Lane for *My Fair Lady*.

Katie continued to defy death with her spirit, insisting on leading a normal social and working life, as far as her strength permitted. We went out and about, and away for weekends, as we had always done, and all the time I had to pretend she was all right. It was far more difficult than any part I've ever played. We went to Dirk Bogarde's house in the country where Katie had stayed every weekend for about five years before she met me and I swept her off. Dirk was an extremely close friend of Katie's and a good one of mine, too, and of course he knew Katie far too well not to know how frail she had become. But, like all of us who loved her, we hid our feelings, and cherished her as much as possible, pandered to her crazy whims – and kept on hoping.

We also went for weekends to Larry and Vivien Olivier's at Notley Abbey, and of course, everyone fell in love with Katie. "She was one of the most enchanting people I have ever met," wrote Godfrey Winn. And added: "Already there hung over her the question mark of the incurable disease that was to cut short her life and her radiance with such tragic cruelty. She gave and received love with such abundance that she had a special quality I have rarely found." Katie and Vivien became very close to each other, which was not at all surprising considering that they had similarly huge appetites for life, and Vivien also lived on the extreme edge of the abyss, her health and strength, both mental and physical, having deteriorated in the years I'd known her, putting enormous and increasing stress on Larry and their marriage. Vivien's energy had always been manic, of course, but now the manic depressive condition was taking its dreadful toll, and she seemed more than ever like a beautiful Dresden shepherdess, exquisite, and only too easily breakable.

Kate and Vivien used to dance to the gramophone together, sending themselves up, laughing and giggling and falling about, doing imitations of all kinds of people. One day they were doing a spontaneous cabaret act to records, as usual, dancing and kicking their legs up – I think they were being the Dolly sisters on that occasion – when Vivien slipped and hit her head. Larry scooped her up and carried her upstairs, for all the world as Clark Gable/Rhett Butler did with Scarlett in *Gone with the Wind*, but when he came down he was in a state of terror, because a slight accident like that could apparently trigger off a bout of her illness, which could last for weeks. We all spent the rest of the evening willing her recovery.

Around this time Katie told me she wanted to do a play she had found called *The Bright One* by Judy Campbell, about a schoolmistress on a tour of the Greek Islands, who changes places with a sprite of magical charms. I was still at Drury Lane doing *My Fair Lady* but I managed to get the Winter Garden Theatre for her, and arranged to direct the play, with Gladys Cooper acting in it with her. Jack Minster produced it for us, and Tanya Moiseiwitsch did the sets. I kept the play running at a loss for her – she was doing some brilliant things in it, though the play itself didn't quite work – and during the short run her health kept up amazingly. She didn't miss one performance. She was, in spite of this, in the last phase of her illness, but of course she didn't know, and insisted on doing another film in Paris called *Once More with Feeling*, a comedy directed by Stanley Donen, with Yul Brynner playing opposite her. Dr Goldman and I decided we could not prevent her from working, because that would be to admit defeat, and Kay herself would never admit defeat.

In order to go with her and attempt to look after her, I hastened the end of my run at Drury Lane, finishing there in April 1959, after almost a year, but *My Fair Lady* occupied the Theatre Royal there for six years altogether – breaking all records. The longest-running musical they'd had previously was *Oklahoma*, which ran at Drury Lane for three years. Edward Mulhare took over my part, and once, Katie and I went to see the show, an extraordinary experience for me. We'd been on holiday, staying in Noel Coward's house in Jamaica, and when we came back, we decided suddenly that we'd like to see the show. There were no seats, of course, so they put a couple of chairs at the back for us, and we sat there and watched, unknown to anybody. Edward Mulhare was very good, and I was completely captivated by the whole performance. The play looked like a jewel, I thought, and I realized that all the time I'd been up there in it, I had never really known how perfect and beautiful it looked from the front.

I went with Katie to Paris, and tried to help her struggle on until she finished *Once More with Feeling*, though she was getting weaker and weaker all the time. From Paris I took her to a clinic at Rapallo, and from there to my villa at Portofino, but nothing was any good, and I was at my wit's end to know what to do to try and save her. In a last desperate bid to do so, Dr Goldman and I took her

166

back into the London Clinic, but to make matters even grimmer through those final days, the Press wouldn't leave her alone, and followed her everywhere. She was almost always breathtakingly rude to them – had been all her life – and, true to form, at the door of the London Clinic she turned on them and said: "Don't think I'm coming here to die. I'm not." A week later, on 6 September 1959, she died. She was thirty-two.

Those two years with Katie were without doubt the most complicated, the most difficult, the most wonderful, the most terrible, and the most rewarding I've ever been through, but when they were over, I was, I suppose, in such a state of shock that I made a lot of rather stupid career decisions without knowing quite what I was doing. I knew without thinking about it that work was the only therapy, and I just wanted to work.

The first of these wrong decisions was to do a play called *The Fighting Cock* by the French playwright Jean Anouilh which I'd seen when it had been a smash hit in Paris under the title *L'Hurluberlu*, while Kay had been filming there. Peter Brook had agreed to direct it in America, first on tour and then in New York, but what neither of us had taken into account was that this was a French satirical play about an old General, sending up the massively important figure – in France – of General de Gaulle, and that in translation, and in America, it didn't mean a thing. I had a lovely time doing it, trying on noses and eyebrows and medieval armour, taking them off again, and trying to make the old buffoon touching and sympathetic without losing any of the play's ironic humour. From the acting point of view, I may have been convincing, for *Variety* said: "If The General isn't Rex Harrison's most successful performance to date, it may conceivably be his finest." However, the play lasted for only 87 performances at the ANTA Theatre, New York.

After that I stumbled into a film called *Midnight Lace* with Doris Day, and the pity of that was, that instead of one of her light comedies, in which I could have played the Cary Grant or Rock Hudson part, the film was a murder mystery based on a London stage play called *Matilda Shouted Fire* by Janet Green.

Apart from Doris Day and myself, the film also starred John Gavin, Myrna Loy, Natasha Parry (Peter Brook's beautiful wife), Herbert Marshall (still going strong), and Roddy McDowall. But we never left the Hollywood studios while shooting the London locations the story called for, and though I did my best to make the villain of the piece seem debonair, there was not much humour in it. Doris Day herself found the proceedings such a strain that she had a nervous breakdown during shooting, which stopped production for a bit, after which she credited me and my "light sense of humour" for helping her keep her sanity while we shot the rest of the picture. That was nice of her, but I'm not sure how well I was hanging on to my own sanity at the time!

I was rescued from all this by a piece of luck. George Devine, director of the Royal Court Theatre in London, asked me to play the title role in a really interesting early play of Chekhov's, which had never been performed, called *Platonov*. The play itself was a tremendous challenge – some people have since pronounced it quite unplayable – because it is so black, and the leading character, of Platonov himself, is such a hopeless drunk and so unredeemingly awful that even I was obviously going to have trouble finding the humour in him. Doing *Platonov* was also a challenge because it meant going over to the other side.

I had better explain what I mean. While I was doing *My Fair Lady* at Drury Lane, I'd noticed, by reading the newspapers, and seeing what was cooking in the theatre, that there had been a distinct change. A new group called the Angry Young Men had appeared, John Osborne and Co., and with them a trend towards the distinctly non-gentleman type of acting. This type of acting meant that if an actor hadn't a Yorkshire or a Lancashire accent or a cockney accent naturally by birth, he put it on. It was very *de trop* to speak proper English.

The Angry Young Men became a very popular movement in the theatre. I never liked it, it was the kind of acting I hated, and I called it "The Scratch and Grunt School of Acting", because all they did was grumble and scratch and grunt. It was a disgusting time in the theatre, in my opinion, and so unlike what I'd seen and loved when I first came to London and saw the acting of Hawtrey and Du Maurier. They were gentlemen actors, they played themselves, up to a point, but that became – oh very old hat indeed! If you had any kind of educated voice in the Sixties you had to disguise it by putting on some sort of regional accent. Well, I wasn't going to do that, but when George Devine, who was at the very centre of the grumble and grunt scene asked me if I'd like to go to the Royal Court, I thought, my God, that would be a change of pace for me.

The Royal Court Theatre in Sloane Square had become the centre for the Angry Young Men. John Osborne's *Look Back in Anger* had started there in 1956, and proved to be a watershed in the theatre. It changed a great many things about theatrical material and style, and also about acting style, in that it introduced to Britain a seemingly "realistic" style of acting known as the Method in America. Nothing could be further from my own naturalistic style of acting, as exemplified by Henry Higgins in *My Fair Lady*, which I'd been doing at Drury Lane, at the same time, and I felt that this young angry brigade despised me and my methods as old-fashioned and reactionary, and affected an attitude of superiority towards me which I found both irritating and amusing. The idea of joining them in their lair, and seeing if I could beat them at their own game, appealed to me a lot.

I don't suppose I had become aware of the rise of the Angries, until I returned to London to do *My Fair Lady* at Drury Lane in 1958. Whilst I'd been in New York for two years doing it, I must have been cocooned to a certain extent from the outside world by the quite extraordinary success of the show. I certainly hadn't realized the strength of the anger about class that had developed in England and was expressing itself with such force in the London theatre. You don't have much time to go to other theatres when you've doing eight shows a week of a big musical, but once I started rehearsing at Drury Lane, I saw as many other shows as I could. I saw *Look Back in Anger*, and went to the Royal Court Theatre several times after that, and got a smell of it.

Of course, "The Scratch and Grunt School of Acting" already existed in New York, what with Stanislavsky and the Method, as practised at the Actor's Studio of Lee Strasberg, so I'd realized that something was going on, but it hadn't made a great impression. You could take it or leave it, rather. Socially conscious themes weren't forced on you in America, as they seemed to be in England.

There were marvellous, socially conscious, plays in America, like Arthur Miller's *Death of a Salesman*, but they took as their subject working-class men, rather than making a terribly obvious statement about the Working

170

Class. *Death of a Salesman* is a great play, but it isn't
saying: "Down with you beastly, rich gentlemen!" or anything like that. It wasn't denouncing what Shaw called
the Members of the Idle Rich Class, it was talking about
the human condition in general. And the Marlon Brando
character of Stanley Kowalski in Tennessee Williams's
A Streetcar Named Desire was making his statement
alongside, and parallel to, much more traditional theatre,
and many more traditional American plays.

People were talking about class and class structure in
the theatre in America, but they were much less angry
about it, whereas in England this new angry young
movement had not only taken over the whole culture,
but was very much confined to talking about "Members
of the Idle Rich Class", from a working-class point of view.
The Angry Young Men's plays were all about the evils of
the bourgeoisie, and what they had done to the working
classes, and the writers were publicly airing their grudges
against them. I was amazed by it, and particularly by the
virulence it showed. I wasn't so much surprised, because
I think the jealousy of the underdog had been around,
festering, for a very long time. But they didn't seem to
realize that you could pull yourself up by your bootstraps
or your knee-breeches, if you wanted to, whatever class
you came from. You didn't have to wallow in despair. I
think it's envy and jealousy, mostly. There's a great deal
of jealousy in England.

For instance, in England, in the late Fifties, middle-
class intellectuals, liberals, seemed to bend over backwards
to want to join in this anti-bourgeois movement, and there
was a whole school of people who pretended that they
weren't middle class, or educated, and, as I've said, even
went to all the trouble of changing their accents – and
down, not up. Preposterous! Now in America that never

171

happened. Class warfare there may have been, but I don't think it ever affected people that way. In America, accents are regional, and not about class at all. You may have a Southern accent, or an Eastern seaboard accent, and this will place you, but it won't necessarily depict your class. In general, it's much more democratic. You never get the snobbism of somebody walking into a club in St James's with a rather overdone posh accent, the sort of thing which used to irritate the hell out of these angry young writers. In America, it wasn't the same kind of gripe.

As it happened, *My Fair Lady* opened on Broadway in 1956, which was the same year that John Osborne's *Look Back in Anger* opened at the Royal Court Theatre in London. It was also the same year as the Suez crisis, which precipitated much discussion and reassessment of Britain's role. So when I came to do the show at Drury Lane, in 1958, I saw all this new-style theatre going on, and though I didn't agree with much of what they were saying, I could see it had a lot of energy to it, which attracted me.

At the Royal Court, they'd taken Chekhov to their bosoms, these chaps. They thought he could provide them with a perfect example of what they ought to do in their own work. They would have loved to write plays just like his. But Chekhov's plays are not really about the class struggle as the Angries see it, so I don't see how they worked that one out at all. Of course, they all got wedded to Stanislavsky, and his Method, and they didn't seem to notice that Chekhov himself had never liked Stanislavsky that much. He wrote comedies, and most of his plays are much funnier than they're generally acted in England. We're much too solemn about Chekhov; we bring out the melancholy in him. The Russians bring out the comedy.

Anyway, in 1960 I decided to do *Platonov*, and I made

a comedy out of it, and it was a great success. George Devine, despite the fact that he had been running the Royal Court all through the Angry period, proved an excellent director for me to work with. And Rachel Roberts was in the play with me, playing Anna Petrovna, the general's widow, who pursues me – in the play – with amorous intent. She was a very good serious actress, daughter of a Welsh Baptist preacher, and, naturally, given her age and her life experience, much more involved in the angry young movement than I was. As far as temperament and experience is concerned, we couldn't have been more different, Rachel and I, and yet a great sympathy grew up between us and we became very close. She was later to become my fourth wife.

Above all, I found *Platonov* great fun, and the reason I enjoyed it enormously was because I managed to get a lot of humour out of the plight of a desperate man. They are so desperate, the Russians, when they get depressed. And they do seem to get depressed a lot. Then they take it out on the bottle. He's a thoroughly unsavoury character is Platonov, he's a drunk and a seducer, and he would have been quite disgusting if he'd been played in the usual manner English actors tackle Chekhov – I mean black and dark. No one could sit in an audience and tolerate a leading character like *Platonov* unless he had humour. I realized this, and my Platonov worked because I managed to make him funny.

Chekhov was writing about Platonov as if he was really Russia, and Platonov was Russia, because Russia was, in Chekhov's view, in the same kind of plight that Platonov was in. He was in such a state, and he drank such a lot, and got into such pickles with all these women he tried, quite unnecessarily, to seduce. He didn't have to seduce them, but he loved being mischievous, and mischievous is the word I cottoned on to in that play, and George Devine helped me to do so. It had to be a raging comedy, but it was very very hard work because it had to be played at an enormous pace, and Platonov finishes up breaking up whole sets and whole schoolrooms. And he drinks glass after glass of vodka does Platonov, so most of the time he's roaring, falling down, drunk. Oh, it was a funny piece! I loved doing it, even though I, of course, was only drinking water. And I think that by my playing *Platonov* for comedy, we were more in the spirit of the real Chekhov than some of these terribly serious arty productions full of long phrases. I don't think that's what Chekhov wanted at all. He meant all his plays to be both black and funny, but with the kind of productions they generally got in England they became black without being funny. Poor man! The arty left-wing got hold of his plays and thought: "This is a bonus, we can do something with this."

I think they thought that as Chekhov was a Russian, and Stanislavsky was Russian, and the Revolution was, of course, Russian, that made it all right. And then I think they thought his plays presaged the Revolution in some way, that he was showing all these people in despair because the Revolution hadn't yet come, and that what they were waiting for wasn't Moscow, or Life, but to be saved. Whatever their political reasons, they also felt *Platonov* was prestigious and something of a coup for them because it was a play Chekhov had written as a young man, and it had never been performed – at least, in English.

I found this attitude particularly funny because *Platonov* is actually a sort of *cri de coeur* on the part of a man who behaves desperately badly. In fact, he is such an unpleasant character it is difficult to get humour out of him. If you look at him on the other side of the coin he is just a total wastrel. There's a big cast, with all the people

174

surrounding Platonov, the doctor, the postman, the Jew, and everybody else in the play behaves very badly, too. There's Jew-baiting, and all sorts of other things in it which are rather unattractive. Yet these Lefties obviously thought all this bad behaviour was all right because it showed what was going on in Russia before the Revolution, and that now the Revolution had come, it had swept all that nastiness away!

I kept myself out of any possible arguments about it, as far as I could, and fortunately, George Devine was a very sensible man, a working director, damn good too, and he wasn't hoodwinked either by any of that stuff. Very matter of fact and feet on the ground was George. We were helped in bringing out the humour in the play by the fact that it had not been tampered with before by the kind of serious and solemn English actors who would have wanted to make it deep and deedy and slow and boring.

I'm not saying that the best actors in the Method style weren't fine actors. I think Brando was the most successful actor in that school. He was a very good actor. I shall never forget him in *A Streetcar Named Desire*. He did convey an immense amount by his scratch and grunt technique, but, in fact, he didn't scratch and grunt all that much. He grunted more than scratched, I think. But he was very effective. He could certainly do real acting, if called upon. He didn't appear on the stage a great deal. He did an awful lot of films, but not many stage productions, which was sad. And then he got enormously fat, he was like a great Buddha, he had to lose 100 pounds once in weight just to do a role. He put on weight extraordinarily. And when he did, he became an unrecognizably vast man, with this beautiful face on top. But he was a wonderful actor, Brando, there's no question about that. He was the greatest, the only one, who was worthy of the cause of grumble and grunt, I thought, and he was *first class*. Of course he had a tremendous lot of imitators. Most of the actors of his school copied him slavishly, but there was no-one like him, no-one to top him.

There were some other wonderful actors around that time who were working with the grumble and grunt actors, in grumble and grunt kind of plays. Lee J. Cobb, the actor who created the part of Willy Lomas in *Death of a Salesman* on Broadway, was marvellous. That was a wonderful perform-ance of real emotional acting. Of course, I don't think for a moment that Lee J. Cobb copied Brando. He was his own man and had his own style. But the younger men coming up in America all copied Marlon Brando unsuccessfully. He was the original, and the key, almost, for the movement. I loved his acting.

On the whole, though, the scratch and grunt style is not acting, it's avoiding the issue. It's much easier to scratch and grunt than it is to say the lines, and to remember them in the order in which they come. The Stanislavsky/Strasberg idea that you didn't have to act a tree, you became a tree, is, to me, absurd. There are all sorts of stories which illustrate what I feel about that, like the incident which happened on the film of *Marathon Man* when Dustin Hoffman regularly knocked himself breath-less by running for hours before he came on set, and when Olivier asked him why he was doing this to himself, he said: "What else can I do? I'm supposed to be a runner. I have to be breathless." And Larry said: "Try acting."

Before the Method became fashionable, there was a famous saying that when actors came on to do auditions they were told: "Don't just stand there – do something." After the Method it was the reverse, and they were told: "Don't do something, just stand there."

But the net result of all this angry acting was that all

176

kinds of standards went by the board. Even audibility was something they didn't find necessary. There were whole productions, and whole films, during the worst of that period, when you couldn't hear anything anyone said – in the name of realism. It drove you *mad*! It really was a dreadful cop out. It is a pity, though, that when I was in the States I was always too busy working to see any members of the Strasberg school, or to go to their studio either. I should, at least, have gone down there to watch. I suppose I thought if I did go down there I'd get roped in, and then I'd find it difficult to extricate myself. And on top of that, I felt that they didn't approve of me. They gave off an air of superiority towards me.

CHAPTER 9

HOLLYWOOD FANFARE II

After my brush with the Angries I decided I was going to go back to Hollywood to make some more films, to support my vineyards and my villa, *San Genesio* in Portofino, so I made a film which was quite famous – or infamous – *Cleopatra*, with Richard Burton as Mark Antony, Elizabeth Taylor as Cleopatra, and myself playing Julius Caesar.

So much has already been written about the making of *Cleopatra* that it is difficult to find anything new or interesting to say. Playing Julius Caesar, the most powerful man the world had ever known at that time – or perhaps at any time – was a challenge I looked forward to, but as usual I was not helped much by anyone, even though the writer/director was Joseph L. Mankiewicz, with whom I had already worked well in *The Ghost and Mrs Muir* and *Escape*. The script gave me verbose and impossibly stilted speeches which I was supposed to deliver in long shot, to enormous crowds, and the make-up, wigs, and clothes were frightful before I cottoned on, and started to supervise my own, getting my own boots made in Rome

179

for me, and getting the colour of robes and togas right by making them dye fabrics with the ancient dyes the Romans had always used.

When Rachel came out to Cinecittà Studios and saw me in full drag, she was at first horrified, and then she started to laugh. I was wearing a funny wig, a costume of dreadful red velvet, and, worst of all, they had somehow managed to erase all the lines from my face. Fortunately, they wanted me to do some tests in this gear and full make-up, and I asked Mankiewicz to look at them and react. "What happened to your face?" he asked me. "All those lines and things, I *want* all of those lines." Vastly relieved, I said that was what I wanted, too, and we began on Caesar's appearance all over again.

When Richard Burton arrived, half-way through the shooting, to play Mark Antony, they palmed him off with boots which were uncomfortable and didn't fit him from a previous film in which Stephen Boyd had played Mark Antony. He was thunderstruck when he heard I'd had my boots made to measure for me. It hadn't occurred to him to complain. I liked acting with Richard Burton very much indeed, he was a great colleague, both on and off the set, but unfortunately in *Cleopatra* I had hardly any scenes with him. My scenes were mostly with Cleopatra before she met Antony, and once Antony had turned up and the two great legends had fallen in love, they didn't really want to know about Caesar, or me. The much publicized love affair often made work pretty trying for me, for at the height of it Elizabeth and Richard kept hitting each other and giving each other black eyes and not turning up at the studio. I had three or four key scenes of Caesar still to play and they wouldn't call me to the studio to make them, because they were keeping me in reserve in Rome, and I hated this. I hated being a stop-gap for Richard and Elizabeth, and being under instructions to wait in case they – the studio – got into any trouble with their shooting schedule, and then they would call me. One day I decided to go back to London and see what was cooking there, and I left Rome, by air. I had something I wanted to do in England. I'd heard of a new speed boat I wanted to try out which was in Poole Harbour, near Southampton, on the south coast of England, so I went there and found the boat and took it out to sea, and gave it a trial. It seemed very nice, twin-engined, big – I was rather enjoying it – and as I came back into Poole Harbour I saw, to my surprise, that a lot of little figures were dancing up and down on shore, waving at me and shouting.

I couldn't hear anything because of the engines. However I came in and docked the boat and they came swarming on board, and they said: "Oh my God! A terrible thing's happened, you're wanted in Rome immediately, you've got to go to Rome. The film company's mad with you." I said: "Oh really, what's happened?" They said: "They want you tomorrow." I said: "How the hell do I get from Poole to Rome tomorrow? I'd better get back to London first, and get to Rome from there." Anyway, when I got back to Rome they were all very angry with me for having gone away, and, in fact, the balloon had gone up, and either Richard or Elizabeth hadn't turned up for work and they wanted old stop-gap Harrison to go in, so I did. I went in.

Joseph Mankiewicz claimed that a lot of the original material he used in his script of *Cleopatra* came from Plutarch, Suetonius, Appian and many of those ancient scholars. There were also two very good books which I myself used and found absolutely fascinating, and a great help with the part of Caesar. These were *The Life and Times of Cleopatra* by an Italian historian, Carlo Maria Franzero, and a novel called *The Ides of March* by

Thornton Wilder. In spite of all this, as well as being such a de luxe movie, shot in Todd AO and every damn thing – a very posh production – it didn't come out too well, I didn't think, though there were a lot of good actors hanging about there in Rome for an awfully long time.

But Caesar was a good part. I enjoyed playing Caesar because he was a fine man and it was worth doing, and there were other compensations.

I loved working with Elizabeth Taylor on the film because she is in every way the consummate film actress and her professionalism on the set and in front of the camera is quite remarkable to see. She was, of course, practically brought up in the studios, and as a result she knows exactly what she's doing with the slightest movement of an eyelash, or curve of a lip. She is always word-perfect, too, something which, on *Cleopatra*, with its convoluted words, I found difficult to be. For those of us – including Richard Burton – who had spent our youthful energies on the stage, Elizabeth's film technique is an eye-opener. A spectacular film like *Cleopatra*, with its combination of huge crowd scenes – for which you have to use something much more like stage technique, make appearances, and even declaim the lines – and intimate two-shot close-ups, is probably the most difficult kind of film to do, and I suppose they'd chosen Richard and myself because we were used to heroic roles in the theatre. Elizabeth, because she was so good in front of the camera, was much more nervous in the stagy scenes, and at one point, when she had to descend a steep flight of steps into the Forum, she had vertigo, and they had a terrible time getting her to go down.

About half-way through the shooting, Fox realized how much money they were spending on all this, and attempted to cut back by removing my trailer dressing room, and sacking my chauffeur. I had to be even more imperious than Julius Caesar – I had to threaten to quit – in order to get both these essentials back.

I did a lot of homework on Caesar, and the more I read, the more fascinated I became. I realized that to play such a powerful man and to suggest being brainy as well as powerful is very hard. You need to be laconic, and slightly dry, as Claude Rains had been in the film of Shaw's *Caesar and Cleopatra*. I think also it has a lot to do with stillness. There must be nothing tentative in movement or in speech. You have to be totally aware, all the time, of the fact that you are a Caesar. It was also important to discover what Caesar's, the man's, weaknesses were. He suffered from a minor form of epilepsy, and he was always terrified that he would have an attack while he was making a public appearance, or speech. No wonder he was terrified. If he had suffered an attack in public, the Romans would have pulled him down into the crowd and torn him limb from limb. A Caesar was not allowed such ordinary, human signs of weakness. This, then, was his constant fear, and I had to hold this somewhere in the back of my head all the time, because although you can't express it, it must condition the way the man behaves.

During *Cleopatra*, Rachel and I were married in Genoa. The immensely long filming of the epic had been something of an endurance test for both of us – but it ended well. It had taken from September 1961 to the end of July 1962 at Cinecittà in Rome and on other locations in Italy and in Egypt, with additional shooting in February 1963 in Almeria, Spain, and was finished at Pinewood Studios, England on 2 March 1963. It was first shown, amidst much ballyhoo, on 12 June 1963 at the Rivoli Theatre, New York, and on 31 July at the Dominion in London. Neither Rachel nor I won an Oscar that year, but both of us were nominated, she for that excellent film *This*

Sporting Life, directed by Lindsay Anderson, and I for my part as Caesar in *Cleopatra*.

It must be said, however, that my making films like *Cleopatra* and the ones that followed was to prove disastrous, in the end, for my relationship with Rachel, who was so much more at home at the Royal Court Theatre, and the working-class theatre in general. She hated the false glamour of film life, and found it very difficult to hang around waiting for me.

One of the most delightful films I've ever made was *The Yellow Rolls-Royce*, written by Terence Rattigan, directed by Anthony Asquith, and produced by Anatole de Grunwald. I had remained close friends with Terry since our *French Without Tears* days, but oddly enough, we had not worked together. Now he came up with *The Yellow Rolls-Royce*. The story was built round different episodes in a yellow Rolls-Royce's life. My leading lady was the lovely sexy French actress, Jeanne Moreau, and she was wonderful to work with. Edmond Purdom was also in it, as the other man, and it was about a man who had just got married, and bought his wife a very handsome present of a yellow Rolls-Royce.

At the beginning of the film he goes and chooses it in Hooper's show window, it is a beautiful touring Rolls, and he takes his wife to Ascot in it, to the Gold Cup, and during the running of the race of the Gold Cup, which he wins, incidentally, he misses his wife, and he goes and wanders about in the paddock and he can't find her anywhere. Then he goes to the car park and he finds her being made love to by Purdom in the back of the Rolls-Royce which he had just bought his wife as a wedding present. Well, that's pretty grim. He actually wins the Gold Cup, and driving back to his palatial home outside Ascot with the Gold Cup, he gets out of the car and tells his man to take the car back.

He says: "It displeases me." He'd written it beautifully, Terry Rattigan, and it made a marvellous short episode, which I loved doing. Sadly, *The Yellow Rolls-Royce* was Anatole (or Tolly) de Grunwald's last film.

I began to think I was liking making films, but then I was persuaded, against my better judgement – and oh, how I wish I'd listened to it – to make *The Agony and the Ecstasy* – about the battle between Michaelangelo and Pope Julius while Michaelangelo is painting the famous Sistine Chapel ceiling.

Although it was based on the successful novel of the same name by Irving Stone, this film was an altogether horrendous experience for me. Poor Michaelangelo kept telling the Pope he was really a pretty good sculptor, rather than an interior decorator, and shouldn't have taken on so ridiculous a project as painting the barrel-shaped ceiling of His Holiness's private chapel in the Vatican. The Pope I played should have been a good character – he was a most un-Popelike Pope, a Renaissance bull of a man, fighting duels, siring illegitimate children – but I felt like saying I was a pretty good, naturalistic stage actor, rather than a ham film star, and shouldn't have undertaken so ridiculous a project as this film. Michaelangelo nearly went blind painting that ceiling, and I nearly went mad from boredom and frustration in *The Agony and the Ecstasy*.

Charlton Heston was playing Michaelangelo, and every day he turned up on set he seemed to loom over me, as if he had grown a little taller. This puzzled me a lot, as I am not particularly short myself, and then it came out that he was having lifts put in his shoes. Without saying anything, I did the same, so that, day by day, there was the spectacle of two very tall, grown-up men, growing taller and taller, in a juvenile attempt to look down on one another! In spite of all this nonsense, I worked terribly hard trying to breathe some life, if not humour, into my part, so hard that the director, my old friend Carol Reed, who was directing it, seemed quite worried about me. I said I always worked that hard and I always do, but however hard I worked on him, there wasn't much I could do with the Warrior Pope. But Carol Reed seemed a very changed man from the days of *Night Train to Munich*, when he had a great sense of humour and was fun to work with. In this instance I found him doggedly trying to please the front office and Charlton Heston, who, I felt, was altogether too wooden to play this great artist. They would have been much better served by someone like Spencer Tracy.

Some time later I discovered with surprise what Charlton Heston had said about me in his diaries, published as *The Actor's Life*. "Rex requires careful handling, but he'll be damned good in the part . . . He has the temperament of a thoroughbred racehorse . . . highly strung, with a tendency to snort and rear and kick at the starting gate." Fortunately, by the end he seemed to think my performance was "worth all the migraines". I thought, on consideration, and if you could crane your neck to see it, his ceiling wasn't half bad, either.

Fortunately for me, the moment the aptly named *Agony* was over, we had to launch the film of *My Fair Lady*, and every day was like a wonderful party. First of all I had to go to New York for the opening there, and then, after that Jack Warner, George Cukor, Audrey Hepburn, Cecil Beaton and myself went off in a private plane to Chicago, and then to Los Angeles. Each opening was a gala evening for a major charity, and after the showing of the film, there would usually be a reception and ball. Hollywood is, of course, the original place where "nothing succeeds like success", and gave us the kind of lavish treatment it only metes out to the super success, but it was not until I had attended the premières in London and Paris that I learned, to my great delight, that I had been nominated for the Academy Award.

Meanwhile, *My Fair Lady* continued to be a passport to everywhere – even managing to get me invited to Moscow, when we took it to the film festival. It was shown in the Kremlin, and I made a speech from the stage. The following day I had to make another speech at a football stadium holding about 50,000 people, who all seemed to think my description of my first day in Russia immensely funny, and howled with laughter at me all the way through. All I said was that I had been to Lenin's tomb, and visited the shops. To this day, I wish I knew what I said or did that so amused those Muscovites.

I also did service as a judge at the Cannes film festival, where I got plenty of amusement watching the in-fighting, particularly on the part of the French writer, Alain Robbe-Grillet, whose new style of novel was very fashionable at the time. M. Robbe-Grillet cocked a snook at the whole operation by insisting that a very silly film about two guys on a night out picking up two tarts was a work of art, but in the end, the British won the award that year with the charming kooky comedy, *The Knack*. Then I was invited to Taormina in Sicily to be presented with the Italian Oscar, the Davide di Donatello Award, which they were giving me for my performances in both *My Fair Lady* and *The Yellow Rolls-Royce*. This was about the most romantic award ceremony I – or any one else – has ever been to. It took place by moonlight in the picturesque ruins of an old Greek amphitheatre in the mountains above Taormina, with Mount Etna erupting away in the distance. Sometimes even I am forced to realize that I have come quite a long way from the Liverpool Playhouse.

During all this partying and ballyhoo, I had been persuaded, unwisely, as it turned out later, to do another film with Joseph Mankiewicz in Rome. Once again, it seemed respectable enough, in fact I liked the idea a lot. Joe wanted to make a modern film version of Ben Jonson's play *Volpone*. Of the Elizabethan playwrights, I have always preferred Ben Jonson to Shakespeare. He goes in for the kind of satire which is much more my kind of thing. "Volpone" in Italian means "Fox", and the modern version was about a foxy character, suitably named Cecil Fox, a man much talked about as a millionaire, though actually penniless, who lives in grand style in a luxurious palazzo on the Grand Canal in Venice, and decides to play a trick on three of his former mistresses. He pretends he is dying, and invites them to visit, so that he can judge their different reactions to the reading of his will. Mankiewicz had lined up a terrific cast, with Susan Hayward, Edie Adams and Capucine playing the three ex-mistresses, a very young Maggie Smith as Susan Hayward's nurse, and Cliff Robertson as the Fox's confidential secretary, who helps him implement the plan.

Three important writers, four if you include Mankiewicz, who is himself a brilliant screenwriter (e.g. *All About Eve*), had worked on the script, for Ben Jonson's original had inspired a novel, *The Evil of the Day* by Thomas L. Sterling, and this had, in turn, inspired a play, *Mr Fox of Venice* by Frederick Knott. My character, Cecil Fox, was a fascinating manipulator, with an obsession about time and a longing to outwit it, as well as a lifelong regret that he never became a ballet dancer. I was given some unusually literate speeches which I enjoyed doing, and all in all it is a wonder that we did not have a success on our hands. I think the trouble was that the film became vastly too long, and in cutting it, they had to cut out many of the funniest fantasy sequences. I suppose they never got the balance right – or the title, which went from *Mr Fox of Venice*, to *Anyone for Tennis*, and finally – though I shall never know why – *The Honey Pot*.

Cecil Fox exited from his troubles in the film by performing a jolly dance of death into the Grand Canal. But I simply went from trouble to more trouble. After playing a man called Fox, in a film made for United Artists, I went to work for Twentieth Century-Fox again, in a little number, called *Doctor Dolittle*, which was eventually to cost the studio seventeen million dollars. Frankly, I'm surprised they ever wanted to speak to me again after *Cleopatra*, which, through no fault of mine, cost an unprecedented sum of money and was commonly supposed to have ruined Fox completely, a mere three or four years before. In between, of course, I'd made the film of *My Fair Lady* for Jack Warner, which probably stung Fox into competition, and I think they planned to reassemble some of the same team besides myself. They certainly asked Alan Jay Lerner to do the book and songs. All in all, *Doctor Dolittle* made a lot of sense in a number of ways, to a number of people. At the outset.

CHAPTER 10

TALKING TO
THE ANIMALS

*S*ince my performance as Higgins in *My Fair Lady*, and the invention of the now-famous sing/speak technique, I, and many others, had been ceaselessly searching for a new musical subject in which I could once more exercise this curious talent I'd developed. The *Doctor Dolittle* books had been tremendous favourites with children both sides of the Atlantic for quite a while, and Twentieth Century-Fox had acquired the film rights to them. Hugh Lofting had started writing stories about this funny little doctor who much preferred animals to people, and whose great gift was that he could talk to them, while he was up to his ears in mud in the trenches during the First World War. I really admire him for that. It is incredible to think of someone with so gentle an imagination managing to keep himself sane in such hellish circumstances by making up bedtime stories for his children, but that is what Hugh Lofting did.

He sent the stories home in instalments to his two sons, and his wife kept them. After the war he was persuaded to make them into a book – the first *Doctor Dolittle*. This was such a success that dozens of other titles followed, and Dolittle became an essential part of a whole generation's childhood. The books came complete with endearing little line drawings, which I believe Lofting did himself, showing the doctor to be a tiny, tubby man with a large, bulbous W.C. Fields nose, and bandy legs – not exactly a physical replica of the actor now asked to impersonate him.

The great originality of the stories, however, apart from the gentle sweetness and oddity of the character, was the idea of a man who could actually communicate with animals *in their own languages*, and who took the trouble to learn how they thought, felt, and spoke. This is where I came in. Dolittle was, in a sense, a kind of Professor Higgins – a much kinder one – whose subjects were animals of all kinds, and to whom he – unlike Higgins – never condescended. Besides all this, I have always loved animals, liked having them around, and got on very well with them. At least I did, until the year I spent as Doctor Dolittle!

Right away, the film ran into trouble. About a year or so into the development period, Fox wanted to replace Alan Jay Lerner by Leslie Bricusse. I got cold feet and tried to get out of the picture. The studio was livid. In his book about Twentieth Century-Fox, *The Studio*, John Gregory Dunne reports Arthur P. Jacobs as saying that when I said "goodbye" they were stuck with "a picture called *Doctor Dolittle*, twelve million going in, and no one to play Dr Dolittle." They "scratched around and came up with Christopher Plummer. The studio liked him, he'd been in *The Sound of Music* . . ." They signed up Christopher Plummer. Some time elapsed before they began to think better of this plan. And the more they thought about it, the more it seemed to them that only Professor Higgins could convincingly play a man who was supposed to know 498 animal languages. So Arthur P. Jacobs, the producer, and Richard Fleischer, the director, tracked me down in Portofino and – after much arguing – persuaded me to stay aboard. They paid off Plummer – "he had us over a barrel with a nice legal contract", reported Jacobs – "But Rex is back, and we're ready to go."

Next – I admit it – I made a mistake, an error of judgement. I suggested they try Michael Flanders and Donald Swann, two very talented British song writers who had their own show on in Shaftesbury Avenue, London, and had become the talk of the town. They wrote brilliant, sophisticated stuff and I wanted them to do the songs for me in *Doctor Dolittle*. Naturally, neither Jacobs nor Fleischer had heard of Flanders and Swann, and I had to dispatch them to London to see their show. They agreed to hire them, but in the event, clever though Flanders and Swann undoubtedly were, the whole idea misfired a few weeks later when they sent me a tape of the first songs they'd written for Dolittle.

With high expectations, I listened to their tapes at San Genesio with Richard Fleischer, then asked him to give me his comments. He took a big breath and told me in no uncertain terms that the songs he'd just heard seemed to him lightweight and precious, the kind of thing you used to hear in pseudo-sophisticated cocktail lounges. There was a long pause – and I was forced to agree with him. The songs did sound rather cheap. Leslie Bricusse was re-hired, wrote the screenplay and the songs, and proceeded to win himself the coveted Oscar for Best Song. And despite my initial lack of faith in him, he and I became firm friends, and have remained so to this day.

Some time after all these shenanigans, the whole zoo

from Twentieth Century-Fox – not to mention the animals themselves – descended on the quiet and picturesque village of Castle Combe, in Wiltshire, England, and set about spreading havoc all around them. They'd gone to Castle Combe in the first place because it was a perfect example of an unspoilt English inland village, about a hundred miles from the sea, and one of the great beauty spots of the beautiful West Country. But then, for reasons best known to their most extraordinary selves, they decided it ought really to be a fishing village, with a pretty little harbour, so they started to dig holes and build dams and import gallons, or is it fathoms, of water, to make it look like one.

Half the villagers were in a state of righteous indignation and wanted us hanged, drawn and quartered. The other half were making a fortune out of us, and had never had it so good. One gallant military type, a young man of impeccable lineage, from one of the oldest and most distinguished families in England, became so incensed by what we were doing to the place that he got hold of some dynamite and mined the dam and the building work Fox had done, expertly setting detonators under a garage and other things he didn't like. Fortunately, someone talked a bit too much in a pub in Bristol, the hero of Castle Combe was arrested, and his plot speedily undermined. I dread to think what would have happened, and how much would have been lost, had he not been stopped in time.

On top of that, it rained. Only Englishmen know that August, being the month of holidays, is always the worst month of the year, and Twentieth Century-Fox is not composed of Englishmen. It rained and rained and rained, for all the world as if we were in for a second Flood. And indeed, Castle Combe had as many animals, and of as many different species, as Noah had. What we

194

didn't have, alas, was Noah's Ark. The fields where the animals were kept turned into seas of mud – they were veritable quagmires – and on the rare days when it actually stopped raining, the animals played up. We had all kinds of problems filming with the animals, and quite a few with the animal trainers, and all of them we could certainly have done without.

I know they say "Never work with children or animals" for fear, I suppose of being upstaged by them. But in this case, the animals behaved well in almost all respects. It was the animal trainers who should have been shot. Several times, during filming, when I had a delicate scene to play with one of my animal co-stars, the whole thing was ruined, and ruined dangerously, by the trainers. When I first met Chi-Chi the chimp, at the beginning of filming, she and I became great friends. She was terribly sweet and affectionate, and never stopped kissing my hands and cuddling me. But one day, later on in the schedule, I was sitting with her on my knee, preparing to do a scene set in my study. Chi-Chi was playing around with the papers on my desk, and suddenly, for no reason at all that I could see, her trainer gave her a wallop on the head. Poor Chi-Chi was so startled she turned on me, instead of on the trainer, and started to maul me, scratch me with her claws, and – worse still – bite me with her teeth.

I was insured by Fox for one million dollars on *Doctor Dolittle*, and it was a jolly good thing I was! Not only was I bitten by the chimp, I was also bitten by a Pomeranian puppy, a duck, and the parrot who played Polynesia, the thinking parrot, who, because she can talk to humans, encourages the good Doctor to learn to talk to animals. Polynesia's bite, which was, once again, the result of interference in our relationship from her trainer, was quite a serious thing, because human beings can get a fatal disease from parrot bites. Nervously, I reported immediately to the nurse on set, who told me cheerfully that there was nothing they could do, but to be sure to let them know if I felt I'd got a fever so they could report the matter to the authorities! During the week that followed, I observed myself closely to see if I was turning into a parrot, and from then on, kept myself slightly aloof from Polynesia.

One trainer was trampled by an elephant – the large animals thought nothing of walking on your feet, or sitting on you, once they'd got used to your presence around the place. Another trainer caught a liver complaint from the chimps. A doe drank a pail full of paint and was rather ill. The whole thing was impossible, really. I don't know how we thought we could cope with it. Imagine trying to get a scene in which a squirrel is supposed to be sitting on a bridge talking to Polynesia, with Doctor Dolittle listening to their conversation. A farmer promised us a tame squirrel to work with, but it didn't seem very tame to me. It wouldn't sit on the bridge, and scratched at anyone who tried to hold it there, which was dangerous because squirrels can sometimes transmit rabies. The handlers tried putting on large gloves, and tying the poor creature to the bridge with bits of wire around its feet. This, understandably, made the squirrel angrier and angrier – I could sympathize with it! – and eventually they were advised by a local vet to give it a fountain-pen shot of gin. Far from sedating the animal, this made it struggle violently, but they gave it another slug. There must be some footage on a cutting-room floor somewhere showing a squirrel swaying around in a drunken manner on a bridge, then finally falling over in an indecent sprawl into a stupefied sleep.

Once Fox was sure it had ruined the beauty of Castle

Combe, and that it would never stop raining, shooting was adjourned, and moved to the studio in Hollywood and to a ranch Fox owned in California, where they rebuilt the village once again. It is hard to decide which of these locations was the worst. In the studio, the set containing my study was as tiny as the front room of a Victorian workman's cottage, and what with the Todd AO cameras, the many different kinds and sizes of lights, a crew of seventy, and the whole of Noah's Ark in attendance, the heat and smells were quite appalling. After every shot, the pick-up men would rush in with shovels and mops to clean up after the animals.

I spent a year of my life, all told, on *Doctor Dolittle*, and by the end of that year my tolerance for film-makers and my love for animals were both at a remarkably low ebb.

As an actor, I have never needed my quite considerable powers of concentration on the job in hand as much as I needed them on *Doctor Dolittle*. There was so much noise and confusion on the set, that at the end of each day's shooting, I would jump with fright when anyone spoke to me unexpectedly. Working with so many animals and the hazards they could represent meant that I had to be on the alert to danger all day long. This made the actual acting very difficult. Like most experienced actors my performance has always been influenced by the responsiveness, or otherwise, of the actor or actress with whom I am playing a scene. I have always found it essential to have eye contact with my partner, especially in a two-shot. What distinguishes a really good actor is that he looks at you and listens to you, in the part. With the animals, however well-trained they are, and however responsive they are to you, you cannot get the necessary eye contact, which is why I would sometimes stop plumb in the middle of a scene in *Doctor Dolittle* and poor Richard

197

Fleischer would have to stop the cameras and ask me what was wrong. According to him, I would always say the same thing. "It isn't *looking* at me!" I'd complain of the poor unsuspecting seal, pig, monkey, Great Pink Sea-Snail, Pushmi-pullyu (the two-headed llama), or whatever.

I was driven half-mad with frustration, but the crew must have thought me the worst, most crochety old perfectionist that ever lived. And at the end of the filming, when I decided that I hadn't sung any of my seven songs as well as I could sing them, and announced that I wanted to re-record them, they thought me a lot worse than that! The head of the music department exploded with fury at the very idea, and said that because I had insisted on recording my songs live, and not, as everyone else always did, and should, to playback, it would be impossible to re-record. Nobody, even the producer and director, actually thought I could improve my performance simply by speaking some of the words I'd sung and singing some of the words I'd spoken. I knew I could. And that is what I did. They cursed and swore at me, but when we started to do the lip-sync-ing, and they saw, apparently to their astonishment, that, after a couple of rehearsals I was perfectly capable of re-voicing a whole song straight through and getting it in sync on the first take, they changed their tune. Sing/speak is such a particular form that no-one really understands how you do it. In this case, no-one believed I could make my songs better, but when I did, they all appreciated it at once. The film was nominated for Best Picture, Cinematography, Art Direction, Sound, Original Score, and Song ("Talk to the Animals"), and won the Oscar for Best Song and Best Visual Effects.

It cannot be said that the many tensions of making *Doctor Dolittle* was helping the survival of my marriage to Rachel Roberts. I suppose we should have realized at the beginning that there were too many real differences between us for us to make it work. Our backgrounds and our attitudes were really diametrically opposed. Rachel was very Welsh – almost belligerently so – her father, a dear man, was a Baptist preacher, who had had to have a serious cancer operation at the age of seventy, and needed a lot of caring for during this time – and she had a lot of puritan anger bottled up in her, which was readily released by the kind of rich, wasteful lives she saw around me in the jungle of Hollywood film-making. Her commitment to the left-wing values of the "Angry Brigade" were not reconcilable with the life she led with me. Perhaps, if I'd gone on working at the Royal Court after *Platonov* and *August for the People*, she might have liked me a lot better!

Anyway, during the period of my big Hollywood films, she had been getting increasingly frustrated by the Hollywood kind of life, and although she had frequently gone off and made films of her own, or done plays, she'd got herself into a pretty depressed and suicidal state, punctuated with periods of wild, rather anti-social behaviour. I could deal with Rachel's wildness – I often found it highly amusing – but the rest of the world regarded it as distinctly rum. I noticed with particularly wry amusement that Richard Burton wrote in his diaries that he thought me terribly tolerant of Rachel's bouts of drunk and disorderly behaviour, adding that if he'd been married to her he would not have put up with it, and would certainly have belted her one after a very short time indeed. As a comment from one wild Welsh person not entirely averse to drink, about another, I thought this was very rich – and "Rich"! – indeed.

Whether I showed it in public or not, I was often very worried about Rachel and her state of mind. She'd been suicidally depressed during the making of *The Honey Pot*,

199

and later on, in Portofino, while Fox were over to discuss the problems of *Doctor Dolittle* with me, she made a scene in a restaurant, The White Elephant, or L'Elefante Bianco, where we were pretty well known, which some people have apparently not forgotten to this day. She used to do a wonderful imitation of a basset hound when she'd had a bit to drink, which was harmless and funny, but she also tried to do idiotic things like stab my hands on the table cloth with a sharp knife, which alarmed a lot of people, including myself.

For a while, on *Doctor Dolittle*, we lived on St Lucia, one of the Windward Islands in the Caribbean, though, naturally – this being that kind of film – the experience was far from idyllic. Even there, the weather played us up, giving us five or six spectacular tropical storms each day, and making sure every biting insect or stinging fly in the whole West Indies knew just where we were. I charted a three-masted schooner, and Rachel and I lived on board, and on windy Sundays we put the sails up and got some reasonable big sailing, which was marvellous. The yacht enabled us to explore the other side of the island, which had a walk-in volcano, which was very exciting – you could climb the shallow slopes until you reached the edge of a molten lake bubbling with sulphur geysers. Behind the volcano, at the mouth of the river where I had to film my scenes with the Giant Pink Snail (an invented character), ran a clear and very tempting river, in which there lived a very real species of tiny poisonous snail. It seems there is always trouble of some sort in Paradise.

When the filming of *Doctor Dolittle* came to an end at last, Rachel and I both hoped that by working together on a film of Feydeau's classic farce *A Flea in her Ear*, we might be able to save our marriage. So many of the people on the film were friends of both of ours – Doc Merman, Richard

Zanuck, Rosemary Harris – and of course we loved the script, in the adaptation of which John Mortimer had had a hand. In retrospect, however, I think there is a tremendous difference between French farce on the stage, and on the screen, and I incline to the view that on the whole it is a form which doesn't work on film. French farce is a very particular comic form and it needs the space of the theatre for its effects. The eye needs to rove around a whole stage, taking in the outlandish situations happening on different parts of it. Without that, the comedy and the timing do not work so well. There is also a case to be made for saying that it doesn't work that well in English, either. Who knows? In any case, things were no better between Rachel and me after the film than they were before, and I, at least, began to accept that our differences were insurmountable.

A film I should not really have done, even to pay for my villa and vineyards, was *Staircase*, based on a bizarre but successful stage play by Charles Dyer, to be directed by the erstwhile comedy and musicals director Stanley Donen, in which I was to star opposite Richard Burton, and the music was to be written by Dudley Moore. The piece was virtually a two-hander between me and Burton, and the gimmick was that he and I – two of the better known heterosexuals in the business – would do our damnedest to play homosexuals without in any way being "camp". I can't imagine now why I agreed to do it, unless it was as a chance to work more closely with Burton, who I'd never had real acting scenes with on *Cleopatra*. Naturally, we did get to know each other better, and got to know each other's way of working, too, and that was fine. It was always great fun to be with Richard, but what on earth we thought we were doing, the pair of us, playing two long-married homosexuals as straight as we could, and trying so hard not to camp the piece up, or appear like a couple of outrageous queens, is beyond me. The whole thing must have been part of the trendy Sixties, I suppose, though it seemed respectable enough at the time: Paul Schofield and Patrick Magee had done the play in London, and Eli Wallach and Milo O'Shea had done it on Broadway.

CHAPTER 11

"THE CURTAIN WILL RISE . . ."

After a long stint in films I was longing to work in the theatre again. I love the theatre, and I feel very much part of the theatre in a way that I've never felt part of films. I've made a lot of films, and very successful films, but I've never felt like a film star. In any case, after *Staircase* I started looking at possible plays to take me back into the theatre, and after a few false starts, found a delightful comedy called *The Lionel Touch* by a writer called George Hulme. It was to be produced by John Gale and directed by John Gorrie at the Lyric Theatre, Shaftesbury Avenue, London, and my co-star was to be Joyce Redman, who had played my Anne Boleyn so beautifully in *Anne of the Thousand Days*. We began rehearsing in London towards the end of 1969, and it was at that time that I met the Hon. Elizabeth Rees-Williams, daughter of Lord Ogmore, who had previously been married to the actor, Richard Harris.

My separation from Rachel had left me exhausted and depressed, so Elizabeth and I started travelling together, and in 1971, when my divorce from Rachel became final she and I were married at Alan Jay Lerner's house on Long Island. We went from there to Portofino, and then she accompanied me to Spain, where I'd been asked to do a very classy TV film of the great Spanish classic novel by Cervantes, *Don Quixote*. There had recently been a stage musical made of it, *Man of La Mancha*, and this had revived interest in the subject. It was to be shot in the glorious plains of La Mancha in Spain during the summer of 1972, with Alvin Rakoff directing, and a cast which included Frank Finlay as Sancho Panza, Rosemary Leach as Dulcinea, Bernard Hepton, Ronald Lacey and Robert Eddison. I accepted the part of Don Quixote, and we were all set, except for one misfortune – just before leaving I slipped on one of the terraces in Portofino, hurtled down about six more terraces and landed hard on my right side. I broke three ribs. There is nothing you can do about ribs, except strap them up, and there is nothing you can do about starting dates except start.

It was awful – a truly ghastly experience for me. I was in absolute agony, but I had, somehow, to wear armour and ride in intense heat, and to put up with primitive accommodation beset by giant horseflies that bite. I am not exaggerating. Elizabeth described my trials and tribulations in her book *Love, Honour and Dismay*: "During the whole time we were in La Mancha Rex was in considerable pain. . . . He had to mount his horse by means of a step-ladder; he would remain in the saddle for hours since it was too painful to dismount between takes." Perhaps I should add that, while speaking of my dedication to my work, which she claimed had always "awed" her, she also reported that "he drives himself as well as others mercilessly." The worst of it was that it didn't come out too well as a film, and I never felt I'd got Don Quixote right.

I had a lot of time to think while making *Don Quixote*, and something that the great Knight Errant himself is made to say stayed with me:

> The truth lies in a man's dreams . . . perhaps in this unhappy world of ours, a wise madness is better than a foolish sanity.

I had often noticed that the actors I'd admired most, especially on the stage, had had a touch, or more than a touch, of madness in them. Wilfred Lawson was one example. Ralph Richardson another. I began to long for a touch of madness in my career, and the chance to do something big in the theatre about the roles of sanity and madness. It was then that I found Pirandello's marvellous play of 1922, *Enrico Quattro* (Henry IV), which is about a twentieth-century man who believes himself to be an eleventh-century emperor – the Emperor Henry IV. The play had been acclaimed a masterpiece, but had rarely been performed in English, in fact, it had not been seen on the London stage since 1927, so I took an option on it, and, together with the director Clifford Williams, commissioned a new translation from a writer called Stephen Rich.

Henry IV was an immensely difficult role for me to play, quite different from anything I'd done before. I could no more have played it when I was young, than I could fly. You need lots of water under the bridge, lots of experience in hundreds of parts before you can tackle chaps like Henry IV. You have to work up to them your whole career. I had reached the stage then when I could choose parts because they *were* difficult, and I knew from the beginning, that Pirandello's *Henry* would be wonderfully challenging to do. In some ways it was an odd role for me to choose, considering my lifelong dedication to naturalism, but the trick lay in playing a fantastical part as naturalistically as possible. I suppose most people thought I must have been mad to do it. Even Elizabeth wrote that I seemed to be pretty terrified of the role: "It is a massive, complex part and a formidable challenge to any actor, even to one of Rex's considerable talent. I know that it often made him physically sick with fear and apprehension. It amazed me. He could have chosen almost any play he wanted . . . yet he drove himself to play the Emperor."

Of course, I didn't know if I could achieve it, and that, together with the subject matter, was what fascinated me. All Pirandello's plays are about madness – different forms of madness, because, poor man, his wife was incurably insane. He didn't want to put her away in a home, and he lived with her, so he had first-hand knowledge of insanity. Naturally, this affected his work, and most of the brilliant plays Pirandello wrote have madness at the root of them. *Enrico Quattro* is a very ingenious play about a group of Italians having a sort of charade. They'd all dressed up, they were having a little party, and the character I played dressed up as Henry IV, a medieval European king. There was a little intrigue going on, a little danger, and one of the characters decides, when I'm riding on horseback in the charade, to jab my horse from behind with his spear, which he does. The horse rears. (This is all before the play starts.) I am thrown from my horse and knocked on the head and, from then on, believe that I am Henry IV. In other words, I go mad. All the people who've taken part in the charade decide that the one thing not to do with me is to lock me away in an asylum, so they acquire a villa in Umbria where they put me and get me these people to wait on me and treat me as if I were Henry IV.

And that is where we are when the curtain rises. We see a man in a villa, surrounded with all his courtiers.

His friends have decorated the villa, and all the windows are shut and the curtains drawn, so that as far as he is concerned, he, Enrico Quattro, is living in medieval times with all the people he would normally have had around him had he been the King. And when these friends of his come in, in modern clothes, you don't know whether he recognizes them or not. In fact, he recognizes them all, and at the end of the play he kills the man who jabbed his horse, and knocked him off it. At the end of the play he says, "Well, here I have to stay forever." He has to remain Enrico Quattro although we the audience know that he is totally sane and rational. A marvellous play, and quite unlike anything I'd tried to do previously. The great examples of Du Maurier and Hawtrey could not be used. It was, in a sense, a bravura part, a great character part, with enormous possibilities for extrovert acting which I made myself do because I felt I owed it to myself. I felt I would like to extend myself from high comedy into this great role, and I managed to do it both sides of the Atlantic and I'm very proud about that.

An American friend of mine, an actor called Paul Hecht, played in the original production with me in America and took the part Baron Tito Belcredi, the man who actually jabbed my horse and who was responsible for the whole period of my presumed madness, and whom I kill at the end. He was excellent. Later, knowing the play so well, he wanted to have a crack at playing Henry IV himself and I went to see him do it. He was terrific, and I realized all over again when I saw this play a second time in New York last year, what a marvellous play it is and what great possibilities it has. All Pirandello's plays are wonderful, and I want to do more of them. There is a great well of plays which have not been produced, but they need to be very well translated. *Six Characters in Search of an Author* was beautifully done at the National not long ago, and there are many of his plays in which I would still want to play.

I was very lucky to find the right director to do *Enrico Quattro*, as good direction in this kind of play is of the utmost importance. Clifford Williams directed both productions, on either side of the Atlantic, with different casts, quite brilliantly. We opened in Toronto in December 1972 and went on to Los Angeles, Boston and Washington before coming into the Ethel Barrymore Theatre, New York, at the end of March 1973. Early in 1974 we brought the play to London for a limited three month season, at Her Majesty's Theatre, opposite my old favourite The Theatre Royal, Haymarket. In the event, I collected some of the best notices of my career, but what I am proudest of is that I introduced this remarkable play to a whole new generation of theatre goers. In London I insisted that good seats should be available at a price within the reach of students, and when those students came round to the stage door, not to praise my performance, but to discuss the play with me, I knew I had been truly successful in what I had set out to do, and I felt fulfilled by it.

A member of the London audience described what he saw me do in *Enrico Quattro*, which is nice to know, as I, of course, have no memory now of exactly how I played the part. "The play starts with the figure of a King, a man with an archaic regal manner – sitting on a high throne in an ermine robe in what seem to be medieval times. Servants scuttle at his feet, and after one imperious command, the King sends his men away. Then a sly look of malicious humour comes over his face, and with one extraordinary, almost simian movement he delves into his voluminous robe and plucks out a large cigar and a box of matches. He handles the cigar as a precious object, holds it up for inspection, lights it very carefully from the box of matches, then puffs out blue clouds of smoke. It was an absolute show-stopper, for with that one little bit of business he conveyed that something very strange was going on, and one at once realized that we were not in medieval times, as we had thought, but in the present day, and that perhaps the regal figure we were contemplating was not as royal as we had supposed. Rex Harrison's genius lay in the fantastic control and timing of that gesture. Had he taken longer it would have spoilt the tension. Had he rushed it, he'd have ruined it. As it was it put a catch in my throat – and judging from the attentive silence in the house – in everyone else's throat as well."

Enrico Quattro was in every way a real challenge to me, and there is a story from that time which proves how much I was enjoying it, and also illustrates my love of jazz. When I was appearing in *Enrico Quattro*, (or *The Emperor Henry IV* as it was known in America) at the Ethel Barrymore Theatre on Broadway, I went one night after the show with Paul Hecht to hear the great vibraphone master Lionel Hampton, and I thought he was marvellous. Next night, after the performance, Paul said to me, "What on earth were you up to tonight, Rex? Your performance was different somehow. It had all kinds of new rhythms in it." I was puzzled by this remark, until I realized that had happened. I had been so influenced by Lionel Hampton and his vibes, that his compelling rhythms had somehow found their way into my performance!

My next venture was to do a new play on Broadway by Terence Rattigan called *In Praise of Love*. Terry had based the play on aspects of my brief and poignant marriage to Kay Kendall, though naturally, he had changed all the details of the two characters' lives, so that only the basic situation – that the wife is going to die – remains similar. In the play the couple have been married for twenty-eight years, and their backgrounds are totally different from Kay's or mine. I played the curmudgeonly husband, a high literary critic, a sort of Edmund Wilson figure called Sebastian Cruttwell. He was rather a Shavian Professor Higgins type, abrupt, rude, and invariably sarcastic towards his wife. In the play she knows she's dying, and thinks *he* doesn't know, but he does know, and is faced with a dilemma. Does he change his spots or continue to behave as badly as he has always done in order to allay suspicion?

Naturally, I was full of trepidation about doing a story which sailed so close to the wind of my own life and my own private pain. I knew it would not be easy to do, yet the memories of Kay were no longer painful ones – I wouldn't have missed a moment of the life we shared.

A member of the audience who'd had a seat in the stalls reminded me of one scene in the play: "The set was of the interior of the critic's apartment – a study/drawing room, with a balcony with books all round it. Rex was on the balcony getting out a book, and his wife was in the downstairs room. The dialogue consisted of him being his usual brutal and sarcastic self, with his back to the audience, and to her, while she sat at a desk not looking at him. And then, after one particularly brutal and sarcastic speech he turned, and you suddenly saw his shoulders slump as though the effort to keep up the pretence were too great for him. It was an enormously poignant and touching moment, and yet it was just a brief gesture, just this sagging of the shoulders – no words – a perfect little bit of business which conveyed far more than words would have done at that point."

It's nice to be reminded of what one did in a performance, and very flattering that members of the audience remember such tiny, but all-important things. To me, they are so instinctive at the time, I rarely remember what I have done in the way of gestures, or little bits of business. This story also reminds me that all through my career, from my parts in *Heroes Don't Care*, *The Rake's Progress*, *Anna and the King of Siam*, and *Henry VIII*, to Professor Higgins in *My Fair Lady*, the desperate drunkard in *Platonov* and the literary chap in *In Praise of Love*, I have been employed for the sole purpose of making people love the villain or the cad. Almost all my major roles have been of self-centred type, who, in Higgins's words, "desire nothing more/ than just the ordinary chance/ to live exactly as he likes/ and do precisely what he wants", and my task has been to get an audience to find something sympathetic in them, so they can identify, and even grow to *like* them. I've no idea what this proves, if indeed it proves anything except that, in my period, people have preferred, on the whole, to identify with the cad than with the hero, at least in drama.

The first production of *In Praise of Love* had been done in London with Donald Sinden and Joan Greenwood. I had the brilliantly talented American actress Julie Harris as my co-star, Fred Coe as director, and Arthur Cantor as producer, and we tried out our production in Wilmington, Delaware, and at the Opera House at the Kennedy Centre in Washington DC, before coming into the Morosco Theatre in New York. *In Praise of Love* collected a lot of praise, was wonderful to do, and was a great success, running to packed houses for nearly six months, and closing before the summer heat in May 1975.

Meanwhile I suppose I must have known that my marriage wasn't going very well, but I didn't enjoy learning that it was actually at an end when Elizabeth told the press in

211

London she was suing me for divorce on the grounds of "irreconcilable differences". Elizabeth got her divorce in December 1975, and she and I have remained friends.

In 1976 I did two more "vineyard and villa" films. One, *The Prince and the Pauper*, with Richard Fleischer as director and Charlton Heston as my co-star, was based on Mark Twain's delightful classic; the other was a re-make of Alexander Dumas' *The Man in the Iron Mask*, which appeared as *The Fifth Musketeer*. But my wish was, as always, to return to the theatre, and in this I was to be aided by two people: Patrick Garland, and George Bernard Shaw. Patrick Garland is a stage director who was working at the Chichester Festival Theatre in Sussex, England, and wanted to put on a little-known French farce, *M. Perrichon's Travels*. This wasn't notable in any way, except that it was great fun to stage, and had me, in a spectacular surprise effect, hanging from the rafters at the back of the auditorium, to represent the fact that I was supposed to have fallen down the Matterhorn! This flying stunt resulted, unsurprisingly, in a back injury, which meant I had to rest up for a while.

Shaw came to the rescue with a new production of *Caesar and Cleopatra* to be done on Broadway, with the extraordinary American actress Elizabeth Ashley as Cleopatra. I trotted out my Caesar again, and my friend Paul Hecht played Rufio. Elizabeth was very good, and we were directed by Ellis Rabb in an excellent production. The following year Shaw came to the rescue again, at the Edinburgh Festival, where Patrick Garland directed me in five afternoon performances of an entertainment entitled *Our Theatres in the Nineties*, taken from three collections of Shaw's dramatic criticism, where he talks about the great actors of the 1890s.

I loved doing it, although it was even more of a challenge than Shaw's plays are, and extremely difficult to remember, as it was not written in dramatic form. Shaw's criticism, like Shaw's plays, is marvellously vigorous stuff, of extraordinarily high quality. Shaw held the theatre very high, he was always hoping for better things. He tried to get the actors to be more honest in their acting but they did nothing about it. He was impatient because he had high ideals. If there was someone like him writing theatre criticism today, then leading actors would certainly take note.

On reviewing these pages, I must say it does look as though I have done a lot of George Bernard Shaw in my life, and it's true. If you count *My Fair Lady*, which we should, considering it was taken straight from *Pygmalion*, I should say I've spent a good half of my life doing Shaw. This is because Shaw's work has always appealed to me very much. He was very erudite, he had humour, he was an excellent writer, and he wrote beautiful prose – clean, easily spoken, brilliant prose, and so lovely to speak that I had great joy in speaking it.

I did a lot of dashing back and forth at this period, Broadway, Edinburgh, Chichester, and then, I went travelling even further afield, for the movies. I went to Southern India for an extravaganza called *Shalimar*, and then to Kenya and Israel for another film for the indefatigable Richard Fleischer, an adventure story called *Ashanti*, in which I starred with William Holden and Michael Caine.

Fortunately, I was given a bit of respite from all this globe-trotting by being asked to do the Broadway version of a lovely, sophisticated English play by William Douglas Home, *The Kingfisher*.

This play had opened in London in May 1977 with

213

Ralph Richardson, Celia Johnson and Alan Webb. The director was Lindsay Anderson, and the designer Alan Tagg. Lindsay Anderson and Alan Tagg were going to take the same production to New York, so of course when they asked me if I'd like to do it in America, I said I'd love to. The play is about two people who have met in their early teens and then re-meet and catch up with all their old experiences when they are the age we are. I had the idea of asking the famous Hollywood film star, Claudette Colbert, if she would like to act on the stage opposite myself and George Rose, and this turned out to be a very good idea indeed. Audiences were as thrilled to see Claudette Colbert on the stage as I had been years and years ago when I first saw her on the screen, and the combination of us two old war-horses proved a powerful box office draw. We ran for six months, from December 1978 to May 1979, after which we took the play on tour around America, and I made a film of it for BBC Television in 1982. A very big part of *The Kingfisher*'s success was due to the direction of my old friend Lindsay Anderson. I admire Lindsay very much, he's done some marvellous things in his career, but he hasn't often done comedy. *The Kingfisher* proves that when he gets hold of a comedy he does it beautifully. He did a wonderful job.

At the beginning of 1979, during the run of *The Kingfisher*, I married my sixth – and last – wife, Mercia Tinker. We live in New York when I work here, and are very happy, but it did not take Mercia long to notice how obsessed I am with my work. In the last week of *The Kingfisher*'s run, she was amazed to see me pacing the stage after a performance, trying to work out whether a scene would be better played another way. I had to explain to her, gently, of course, that I like to go on exploring the possibilities of a play until the very last night . . .

214

CHAPTER 12

A SERIOUS BUSINESS

*I*n 1981, to celebrate the anniversary of twenty-five years since we first did *My Fair Lady*, I was asked to do a revival. This was a tremendous risk; there is always a tremendous risk involved in doing something considered perfect, again. But other actors had revived their musical successes – Yul Brynner with *The King and I*, Richard Burton with *Camelot* – to public, and even critical, acclaim, and I had a whole lot of new ideas I wanted to try out on *My Fair Lady*. In short, it was my old favourite – a challenge. Could I do it better than I had done before?

I was given the final word on everything – director, casting, decor – and we were to tour to a lot of places where people had not viewed the original, and would have a chance to see the show for the first time. We began in New Orleans, went to the Golden Gate Theatre, San Francisco, and the Pantages Theatre, Los Angeles, then to Chicago, St Louis, Miami Beach, Boston – and finally, New York – and the nice thing is that I am still getting ecstatic reactions from people who saw the show in their home towns.

The most important thing for me, however, was the way I felt about the play. I felt that, however splendidly we'd honoured the spirit of Shaw the first time round, the virtues of Shaw's *Pygmalion* could have been brought out even better. In spite of everything we achieved in the first production, I didn't think Shaw was done total justice, and part of that was because we engaged singers rather than actors for the show. I thought that as Patrick Garland had worked so well with me on *M. Perrichon's Travels*, and particularly, on the Shaw one-man show *Our Theatres in the Nineties*, he would understand what I felt about Shaw, so I engaged him to direct, explaining that this time I wanted to tip the balance of the production towards actors who could sing, rather than singers who could act.

This time was also wanted Eliza to be a real London girl, a cockney, and much tougher than the earlier Elizas, so Patrick and I started a search for her all over London. My reason for doing this was, once again, to have a challenge. By making her tougher and rougher, so to speak, it would be more difficult for Higgins to turn her into a lady. The play isn't usually done like that, and I thought it would give it a different edge. Eventually we chose Cheryl Kennedy, but almost immediately ran into trouble with American Equity. Since I was still a British subject, and so was darling ninety-one-year-old Cathleen Nesbit, whom I'd chosen to play Mrs Higgins – again! – American Equity wouldn't grant us another green card for Eliza, so we had to audition hundreds of American girls to prove we couldn't get anyone better for the part. Predictably, they could all sing like dickie birds, but none of them could do the cockney accent, which I considered vital.

Eventually, I had to fly to New York from Florida, where I was playing in *The Kingfisher*, and plead the case before the Equity Council, but they still refused to give Cheryl Kennedy a permit. This being the case I decided, regretfully, not to proceed with the revival. The case went into arbitration, and Cheryl Kennedy was at last accepted because of what they call "unique circumstances" – a formula which gets them off the hook by making sure that no precedent is being established.

Another difficult decision was the look of the show. I wanted it to be more realistic, less stylized, than the first production, and boldly decided we should jettison some of Cecil Beaton's prize-winning costumes, in favour of more realistic ones which people could actually have worn, in earthier colours. This was, after all, a grimy London of 1907. We took on Oliver Smith again to do new settings, and he did give me the darker, more realistic look I was searching for.

Surprisingly, considering the pitfalls, the show was an unmitigated joy to do. In my whole career, I have never had a vehicle which gave me – or the audience – so much. My performance was a little less edgy than it was the first time. It may have just come out that way, because I was personally less edgy, because I was enjoying it so much. I don't know of anything more rewarding with an audience than *My Fair Lady*. The standing ovations we got for it made life very much easier than fighting audiences with plays that have material which is not always understandable, too light or too dark or whatever. It's a long show, longer than the average, and it's a very long part. But I love it, and I loved doing it all over again.

I also found the part wasn't as exhausting as it had been, and told Roderick Mann: "I think I'm finding this one easier because my life is organized at last, and Mercia, my wife, is making sure that I eat properly. She is a keen nutritionist. Also, I'm pacing myself better. When I did the original show I seemed to spend my time running round the theatre like a rabbit. In those days I was always anxious to get back on stage. Now when someone else is on stage and I'm not, I'm delighted. In general, I'm not in favour of revivals, but everything to do with *My Fair Lady* proves exceptional, and breaks the rules." Our run in New York was supposed to be limited to three months, but was so successful it over-ran its time.

After that I did *The Kingfisher* for British television, with Wendy Hiller and Cyril Cusack, then I was able to go into another of those major parts, like that of Pirandello's Henry IV, a role which, in a sense, I'd been waiting for all my career to be old enough and experienced enough to play. This was the part of Captain Shotover in Shaw's *Heartbreak House*.

I'd always thought Shotover was a marvellous part, but he is meant to be eighty-eight years old, and I had been too young to play him. He's a wise old bird with quite a lot of humour to him, though possibly slightly mad humour. But the play is really a team play. They are all damned fine parts and everyone has their scene. In the London production, at my old favourite, the Theatre Royal, Haymarket, we had Diana Rigg and Rosemary Harris and Mel Martin, and the play was directed by John Dexter. I much preferred the production we took to the States, in which we had the beautiful and subtle film-actress Amy Irving, as well as Rosemary Harris, playing a different role from the one she played in London, and the excellent American actress, Jan Miner, playing the old nurse. The American production was directed by another English director, Anthony Page, and he brought far more humour into the play. I thought it worked much better.

Heartbreak House is supposed to be Shaw's attempt at

a Chekhovian type of play, and, sure enough, John Dexter's London production brought out the melancholy in it, as the British tend to do with Chekhov, and not the humour. About the New York one, Richard Findlater wrote, in *Plays and Players*: "There is enough humour and humanity in the role for Mr Harrison to feed on it, and for his admirers in the audience to feast on Mr Harrison: his performance was, within its limits, finely accomplished, and soared above the limits in some of the major speeches with surprising effect." Decent of him, I must say! Sheridan Morley was a lot less grudging: ". . . so mesmeric was Harrison in his flamboyant and marvellously quirky theatricality that he managed to hover over the play like some benign Prospero, neither coming or going but merely trying to make sense of a British isle that is still full of noises but no longer so very magical. All of that is of course a perfect role-description of Shotover himself, and when Harrison got himself into that last great speech about England ('The Captain is in his bunk drinking bottled ditchwater and the crew is gambling in the forecastle; she will strike and splint. Do you think the laws of God will be suspended in favour of England because you were born in it?'), it was to be reminded with a sudden shock of what an extraordinary talent we have allowed to disappear over the Atlantic."

I can't think now why I got John Dexter to direct *Heartbreak House* in the first place. He was inclined to be rather grumpy and bad-tempered, and not always particularly articulate. Certainly his ill-humour and sarcasm failed to promote the kind of working relationship which brings out the best of an actor's talent. If the play worked in London, and got a good press, it was scarcely a tribute to the director, but because it's a good play. The fact that Shaw had said it was his attempt to write a play in the Russian style, laid it open, I suppose, to the sort of treatment the English habitually dish out to poor old Chekhov. It's awfully interesting to do the same play twice in the same year (1983), in different parts of the world with different directors and different casts. It is extraordinary the different colours which can be found in it by different personalities. As far as actors were concerned, I was the only continuity between the two productions, (Rosemary Harris was in both, but she switched roles), and because Anthony Page is witty, and is in himself an amusing man, he found humour where Dexter had not found any humour at all, so in the New York production we found all sorts of beautiful things in it which we hadn't found with Dexter.

Fortunately, I was able to put *Heartbreak House* on film for television, and so all our performances are preserved.

After this I revived a play by a writer of the first part of the century, a man who used to be one of the very best and most amusing of my companions in Portofino. He was Frederick Lonsdale, and the play, a comedy written in 1908 as *The Best People*, was *Aren't We All?* It had been produced under the new title in New York in 1923, Gertrude Lawrence did it on film in 1932 – her first picture – and it was revived in the West End of London in 1934. Now I brought my glamorous co-star from *The Kingfisher*, Claudette Colbert, with me to London for it, and we opened at – of course – The Theatre Royal, Haymarket, where we ran for six months, to happy audiences. After which we took it to New York where it was similarly successful, and had, among others, Jeremy Brett and Lynn Redgrave in it with us. And, as with the other recent plays, we plan to put this on film for television too.

Aren't We All? is a lovely play, and Freddie Lonsdale was a great friend of mine, whom I knew long before I'd ever done any plays of his. I once picked him up in Cannes and drove him down to my villa in Portofino, and he stayed with me for a couple of weeks. He was a great house guest, a great raconteur, and a wonderful playwright, and everyone who came to the port in their boats wanted to come up and see Freddie. He was a magnificent man and I loved him dearly. His daughters came to see the play and enjoyed it. Apart from myself and Claudette, the rest of the casts were different in London and New York. In London we had Francis Matthews playing the young man, Willie Tatum, and in New York Willie Tatum was played by Jeremy Brett. Lynn Redgrave played the Hon. Mrs Tatum in it in New York, and Nicola Paget in London.

Later on, when we took *Aren't We All?* to Australia, we had to get an Australian cast because of Australian Equity, but Australia is practically a book in itself

Australia is a strange and rugged continent, not overpopulated, and Freddie had written the play for the West End of London. It was a sophisticated comedy in which there was an Australian playing rather a naive role. He never thought the play was going to be played in Australia, and I must say I would never have taken it to Australia had I known exactly what Australia was like because I was there for six months, and they didn't really ever like it, except in Sydney. In Sydney they sort of understood it. Sydney is by far the most sophisticated spot in Australia. We went to Melbourne, we went to Brisbane, and we flew right across the continent to Perth.

We were in Perth at the same time the Americas Cup was being competed for, and that was very exciting, as I was able to follow it in friends' boats, and it's rough out there in that part of the Pacific. But what amazed me most was how totally unpopulated the West Coast of Australia is. I thought it quite wonderful! We were taken down by helicopter one day to the farthest south-western tip of Australia where there is a wonderful vineyard, and we were given lunch at the vineyard-keeper's house, and he told me how complicated his job was because the kangaroos down there are so huge that they were able to spring over practically anything he put up in the way of fences, and gorge themselves on the grapes. He had great trouble, until he finally found a way of electrifying the fences, so the kangaroos got a shock every time they came near them, and that way he managed to keep them out.

But coming down by helicopter and looking at these stretches of wonderful white sand, absolutely deserted, not a house, not a human being in sight, just mile after mile of beautiful beaches, completely unpopulated, was an experience. So much of Australia is still just desert, populated round the edges, that it stands to reason the Australians wouldn't like or understand a play like *Aren't We All?*. I played a character called Lord Grenham, who had a butler in London and a butler in the country, and the Australians didn't like this idea at all. It irked them that an Englishman should have two sets of servants because menservants are unheard of in Australia, and although the Australians were wondrously good when the British were in trouble – they were magnificent during the war – basically they don't love the English, the English way of life, or the English class system. Why should they? They've probably always felt slightly neglected, and a lot of them feel that they may be descended from the convicts we cluttered them up with at one point when our prisons were so full of petty thieves that we took them all and dumped them in Australia. They've certainly got no reason to love us, and once I was there I wished I'd thought of all this beforehand and not taken Freddie's play there because it wasn't a suitable play for Australia. I would like to go to Australia as a civilian and enjoy it, and not to have to act there.

Anyway *Aren't We All?* was a great success in London and New York, directed by Clifford Williams, who had directed *Enrico Quattro* so beautifully. The Lonsdale play was a very different type of production from the Pirandello – you couldn't find a bigger switch of type of play, or the environment of a play than with these two – but Clifford Williams did a brilliant job with both of them, and I was glad for Freddie, and as he's been dead now for many years, I was glad for Freddie's descendants, and particularly for his daughter, Frankie Donaldson, who is a chum of mine, and a very good writer and biographer in her own right.

I'd like to take a moment now to explain to the reader that when you read "And then I did . . . and after that . . ." it all seems fairly simple, as if I just go from one thing to another, but of course it's not so easy as that. Each play that I do takes a lot of preparing, the rights have to be acquired, and it has to be cast. You have to get the right director and the right theatre, and tours have to be booked. It's a long process, and I don't know that the public understands, really, what goes into the production of a play. If it's done immaculately and looks as though it hasn't been any trouble, that's when it has been the most trouble. If it looks a hell of a sweat, that's when it hasn't been taken care of very well.

It is very important, I think, for people to realize this, because I feel that in this book, so many plays that I did have been mentioned, and I'm afraid that it may seem as though it's all very easy. God knows, it isn't. A great deal of care has to go into every single production. This problem is probably compounded by the fact that what I do best is

223

high comedy, and what I do best in high comedy is to make it look easy. What I'd like people to understand about a career like mine, is that the easier it looks, the harder it has been to do, and the more it has taken out of me. My granddaughter Katharine, who is my son Noel's daughter, is an actress herself, and she distinguished herself when she first started out on the stage by proclaiming that, unlike her grandfather, *she* was going to be a *serious* actress!

I'm sure she will be, but I humbly submit that the success of plays like *Aren't We All?* and J.M. Barrie's *The Admirable Crichton* with which I followed it at the Haymarket, in 1988 and Somerset Maugham's *The Circle*, which I am in now, as I come to the end of this book, does rather prove that these "trivial" comedies, and this frivolous high comedy style of mine, still works, even in the last decade of the century.

Having said this, however, I must admit I am frankly amazed at the rapturous reception from critics and public *The Circle* has received in New York, the more particularly because Maugham wrote essentially English plays, and you can't have American attitudes or American accents in them. They are very English, deeply English-rooted people, in all Maugham's plays. They are also very light and very witty and very amusing, but Maugham can have quite deep sentiments behind his lightness. *The Circle* is based on the idea that things repeat themselves, as in *La Ronde*, and that human behaviour – particularly the behaviour of the young in love – repeats itself regardless of the bad examples of their elders, but not necessarily betters.

A young girl is just about to leave her husband for her lover. Then an older couple comes in, who have done exactly the same thing. Years before, they'd run off together, when they were young, and lived in Florence, and ruined each other's lives. So the young couple have this example in front of them but, of course, they repeat the fatal pattern, in spite of the example – it's that very moving and dramatic thing, an echo – and it raises the whole question, would we do the same thing again? Would you? What is love? Does love last? Is it worth while breaking up marriages for love? And even if you don't think it is worth while, nevertheless, you still do it. All the old questions are brought out in this comedy. It's very funny, and very true. He was a great observer of life, Maugham, and it's a very good play, *The Circle*.

The fact remains, though, that it is an English drawing-room comedy of 1921 and I can only think that its current success in New York must be due to a tremendous need for Americans to escape from the harsh unmannerly lives they live now into a more gracious atmosphere where charm and civilized behaviour were the norm.

The reviews were very flattering, but I confess I am somewhat mystified when magazines like the *New Yorker* proclaim that "greatness" descends at the moment in the script where I am called upon to declare an antique chair a fake. And it totally baffles me when critics profess amazement to see me doing what I've been doing on the stage for sixty-five years or so. You'd have thought they'd have grown used to it by now, and just thought, Oh, that's just Rex Harrison being Rex Harrison. I'm not knocking it, of course. It's lovely, and very lucky, to be in a hit on Broadway, with packed houses and enthusiastic audiences. Anyway, I'd been looking forward to doing *The Circle*, for quite a while, and I'd spent some time, while I was in *The Admirable Crichton* in London trying to get it set up, because I like the play, and it is not very often that I find such a good part for me in a play I like these days.

Elliot Martin, who had produced so many of my more

recent plays on Broadway, wanted to do it, and he and I both wanted Glynis Johns for the part of my wife, Lady Kitty – we thought she'd be just right. I like working with Glynis very much – she's a good actress and she knows her business, and I think we make a good duo. It's a very sweet relationship between Lord Porteous and Lady Kitty, and the scenes between us are very touchingly written. We set about casting the other parts when I came back to New York but we still hadn't found the husband Kitty had run away from when she went off, thirty years ago, with me. I think it was Elliot Martin's wife, Marjorie, a casting director, who had the idea of Stewart Granger, which was an unusual idea, to say the least, since nobody knew what he'd be like. He hadn't been on the stage for thirty years, if ever – he was really a film actor – and he was very nervous. Well, he's still nervous, but he has so much charm he seems to get away with it, and the audience seem to warm to him.

We rehearsed in the most dreadful rehearsal room I have ever worked in, in an area of New York, sordid beyond belief, on West 16th Street, a shambles of a place, full of factories and vans making deliveries, a very rough and frightening place. To make matters worse we had to climb twenty-nine steps to our rehearsal room – which wasn't showing much respect for our combined ages, since those, according to a waspish article in *The New York Times*, added up to 222 years together! If I hadn't been driven to the door, I'd probably have been scared to go there – and then I had to climb those steps. It wasn't much fun, either, trying to get Lord Porteous's white linen suit and impeccable dinner jacket made on 16th Street. After all, it's not Savile Row. It wasn't very well cut, in fact it was put together with a knife and fork, but we were having trouble with our stage designer just then, and I didn't dare send for my English tailors. We rehearsed for four weeks on West 16th Street, and then we went to Duke University, where we were confronted by a set so vast it was unplayable in.

Elliot Martin had hired a very classy designer called Desmond Heely, who'd worked for the National Theatre and Covent Garden Opera, and he proceeded to build this absolutely gigantic set, with huge, tall doors which dwarfed the actors – giraffes or giants would have been okay, but normal-sized actors, even tall actors like myself, were lost in it. There were also enormously tall windows which dragged the eye up way past the actors' heads, and from the moment we walked into that set we had trouble. We couldn't even open the giant doors or windows, and to make matters worse, he had painted the whole thing *salmon pink*, so all our make-up and clothes disappeared into it. For a while, at Duke, we made do with drapes, and then in Baltimore the entire thing was repainted using green – a rather suitable Georgian drawing-room green – for the bottom half, and blue to shadow the top so that the eye wouldn't go up, and the height would be disguised. This improved things tremendously – for one thing, green was a much better colour for our faces – we didn't disappear into it.

We also brought in some statuary and some foliage to indicate the garden outside the windows, and covered the window frames with ivy on the outside, so the drawing room seemed to be in any ivy-covered country house, and now the set looked pretty good.

As if there weren't enough production problems in the early days of *The Circle*, I had physical battles to overcome with my eyes and my teeth – I had to be taken straight off the plane to the dentist at one point, and it's a strange coincidence that in *The Circle*, Lord Porteous actually has the same kind of trouble with his "damn new teeth" as I was having while I was playing him! No wonder I ground them convincingly. As for the eye problem, during rehearsals, my "good eye" haemorrhaged, and for five days I was blinded and had to lie still with my head up until the blurring caused by the layer of blood in the back of the eye dispersed. As a result of this I missed five days of rehearsal, and it was very fortunate that I had already read the part a dozen times or more, and absorbed it, in the way I do, because this method of absorbing a part, rather than learning it, enabled me to continue despite missing those five crucial days. I had also already decided how Lord Porteous should look – I generally create a character from the outside in, beginning with the physical look – and this also helped enormously. I'd modelled Lord Porteous on Max Beerbohm, whom I used to see in Portofino – it was Max who had originally given me the name "San Genesio" for my villa, after the patron saint of actors in Italy. Even in his old age, Beerbohm always wore a wonderful white linen suit and a straw hat, and walked in his own particular way. He lived in Rapallo, and was a perfect example of the type of Englishman who has lived in Italy for many years, so I modelled Porteous's appearance, his clothes and his walk, on Max.

At Duke University where we began our tour, I was fortunate to discover that the university is a hot-bed of eye specialists, and I went to a specialist in glaucoma there, who gave me laser treatment which was very good. Mercia accompanied me most of the time, which helped tremendously. Duke, in North Carolina, is a very popular place to open in now, because there's a big, new theatre there, and good, intelligent audiences connected with the university. Unfortunately I didn't get a chance to see any of the countryside of North Carolina, what with my eyes and my teeth.

In Baltimore, I had to contend with the problems of a hotel so ultra-modern that everything kept going wrong. I had a bath-tub like a swimming pool. It was so vast I couldn't lie in it – I'd have drowned. On top of that, the toilet didn't work, and there was a vast and very uncomfortable double bed. They thought it was the absolute answer to a maiden's prayer, but I'm not a maiden, and I wasn't praying. At least, not for that. I was praying for a nice, normal bath, and a toilet which flushed in the usual way.

The play went well in Boston. We got good notices from the critic of the *Boston Guide*, and the audiences were full of bright people who understood the play well and enjoyed it enormously. Things looked set fair for New York by this time, and Elliot Martin had got the Shubert Management in on the production, and also the Japanese company, Suntory. But nothing in the theatre is ever as smooth as it looks. The Ambassador Theatre in New York is not like the nice, long, intimate shape of London theatres – it is a cinemascope shape, which I don't like nearly so much. And I've never been in a place that had so much piercing light on the stage, even in *My Fair Lady* there was less light, although it was a musical and had footlights and front of house lights. I had to get used to a great glare when I first went on, and could see very little, so it was lucky my part didn't call for me to move around the stage too much.

The Ambassador Theatre is built on such strange angles, that my dressing room came to a point. The building is an elongated triangle, and the back stage is in the point of the triangle, which meant there was very little off-stage room. The steam heat was stifling and I couldn't seem to get it to the right temperature, so I often had to cut it off altogether. Steam heat is very difficult to work in. It makes you feel comatose, half the time. I always try to come home in the break between shows, sleep, have a meal, and get a car to go back, but to get to the Ambassadors from where I live I had to drive right across the island, and mid-town is always tangled up, so I had to allow a lot of time. It helps a great deal with this kind of thing that I have my own dresser who has worked with me for ten years, an awfully nice fellow called Walter Massey.

At the end of all these trials and tribulations, I would not have been surprised to hear the critics and the public say *The Circle* was a lot of old-fashioned rubbish, but they thought it was a gorgeous piece of "verbal chamber music". Most of the credit for this should go to Mr Maugham, for the subtlety and wit with which he depicted the delicious society of his day, and I was both amused and flattered when one of the critics wrote that he wasn't sure whether Rex Harrison had invented Maugham, or Maugham had invented Rex Harrison.

AFTERWORD

People often ask me how I keep going at this stage of my life, and I must say that when I'm exhausted after several months of a show like *The Admirable Crichton*, which I did in 1988 at the Haymarket, I hardly know myself. One's life is certainly very much curtailed by having to do eight shows a week.

The point is that one has to give one's entire life to acting, otherwise it's no good, so I don't waste my energies on socializing. I'm very careful what I eat and drink. I don't smoke. One has to be like an athlete, in training. There are times, naturally, when I resent it, and I become a bit bored by it at times, but then – not really bored, because mentally I'm always heading towards the theatre, and I know I've got to be on top form when I get there, and do it to the best of my ability, every night. And that stops me being bored, and makes me feel rather confined, instead.

The only thing I find rather saddening is that I don't see enough theatre when I'm working in the theatre myself. I don't see enough of other people's plays. Even going to a matinée is too much when you've got an evening performance to give, and if I do go, I find that I come home exhausted. When I go to see a long performance in the afternoon and get stared at and asked for autographs in the auditorium, and then come home and have some tea, I feel that as far as I'm concerned I've done my performance, but then I have to go on in about an hour and do the real performance. So the result is that I don't go to the theatre as much as I'd like to, which is maddening, especially if I go out amongst a lot of actors and they're all talking about performances I haven't seen.

Generally speaking, though, I find it much more interesting to be in training, and to work hard, than to be on holiday or have an ordinary social life. I'd be dead bored by that. That's why I have to go on working. I have no alternative. Acting is the only thing that really engages me. I love painting, and find it both relaxing and engaging to do, but painting doesn't absorb me or stimulate me enough, not the way a challenging part in the theatre does. But acting creates social problems for actors which are not always easy to overcome. When you've always worked hard in the theatre, you find that, when you stop playing, at the end of a run, the evenings seem very long indeed. You have to find something to keep yourself occupied with because you're so used to gearing yourself up to that eight o'clock curtain, but to find any kind of real, absorbing alternative is impossible.

Nobody is as interesting to spend an evening with as a really good part.

If I'm not working, though, it's marvellous to spend an evening with a truly creative director, just chatting about nothing at all except what he likes to do. Other actors, too. I've got lots of chums in New York, whom I like spending evenings with, more in New York, strangely enough, than in London. But the thing is that if you're in training you can't allow yourself this convivial kind of evening because all such discussions lead, eventually, to the bottle, so that to spend an evening with one of these chaps and not have a drink becomes impossible. I can only do it, therefore, if I'm not in the theatre, or when I'm between shows, and then I can behave – for a short while – like a normal human being. I can drink in the evening, and catch other people's shows. When one of my plays comes off, I try to catch up on the plays I haven't seen. I like to see most things; otherwise I can get out of touch so easily. For an actor, seeing other people's work is not just pleasant, it's absolutely essential.

None of this explains, however, what you've probably been wondering – how I manage to totter on at the advanced age of eighty-two, which I am. Well, it's largely to do with my wife, Mercia, who is a great believer in exercise. Also, I have a trainer in twice a week in New York who puts me through my paces, and I've been taught wonderful Indian Yoga exercises. You can do them at any age, providing you can stand up. They aren't very energetic, but they are wonderful for stretching, and keeping your body in trim. I do them a lot and I think they are one of the reasons I'm still going, and fairly active.

I have problems with my legs, of course. I mean, I haven't got the energy I had when I was forty, fifty, sixty, but I have enough energy in my old bones to keep going and wish to do new plays, and I'm always excited about the one I'm going to do next. When I am working in New York, our apartment there is an important factor in all this. We both love the place, and I do think having a place you love to live in is important to relaxation and peace of mind. I've got a studio there where I can paint, with a wonderful light – it all faces the East River – and it's very pretty at all times of the day, or night, with the

233

bridges and the barges and the sense you get in New York of people working like mad and making their own living.

I believe very much in walking, too, and I try to do as much walking as possible, wherever I find myself. Despite certain problems I've had with arteries in my legs, due to smoking too much for much too long, I still enjoy a good walk very much indeed. While I was playing in *The Admirable Crichton* in London I was staying at the Ritz Hotel, which adjoins Green Park, so I walked every day in the park, watching the seasons change, which was lovely. Walking also means that you are out in the fresh air, and I believe in the importance of getting as much fresh air as possible. This can sometimes be difficult in winter, given the prevailing climates in London and New York, so we try to go to Barbados in the Caribbean and to our home in Monte Carlo whenever work permits. There, I can walk, and breathe in the beautiful unpolluted air, and even paint my landscapes out of doors, and soak up plenty of sun with the ozone.

Mercia and I both believe very much in the importance of good food supplemented with the right vitamins. And, of course, in being moderate about alcohol. I have to admit that I've cut down my alcohol intake a lot in the last few years. Actors generally have to have a few stiff drinks after a show in order to unwind – you can't just stop when you come off stage – which is no doubt the reason why so many actors appear to be practically alcoholics to the ordinary public. But nowadays I drink Guinness to unwind instead of the hard stuff – mostly Scotch – I used to knock back. I find that Guinness is an excellent drink for my purposes, and it seems to be better for my system in every way.

People – even actors – have become much more health-conscious lately, and I think it's an excellent thing. The cancer scare changed a great deal about the use of cigarettes by actors, both on and off the stage, and I should think that, after the cancer scare, young actors must have found it much more difficult to know what to do with their hands in the cigarette kind of plays. In those days cigarettes were smoked by all and sundry on the stage. We never stopped smoking cigarettes, and it seemed both a popular and stylish thing to do. Du Maurier even had cigarettes named after him, he smoked so much, and his name brand was a great success, but later, when they tried to launch a cigarette called Olivier, the campaign failed. Does anyone remember Olivier cigarettes?

As I mentioned earlier in the book, I gave up smoking thirty seven years ago, which was pretty difficult to do, because I used to smoke like a chimney. Giving it up meant several weeks of hell, but I was given no alternative by the medicos. The use of the weed was affecting the arteries in my legs, and I was getting a lot of pain. I still have certain pains in my legs when I walk a long way, but luckily I'm very agile for my age. I'm sure I'd be dead by now if I hadn't given it up. I'd like to be able to advise young actors to do so, too, but I'm afraid that no-one takes any notice of advice of that kind. You have to experience the effects at first hand before you are shocked into taking action.

I see what happens, even today, in the theatre, and I know that when you are an inveterate smoker, you can't easily stop. The younger members in the cast of *The Admirable Crichton* at the Haymarket couldn't smoke cigarettes on stage, as the dictates of the play meant we were supposed to be on a desert island rather longer than we were in a drawing room, but I saw them stubbing out their cigarettes before they reached the side of the stage. I suppose it is something of an advance that they have to do that. Actually, there's a new rule now that no smoking

235

must take place in the theatre, even on the side of the stage, let alone *on* the stage. Unfortunately, however, this sensible measure simply means that they crush their cigarettes out before they go on, and continue to smoke like chimneys in their dressing rooms. It doesn't actually stop them doing it. In fact, neither rules, nor scarifying facts from doctors, nor the experience of older actors like myself seem to affect the amount young actors continue smoking off stage – I still see them smoking themselves to death.

Thank God smoking didn't affect my voice, and thank God it didn't affect my lungs, so that I still have the all-important instrument with which to go on. I've no way of knowing, of course, how long I'm going to be able to go on, how long I'm going to be able to keep it up. We'll see . . . I still like to have a whole year's work planned, though I do worry, nowadays, that I will be able to cope with the strain. At first I demurred, rather, about the tour of *The Circle*, because of the conditions of hardship – I don't think that's too strong a word – on a long and arduous American tour. I know I've got to conserve myself at this stage, but it's a damned good play and I wanted to do it. Whether you've a long run, or a short run, you must as an actor have a routine to your day. It's eight shows a week. You're there Monday, Tuesday, two shows Wednesday, Thursday, Friday, two shows Saturday, normally. You've got to be there, and you've got to be fit and you've got to be feeling well, so you have to be careful what you eat, and you have to be reasonably careful what you drink. You should wake up late, and have a good breakfast. And in the middle of the day around two o'clock you should have a good lunch – that's the trick, to have a very good lunch midday. Then you don't need to have anything except a cup of tea and a piece of toast before you go to the night show, because it's no good trying to act a show on a full tummy. You've got to have an empty one.

You've got to get down there and do the show, and at half past eleven when you've finished, you have to have a *light* supper – perhaps a steak, or scrambled eggs, and whatever you like to drink, a whisky and soda, perhaps – because you don't want to be up all night digesting your food, at least, I don't. Wednesday and Saturdays being matinée days you wake late, and have a brunch, a very good big meal at twelve o'clock. Then you do the matinée. And you go home, have a sleep and then, not too near the night show, you have to eat again, so you eat at twelve and six thirty, then you do the night show, and you eat again, lightly, afterwards.

I always try to get to bed early on Tuesdays and Fridays before two-show days, so I'm feeling well enough for the Wednesday and Saturday matinées. The days you have to do it twice are tiring, so that's what I have to do, and what I've always done all my life since I was fifteen. Long runs are, of course, progressively tiring, especially big musicals like *My Fair Lady*, which are more exacting than straight plays because you have the singing, you have the orchestra, you have the additional energy levels that you have to keep up.

My training, and Mercia's care of me, must work, because without it I'd be falling apart, I think. I mean, having to keep oneself fit and having to keep one's legs going and having to get out to the park and walk is very good, and very positive. I do as much of that as I can, but you have to have the spirit and the motivation to do it. You must do it because you really want to do it. It seems to me very unwise after an active life for anyone to stop working, or exercising. It's when you stop that your whole metabolism, and the framework, or routine, that keeps you going, is likely to collapse, and you may succumb to a lot of diseases you wouldn't get otherwise. I'm lucky because, although when I'm doing eight shows a week I get exhausted and fed up, I do have a strong motivation for keeping fit – *I want to go on working as long as I can.*

ENVOI

*R*ex Harrison's sixty-five years' contribution to the English-speaking theatre was honoured on 25 July 1989 when he was knighted by Queen Elizabeth II at Buckingham Palace, and became Sir Rex Harrison.

As the sword descended to dub the new Knight's shoulder, the Queen asked him: "Is it very hard work, the theatre?"

Sir Rex did not hesitate in his reply.

"Yes, ma'am, it is," he said.

* * *

Sir Rex died on 2 June 1990, three weeks to the day after his last appearance on stage. He was still putting the finishing touches to this book, which remains exactly as he left it.

239

POSTSCRIPT BY
DAME MAGGIE SMITH

When the great actor Edmund Kean was dying, a young admirer visited his bedside. The young man was terrified and at a loss for words.

Eventually he managed to stammer nervously, "It must be difficult to be dying."

Kean smiled. "No," he said. "Dying is not difficult. But comedy . . . *that* is difficult!"

The craft of acting is a most secret, subtle and complicated mystery, and the art of comedy perhaps the most difficult and mysterious quality to describe or define. But Rex Harrison somehow managed – in his long career – to master the difficulties and understand the mysteries. He was the direct descendant of the naturalistic school of Gerald Du Maurier, but invested that technique with his own unique blend of charm, elegance and wit.

And his timing was, of course, impeccable. Born in 1908, he was able to move into the plays of Shaw, Maugham, Lonsdale and Coward almost as if the authors had all written the plays with Rex in mind.

241

And he was loyal to his authors. I suppose it *is* sad that we never saw him in Molière or Shakespeare – he would have been a superb Tartuffe – and surely, a marvellously testy Prospero or an arrogant, dangerous King Lear. But even more than sixty years in the the theatre is not long enough to accomplish *everything*.

Let us remember then those performances we *were* priviledged to see, and remember with enormous affection the charm, the elegance and the wit. The charm, of course, was not always evident off stage; he seldom suffered fools gladly, and his relationships with certain pompous directors and many overbearing leading ladies were often stormy. He could be exceedingly sharp! But to the general audience, whether in London or New York, he was the total "matinée idol", a description he professed to dislike, but which his seemingly effortless characterization of the "eccentric English gentleman" only continued to confirm.

The elegance was again in the tradition of Du Maurier, continued by Ronald Colman, Leslie Howard, Jack Buchanan, and brought to perfection by Rex. On one of his few excursions to the radical Royal Court Theatre in London, in Nigel Dennis's satirical comedy *August for the People*, he played a lord and insisted on three suits, one for each act, from his own tailor, Mr Brown of Savile Row. The director George Devine was heard to lament that the three Savile Row suits had cost more than the three sets and the entire wardrobe for the rest of the cast.

As to the wit, that is impossible to analyse, as is timing. He gave every line, every *thought*, a freshness – an elusive immediacy that every actor would love to possess. It is something drama schools cannot teach. It is instinctive, and, I always think, destructive to try and

242

define – like reading a review which describes how you got a laugh on a certain line. And then, on the second night, inexplicably the laugh has gone, not to return for many performances, even weeks to come. Happily, the wit and perfection of timing of Rex Harrison is present in his many movie performances. Perhaps not so magical as in the theatre, but they are there, and I would suggest that any student, would-be actor, anyone anxious to learn, could not do better than sit and watch, over and over again, the master at work. It's all there – the charm, the elegance, the wit – possibly one of the finest, most professional performers of our time, not just a lesson to Eliza Doolittle, but a lesson to us all.

Delivered at the Rex Harrison Memorial
18 June 1990
Little Church Around the Corner
New York City

APPENDIX

*T*he following is a complete list of stage and screen performances by Rex Harrison from his first appearance with the Liverpool Repertory Company in 1924 to his last theatrical triumph in New York with Somerset Maugham's *The Circle*, in 1989/90.
   The credits are arranged chronologically.

LIVERPOOL REPERTORY COMPANY (1924–27)

Rex Harrison is known to have appeared in *Thirty Minutes in a Street* (September 1924; as the Husband); *Old English* (by John Galsworthy; as a footman); *Links* (by Herman Heijermans; in September 1926); *Doctor Knock* (by Jules Romains); *Gold* (by Eugene O'Neill; opened 9 November 1926; as Jimmy Kanaka); *A Kiss for Cinderella* (by James M. Barrie); *Milestones*; and *Abraham Lincoln* (by John Drinkwater; 1927; as a messenger).

TOURING (1927–30)

Rex Harrison appeared in the following plays outside the West End:

Charley's Aunt (by Brandon Thomas; 1927 in Hull and elsewhere; as Jack); *Potiphar's Wife* (by Edgar C. Middleton); *Alibi* (by Agatha Christie and Michael Morton); *The Chinese Bungalow* (by Marion Osmond and James Corbet); and *A Cup of Kindness* (by Ben Travers).

RICHARD III (1930)

Author: William Shakespeare. *Directors:* Caspar Middleton, John Counsell, Barbara Curtis.
Producer: Baliol Holloway.
First night: 1 September 1930 (New Theatre, London).

GETTING GEORGE MARRIED (1930)

Author: Florence Kilpatrick. *Director:* Malcolm Morley.
First night: 26 November 1930 (Everyman Theatre, Hampstead, London).

THE NINTH MAN (1931)

Author: Frederick Jackson. *Director:* Campbell Gullan.
First night: 11 February 1931 (Prince of Wales Theatre, London).

THE GREAT GAME (1931)

Director: Jack Raymond.
Film generally released: 23 February 1931.

REPERTORY IN CARDIFF
(May–September 1931)

TOURING (October 1931–1933)

Rex Harrison is known to have appeared in *After All* (by John Van Druten; October–December 1931; as Ralph); *Other Men's Wives* (1932); *For the Love of Mike* (by H.F. Maltby; 1932; as Conway Paton); *Mother of Pearl* (1933); and *The Road House* (by Walter Hacket; 1933).

NO WAY BACK (1934)

Author: Graham Hope. *Director:* A.R. Whatmore.
First night: 17 May 1934 (Whitehall Theatre, London). Closed 19 May 1934 after four performances.

THE SCHOOL FOR SCANDAL (1931)

Director: Maurice Elvey.
Film generally released: 8 June 1931.

OUR MUTUAL FATHER (1934)

Author: John Beanes. *Director:* Reginald Tate.
First night: 4 November 1934 (Piccadilly Theatre, London, for a single performance only).

ANTHONY AND ANNA (1934)

Author: St John G. Ervine. *Director:* Jack Minster.
Producer: John Y. Smart.

First night: 12 November 1934 (Shilling Theatre, Fulham, London).

MAN OF YESTERDAY (1935)

Author: Dion Titheradge. *Director:* Campbell Gullan.
Producer: Alec Rea.
First night: 19 February 1935 (St Martin's Theatre, London). Closed late May 1935.

TOURING (1935)

Rex Harrison appeared in *Not Quite a Lady*; and *The Wicked Flee.*

GET YOUR MAN (1935)

Director: George King.
Film generally released: 25 February 1935.

LEAVE IT TO BLANCHE (1935)

Director: Harold M. Young.
Film generally released: 25 March 1935.

SHORT STORY (1935)

Author: Robert Morley. *Director:* Tyrone Guthrie.
First night: 2 November 1935 (Queen's Theatre, London).

APPENDIX

CHARITY BEGINS (1936)

Director: Henry Kendall.
First night: 12 January 1936 (Aldwych Theatre, London, for a single performance only).

SWEET ALOES (1936)

Author: Jay Mallory [*i.e.* Joyce Carey]. *Director:* Tyrone Guthrie.
Producer: Lee Ephraim.
First night: 4 March 1936 (Booth Theatre, New York). Closed with matinée on 25 March 1936 after 24 performances.

ALL AT SEA (1936)

Director: Anthony Kimmins.
Film generally released: 10 February 1936.

MEN ARE NOT GODS (1936)

Director: Walter Reisch.
Film first shown: 14 December 1936 (London Pavilion).

HEROES DON'T CARE (1936)

Author: Margot Neville. *Director:* Claud Gurney.
First night: 10 June 1936 (St Martin's Theatre, London). Closed early October 1936.

FRENCH WITHOUT TEARS (1936)

Author: Terence Rattigan. *Director:* Harold French.
First night: 6 November 1936 (Criterion Theatre, London).
Harrison also toured Europe with *French Without Tears*, entertaining the troops, in May–June 1945.

STORM IN A TEACUP (1937)

Directors: Victor Saville, Ian Dalrymple.
Film first shown: 7 June 1937 (Leicester Square Theatre, London).

SCHOOL FOR HUSBANDS (1937)

Director: Andrew Marton.
Film first shown: 26 December 1937 (New Gallery, London).

ST MARTIN'S LANE (1938)

Author: Clemence Dane. *Director:* Tim Whelan.
Film first shown: 19 October 1938 (Carlton, Haymarket, London).
American release title: Sidewalks of London

THE CITADEL (1938)

Director: King Vidor.
Producer: Victor Saville.
Film first shown: 28 October 1938 (various American cities).
British première: 22 December 1938 (Empire, Leicester Square, London).

DESIGN FOR LIVING (1939)

Author: Noel Coward. *Director:* Harold French.
Producer: John C. Wilson.
First night: 25 January 1939 (Theatre Royal, Haymarket, London).
Closed 2 September 1939 by outbreak of war. Provincial tour: 13
November 1939 & week (Prince of Wales, Birmingham), 20 November
1939 & week (Royal Court, Liverpool), 27 November 1939 & week
(Lyceum, Edinburgh), 4 December 1939 & week (King's, Glasgow),
11 December 1939 & week (Theatre Royal, Newcastle).

THE SILENT BATTLE (1939)

Director: Herbert Mason.
Producer: Anthony Havelock-Allan.
Film first shown: 14 April 1939 (Plaza, Piccadilly Circus, London).
American release title: Continental Express.

OVER THE MOON (1939)

Directors: Thornton Freeland, (*uncredited*) William K. Howard.
Producer: Alexander Korda.
Film first shown: 14 November 1939 (Odeon, Leicester Square,
London).

TEN DAYS IN PARIS (1940)

Director: Tim Whelan.
Producer: Irving Asher.
Film first shown: 18 April 1940 (Regal, Marble Arch, London).
American release title: Missing Ten Days.

251

NIGHT TRAIN TO MUNICH (1940)

Director: Carol Reed.
Producer: Edward Black.
Film first shown: 25 July 1940 (Empire, Leicester Square, London).
American release title: Night Train.

MAJOR BARBARA (1941)

Director/Producer: Gabriel Pascal.
Author: George Bernard Shaw.
Film first shown: 7 April 1941 (Odeon, Leicester Square, London).

NO TIME FOR COMEDY (1941)

Author: S.N. Behrman. *Director:* Harold French.
First night: 27 March 1941 (Theatre Royal, Haymarket, London).
Closed 24 January 1942.

BLYTHE SPIRIT (1945)

Author: Noel Coward. *Director:* David Lean.
Film first shown: 5 April 1945 (Odeon, Leicester Square, London).

I LIVE IN GROSVENOR SQUARE (1945)

Director/Producer: Herbert Wilcox.
Film first shown: 19 July 1945 (Empire, Leicester Square, and Warner, Leicester Square, London).
American release title: A Yank in London.

THE RAKE'S PROGRESS (1945)

Director: Sidney Gilliat.
Producers: Sidney Gilliat, Frank Launder.
Film first shown: 7 December 1945 (Odeon, Leicester Square, London).
American release title: The Notorious Gentleman.

ANNA AND THE KING OF SIAM (1946)

Director: John Cromwell.
Producer: Louis D. Lighton.
Film first shown: 20 June 1946. (Radio City Music Hall, New York).
British Première: 11 August 1948 (New Gallery, and Tivoli, Strand, London).

THE GHOST AND MRS MUIR (1947)

Director: Joseph L. Mankiewicz.
Producer: Fred Kohlmar.
Film first shown: 25 May 1947 (New Gallery, London).
American première: 26 June 1947 (Radio City Music Hall, New York).

THE FOXES OF HARROW (1947)

Director: John M. Stahl.
Producer: William A. Bacher.
Film first shown: 20 September 1947 (Saenger Theatre, New Orleans).

British première: 14 October 1948 (New Gallery, and Tivoli, Strand, London).

ANNE OF THE THOUSAND DAYS (1948)

Author: Maxwell Anderson. *Director:* H.C. Potter.
Producer: Leland Hayward.
First night: 8 December 1948 (Shubert Theatre, New York). Closed 8 October 1949 after 288 performances (with summer break from 25 June to 22 August 1949). Subsequently toured Midwest and Canada.

ESCAPE (1948)

Director: Joseph L. Mankiewicz.
Producer: William Perlberg.
Film first shown: 28 March 1948 (Gaumont, Haymarket, and Marble Arch Pavilion, London).

UNFAITHFULLY YOURS (1948)

Writer/Director/Producer: Preston Sturges.
Film first shown: 6 November 1948 (Roxy, New York). *British première:* 17 February 1949 (New Gallery, and Tivoli, Strand, London).

THE WALKING STICK (1950)
(for American TV)

First transmission: 20 March 1950 (NBC TV Chevrolet Tele-Theatre).

THE COCKTAIL PARTY (1950)

Author: T.S. Eliot. *Director:* E. Martin Browne.
First night: 3 May 1950 (New Theatre, London).

BELL, BOOK AND CANDLE (1950)

Author and director: John Van Druten.
Producer: Irene Mayer Selznick.
First night: 14 November 1950 (Ethel Barrymore Theatre, New York).
Closed 2 June 1951 after 233 performances.

ANTA ALBUM (1950)
The Dark Lady of the Sonnets

Author: George Bernard Shaw. *Director:* Sir Cedric Hardwicke.
Producer: Robert Breen for the American National Theatre and Academy.
Special performance: Sunday, 29 January 1950 (Ziegfeld Theatre, New York).

THE LONG DARK HALL (1951)

Directors: Anthony Bushell, Reginald Beck.
Producer: Anthony Bushell.

Film first shown: 9 February 1951 (Leicester Square Theatre, London).

THE FOUR POSTER (1952)

Director: Irving Reis.
Producer: Stephen Bosustow.
Film first shown: 15 October 1952 (Sutton and Victoria Theatres, New York).
British première: 21 November 1952 (Carlton, Haymarket, London).

VENUS OBSERVED (1952)

Author: Christopher Fry. *Director:* Laurence Olivier.
First night: 13 February 1952 (Century Theatre, New York). Closed 26 April 1952 after 86 performances.

OMNIBUS (1952)
(for American TV)

Director: Andrew McCullough.

Trial of Anne Boleyn

Director: Alex Segal.
Producer: Alan Anderson.
Also included: The Mikado, The Bad Men, Witch Doctor.
Producer: William Spier.
First transmission: 9 November 1952 (CBS TV).

MAIN STREET TO BROADWAY (1953)

Director: Tay Garnett.
Producer: Lester Cowan.
Film first shown: 13 October 1953 (Astor Theatre, New York). *Generally released in Britain:* 11 January 1957.

MAN IN POSSESSION (1953)
(for American TV)

Director: Alex Segal.
First transmission: 8 December 1953 (ABC TV US Steel Hour).

THE LOVE OF FOUR COLONELS (1953)

Author: Peter Ustinov. *Director:* Rex Harrison.
First night: 15 January 1953 (Shubert Theatre, New York). Closed 16 May 1953 after 141 performances. Subsequent tour: 2 to 4 October 1953 (Community Theatre, Hershey, Pennsylvania), 5 to 10 October 1953 (Nixon Theatre, Pittsburgh), 12 to 24 October 1953 (Shubert Theatre, Detroit), 26 to 31 October 1953 (Royal Alexandra Theatre, Toronto), 2 to 14 November 1953 (National Theatre, Washington).

KING RICHARD
AND THE CRUSADERS (1954)

Director: David Butler.
Producer: Henry Blanke.

Film generally released: August 1954.
British première: 21 October 1954 (Warner, Leicester Square, London).

BELL, BOOK AND CANDLE (1954)

Author: John Van Druten. *Director:* Rex Harrison.
First night: 5 October 1954 (Phoenix Theatre, London).
Joan Greenwood replaced Lilli Palmer during the run; Harrison himself was replaced later on.

NINA (1955)

Author: André Roussin. *Director:* Rex Harrison.
First night: 27 July 1955 (Theatre Royal, Haymarket, London).

THE CONSTANT HUSBAND (1955)

Director: Sidney Gilliat.
Producers: Sidney Gilliat, Frank Launder.
Film first shown: 22 April 1955 (London Pavilion, Piccadilly Circus).
Opening night selection at Berlin Film Festival, 24 June 1955.

MY FAIR LADY (1956 New York production)

Book: Alan Jay Lerner (*from the play* Pygmalion *by* George Bernard Shaw *and the 1938 film version.*) *Director:* Moss Hart. *Music:* Frederick Loewe. *Lyrics:* Alan Jay Lerner.
Producer: Herman Levin.

First night: 15 March 1956 (Mark Hellinger Theatre, New York). Rex Harrison left the production after the performance on 28 November 1957.

CRESCENDO (1957)
(for American TV)

Director: Bill Colleran.
Producer: Paul Gregory.
First transmission: 29 September 1957.

MY FAIR LADY (1958 London production)

Book: Alan Jay Lerner (*from the play* Pygmalion *by* George Bernard Shaw *and the 1938 film version*).
Director: Moss Hart. *Music:* Frederick Loewe. *Lyrics:* Alan Jay Lerner.
Producer: Herman Levin.
First night: 30 April 1958 (Theatre Royal, Drury Lane, London). Harrison left the production on 28 March 1959 to be succeeded by Alec Clunes.

THE RELUCTANT DEBUTANTE (1958)

Director: Vincente Minnelli.
Producer: Pandro S. Berman.
Film first shown: 14 August 1958 (Radio City Music Hall, New York).
British première: 26 December 1958 (Empire, Leicester Square, London).

THE BRIGHT ONE (1958)

Author: J. M. Fulton [*i.e.* Judy Campbell].
Director: Rex Harrison.
Producer: Jack Minster.
First night: 10 December 1958 (Winter Garden Theatre, London).
Closed after 12 performances.

THE FIGHTING COCK (1959)

Author: Jean Anouilh.
Director: Peter Brooks.
Producer: Kermit Bloomgarden.
First night: 8 December 1959 (ANTA Theatre, New York). Closed
20 February 1960 after 87 performances.

MIDNIGHT LACE (1960)

Director: David Miller.
Producers: Ross Hunter, Martin Melcher.
Film first shown: 13 October 1960 (Radio City Music Hall, New York).
British première: 19 January 1961 (Leicester Square Theatre,
London).

THE FABULOUS FIFTIES (1960)
(for American TV)

Director: Norman Jewison.
Producer: Leland Hayward.
First transmission: 31 January 1960 (CBS TV from New York).

DEAR ARTHUR (1960)
(for American TV)

Director: Bretaigne Windust.
Producer: Bretaigne Windust.
First transmission: 22 March 1960 (NBC TV Ford Startime).

THE DATCHET DIAMONDS (1960)
(for American TV)

Director: Gower Champion.
Producer: Robert Saudek.
First transmission: 20 September 1960 (NBC TV Dow Hour of Great Mysteries).

PLATONOV (1960)

Author: Anton Chekhov.
Directors: George Devine, John Blatchley.
First night: 13 October 1960 (Royal Court Theatre, London). Closed after a limited run of 44 performances.

THE HAPPY THIEVES (1961)

Director: George Marshall.
Executive producers: James Hill, Rita Hayworth.
Film first shown: 20 December 1961 (Woods Theatre, Chicago).
British première: 23 February 1962 (London Pavilion, Piccadilly Circus).

AUGUST FOR THE PEOPLE (1961)

Author: Nigel Dennis.
Director: George Devine.
First night: 4 September 1961 (Lyceum Theatre, Edinburgh, for one week).
London performance: from 12 September 1961 (Royal Court Theatre).
Withdrawn after 11 performances in London.

CLEOPATRA (1963)

Director: Joseph L. Mankiewicz.
Producer: Walter Wanger.
Film first shown: 12 June 1963 (Rivoli Theatre, New York). *British première:* 31 July 1963 (Dominion, Tottenham Court Road, London).

MY FAIR LADY (1964)

Director: George Cukor. *Writer:* Alan Jay Lerner.
Producer: Jack L. Warner.
Film first shown: 22 October 1964 (Criterion, New York). *British première:* 21 January 1965 (Warner, Leicester Square, London).

THE YELLOW ROLLS-ROYCE (1964)

Director: Anthony Asquith.
Producer: Anatole de Grunwald.
Film first shown: 31 December 1964 (Empire, Leicester Square, London).

262

American première: 13 May 1965 (Radio City Music Hall, New York).

GOLDEN DRAMA (1965)
(for British TV)

Director: Bill Ward.
Producer: Cecil Clarke.
First transmission (live): 31 January 1965 (from Queen's Theatre, London).

THE AGONY AND THE ECSTASY (1965)

Director: Carol Reed.
Producer: Carol Reed.
First shown: 7 October 1965 (Loew's State, New York). *British première:* 27 October 1965 (Astoria, Charing Cross Road, London).

THE HONEY POT (1967)

Director and writer: Joseph L. Mankiewicz.
Producers: Charles K. Feldman, Joseph L. Mankiewicz.
Film first shown: 21 March 1967 (Odeon, Marble Arch, London).
American première: 21 May 1967 (Trans-Lux West, New York).

DOCTOR DOLITTLE (1967)

Director: Richard Fleischer.
Producer: Arthur P. Jacobs.
Film first shown: 12 December 1967 (Odeon, Marble Arch, London).

American première: 19 December 1967 (Loew's State, New York).

A FLEA IN HER EAR (1968)

Director: Jacques Charon.
Producer: Fred Kohlmar.
Film first shown: October 1968 (various cinemas in Paris).
British première: 14 November 1968 (Carlton, Haymarket, London).
American release: November 1968.

THE LIONEL TOUCH (1969)

Author: George Hulme. *Director:* John Gorrie.
Producer: John Gale.
First night: 5 November 1969 (Lyric Theatre, Shaftesbury Avenue, London).

STAIRCASE (1969)

Director/Producer: Stanley Donen.
Film first shown: 20 August 1969 (various theatres, New York). *British première:* 22 October 1969 (Carlton, Haymarket, London).

PLATONOV (1971)
(for British TV)

Author: Anton Chekhov.
Director: Christopher Morahan.
Producer: Cedric Messina.
First shown: 23 May 1971 (BBC 1 Play of the Month).

THE BURT BACHARACH SHOW (1972)
(for American TV)

[In March 1972, Rex Harrison recorded the number "If I Could Go Back" from the musical version of *Lost Horizon* at Elstree for transmission at a subsequent date not known.]

THE ADVENTURES OF DON QUIXOTE (1973)
(for British TV)

Director: Alvin Rakoff.
Producer: Gerald Savory.
Film first shown: 7 January 1973 (BBC 1, Great Britain), 23 April 1973 (CBS, United States).

EMPEROR HENRY IV
(1973 New York production)

Author: Luigi Pirandello.
Director: Clifford Williams.
Producer: Elliot Martin.
First night: (following three previews): 28 March 1973 (Ethel Barrymore Theatre, New York). Closed 28 April 1973 after 37 performances.

ENRICO QUATTRO (1974 London production)

Author: Luigi Pirandello.
Director: Clifford Williams.
Producers: Bernard Delfont, Richard M. Mills.

First night: 20 February 1974 (Her Majesty's Theatre, Haymarket, London). Limited season ended 18 May 1974.

IN PRAISE OF LOVE (1974)

Author: Terence Rattigan. *Director:* Fred Coe.
Producer: Arthur Cantor.
First night (following previews): 10 December 1974 (Morosco Theatre, New York). Closed late May 1975.

SHORT STORIES OF LOVE (1974)
(for American TV)

Presenter: Rex Harrison. *Music:* David Shire.
Epicac
Director: John Badham.

Kiss Me Again, Stranger
Director: Arnold Laven.

The Fortunate Painter
Director: Jeannot Szwarc.
Producer: Herbert Hirschman.
First transmission: 1 May 1974 (NBC).

MONSIEUR PERRICHON'S TRAVELS (1976)

Authors: Eugène Labiche and Martin. *Director:* Patrick Garland.
First night: 3 August 1976 (Chichester Festival Theatre, West Sussex).

266

CAESAR AND CLEOPATRA (1977)

Author: George Bernard Shaw.
Director: Ellis Rabb.
Producers/production companies: Elliot Martin and Gladys Rachmil, John F. Kennedy Center for the Performing Arts, in association with James Nederlander.
First night: 24 February 1977 (Palace Theatre, New York). Closed after 12 performances.

THE PRINCE AND THE PAUPER (1977)

Director: Richard Fleischer.
Producer: Pierre Spengler.
Film first shown: 2 June 1977 (Carlton, Haymarket, London). *American première:* 2 March 1978 (Radio City Music Hall, New York).
American release title: Crossed Swords

OUR THEATRE IN THE NINETIES (1977)

Author: George Bernard Shaw.
Director/deviser: Patrick Garland.
First performance: 30 August 1977 (St Cecilia's Hall, Edinburgh). Limited run of five afternoon readings ending 3 September 1977, as part of Edinburgh Festival.

THE KINGFISHER (1978)

Author: William Douglas Home. *Director:* Linsday Anderson.
Producers: Elliot Martin, with Hinks Shimberg, in association with John Gale.

267

First night: 6 December 1978 (Biltmore Theatre, New York). Closed 13 May 1979.

Harrison took the play on an American tour in late 1979 and made a film of it for British television in 1982.

SHALIMAR (1978)

Director: Krishna Shah.
Producer: Suresh Shah.
Film first shown (Hindi version): circa December 1978 (India).

ASHANTI (1979)

Director: Richard Fleischer.
Producer: Georges-Alain Vuille.
Film first shown: 25 January 1979 (Odeon, Leicester Square, London).
American release (through Warner Bros.): April 1979.

THE 5TH MUSKETEER (1979)

Director: Ken Annakin.
Producer: Ted Richmond.
Film generally released (United States): September 1979.

MY FAIR LADY (1980)

Book: Alan Jay Lerner.
Director: Patrick Garland.
Producers: Don Gregory, Mike Merrick.

First night: 23 September 1980 (Saenger Performing Arts Center, New Orleans). Then on tour.

THE KINGFISHER (1982)
(for British TV)

Director: James Cellan Jones.
Producer: John Rosenberg.
Film first shown: 23 December 1982 (ITV network).

A TIME TO DIE (1983)

Directors: Matt Cimber [Matteo Ottaviano], *(additional scenes and action sequences)* Joe Tornatore.
Producer: Charles Lee.
Film generally released (United States): circa September 1983.

HEARTBREAK HOUSE
(1983 London production)

Author: George Bernard Shaw.
Director: John Dexter.
First night (following two previews from 8 March 1983)*:* 10 March 1983 (Theatre Royal, Haymarket, London). Limited run ended 11 June 1983.

HEARTBREAK HOUSE
(1983 New York production)

Author: George Bernard Shaw. *Director:* Anthony Page.
First night (following previews from 18 November 1983)*:* 7 December

1983 (Circle in the Square Theatre, New York). Limited run ended after 66 performances on 5 February 1984.
Taped for cable TV transmission and shown on *Broadway on Showtime* in the United States in April 1985.

AREN'T WE ALL? (1984 London production)

Author: Frederick Lonsdale.
Director: Clifford Williams.
Producer: Duncan C. Weldon with Paul Gregg and Lionel Becker in association with Jerome Minskoff.
First night (following nine previews from 12 June 1984): 20 June 1984 (Theatre Royal, Haymarket, London). Limited run ended 3 November 1984 after 134 performances.

AREN'T WE ALL? (1985 New York production)

Author: Frederick Lonsdale. *Director:* Clifford Williams.
Producers: Douglas Urbanski, Karl Allison, Bryan Bantry and James M. Nederlander in association with Duncan C. Weldon, Paul Gregg, Lionel Becker and Jerome Minskoff.
First night: 29 April 1985 (Brooks Atkinson Theatre). Limited run ended 21 July 1985. Tour announced from 23 September 1985 (Curran Theatre, San Francisco).

THE ADMIRABLE CRICHTON (1988 London production)

Author: J.M. Barrie. *Director:* Frith Banbury.
First night: 8 July 1988 (Theatre Royal, Haymarket, London).

270

THE CIRCLE (1989 New York production)

Author: W. Somerset Maugham. *Director:* Brian Murray.
Producer: Elliot Martin.
First night: 20 November 1989 (Ambassador Theatre, New York).
Last night: 11 May 1990.

PHOTO CREDITS

INDEX

INDEX